KURSK

THE VITAL 24 HOURS

KURSK

THE VITAL 24 HOURS

WILL FOWLER

amber
BOOKS

First published in 2005

Published by
Amber Books Ltd
Bradley's Close
74–77 White Lion Street
London N1 9PF
United Kingdom
www.amberbooks.co.uk

Project Editor: Michal Spilling
Copy Editor: Stephen Chumbley
Design: Hawes Design
Picture Research: Natasha Jones

ISBN 1-904687-36-9

Printed in Italy

PICTURE CREDITS

ART-TECH/AEROSPACE: 17
IAN BAXTER: 51, 106, 112–113, 117, 121, 133, 143, 147, 176
NIK CORNISH: 9, 28–29, 33, 34, 35, 36–37, 49, 52, 76, 78, 90, 94, 114, 118–119, 131, 136–137,
    139, 148–149, 156–157
WILL FOWLER: 8, 13, 23, 39, 46–47, 56–57, 58, 64, 66, 84, 104, 106, 109, 134, 144–145,
    152, 160, 166–167, 175
POPPERFOTO: 32
SÜDDEUTSCHER VERLAG: 6–7, 16, 20, 25, 30, 42, 53, 81, 88, 97, 98–99, 124, 128, 153, 168, 172, 181
TRH PICTURES: 14, 18, 19, 45, 54, 59, 61, 63, 71, 72, 73, 74, 75, 80, 83, 86, 87, 91, 93,
    100, 101, 102, 111, 116, 120, 122, 125, 132, 142, 150, 155, 158, 165, 169, 180, 183
UKRAINIAN STATE ARCHIVE: 40, 62, 105, 108, 115, 129, 138, 140, 164, 170, 177

MAPS

CARTOGRAPHICA: 10, 11, 67, 126–127, 135, 179
PETER HARPER: 50, 68, 69, 70, 79, 154, 163, 171

ALL ARTWORKS © ART-TECH/AEROSPACE

Contents

CHAPTER ONE

KHARKOV: ARMOURED ANVIL

The battle for Stalingrad was over.
But now, on 3 January 1943, the Germans
began an urgent retreat from the Caucasus.
Stalin had ordered his generals to drive for
Rostov to trap the German forces of Army
Groups A and Don, which were out on a limb,
having driven southeast to capture the oil fields
in 1942. Operation 'Leap', proposed by
Lieutenant-General Nikolai Vatutin commanding
the South West Front, would have locked
the Germans into a huge pocket in the
Donets Basin.

IN FIERCE FIGHTING on the Don River on 14 January, the men of the Second Hungarian Army suffered 70 per cent casualties. Despite these losses, Hitler demanded that Hungary should provide more troops for the Eastern Front.

Vladimir Farberov, a veteran of the harsh fighting on the Eastern Front, recalled in an interview in 1974: 'At the beginning of the war, there was still some complacency. "We are sure to win" was the general belief and this confidence had a certain negative effect. For since victory would be ours, since we would win anyway, perhaps there was no need for a

Left: Waffen-SS *grenadiers of* Das Reich *ride on a StuG III on its way to Kharkov. Just visible on the skyline to the left are the tower blocks around Dzerzhinsky Square, known to the Germans as 'Red Square' and later renamed by the* Leibstandarte *'Platz der Leibstandarte'.*

superhuman effort on our part, perhaps things would work out without us. But the Germans poured on the lead without looking. A bitter joke in circulation from Stalingrad times told of a soldier going into battle carrying 150 rounds; when he was carried into the field hospital, he had 151 – he hadn't even had a chance to fire his rifle. There was another extreme – contempt of death. This was written about and acclaimed as valour. But by mid-1942, there was too much of this contempt around, and yet the distance to victory was as great as ever … Sometimes the going gets so hard that death seems a welcome deliverance. Those are no empty words. Gradually they stopped writing about this contempt of death. The mission of the soldier was not to die with dashing defiance, but to kill the enemy.'

On 25 January, Stalin issued an Order of the Day to his troops, congratulating them and exhorting them 'Onward to defeat the German occupationists'. He had promoted Zhukov to the rank of Marshal a week earlier – at the same time, Stalin, despite having no military training, decided that he himself would also become a Marshal.

Opposite: Rumanian infantry climb onto a StuG. Rumanian troops had fought well during the early years of the war in Russia, but now poor equipment and leadership were sapping their morale. Knowing this, Soviet commanders focused their attacks on Germany's allies.

KHARKOV

On 4 February, the Soviets had reached the eastern bank of the Donets, only 20km (12.4 miles) east of Kharkov, and also bypassed it with their left wing. On 5 February, the First Guards Army captured Izyum 100km (62 miles) southeast of Kharkov and were threatening to cut deep into the German Army Group's supply lines. Hitler ordered the II *SS-Panzerkorps* to strike in the rear of the Soviet spearhead at Kupyansk, just behind Izyum. This was unrealistic, as they were busy digging in on the Donets to hold the Soviet right wing and protect Kharkov. While most of the *Leibstandarte SS Adolf Hitler (LAH)* stayed east of Kharkov, *Oberst-Gruppenführer* 'Sepp' Dietrich detached *SS-Sturmbannführer* Fritz Witt's 1st *Panzergrenadier* Regiment to proceed south via Malinovka for the counter-attack.

Meanwhile, the LAH, who held the high western bank of the Donets, inflicted heavy losses on Rybalko's Third Tank Army, but were forced back into Kharkov with the SS-Division *Das Reich*. By 14 February, the Soviets were fighting in the eastern suburbs of Kharkov.

Below: Thundering through the snow with their shashka *– sabres – drawn, Cossack cavalry demonstrate their intimidating tactics. Though mounted troops were very vulnerable to automatic weapons, they could operate in snow and mud that was impassable to vehicles.*

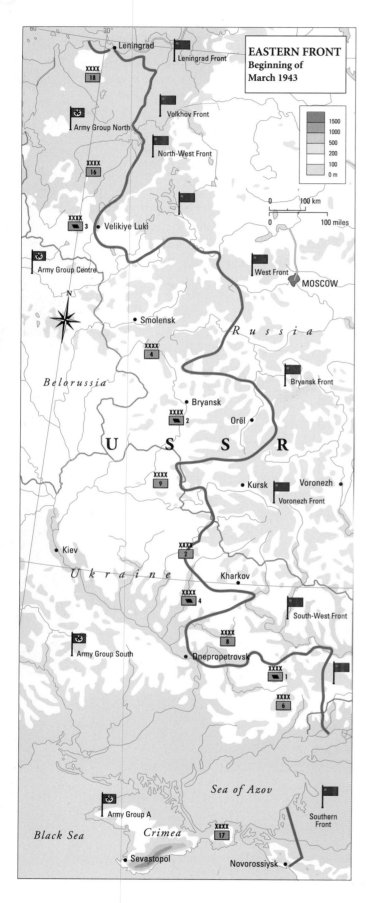

EASTERN FRONT
Beginning of
March 1943

1500
1000
500
200
100
0 m

0   100 km

0   100 miles

Left: The Eastern Front in March 1943. The fall of Stalingrad had released Soviet forces for further operations. Before the muddy season set in, STAVKA planned to drive south towards the Black Sea and cut off Army Group A in the Crimea.

Hitler had declared that Kharkov, the third most important city in the USSR, was a fortress 'to be defended under all circumstances' and ordered that the city should be held by three *Waffen-SS* panzer divisions. However, the hugely experienced *GenObst der Waffen-SS* Paul 'Papa' Hausser ignored the order and pulled his troops out to the south. Hausser said that he would 'rather lose a city than his SS Panzer corps'. He withdrew from Kharkov on 15 February: a day later, the city fell to General Filip Golikov's Voronezh Front and Vatutin's South West Front. Hitler was 'white with fury' at Hauser's disobedience. After driving 186km (115.6 miles), the *Panzerkorps* linked up with General Herman Hoth's Fourth *Panzerarmee*.

Meanwhile, Field Marshal Erich Manstein, commanding Army Group South, had followed the situation map and prepared to strike when the Soviets were deep into the gap between his armies. In what would be called 'Manstein's Miracle', he destroyed Popov's armoured group at Izyum and the Soviet Sixth Army. He then used the II *SS-Panzerkorps* (which Hausser had saved) to recapture Kharkov and destroy the Soviet's Sixty-Ninth Army and their Third Tank Army. Manstein had stopped the great Soviet drive from Stalingrad and removed the threat of annihilation of the Germans on the Eastern Front.

Hausser's II *SS Panzer Korps* advanced from Krasnograd in the southwest with the aim of surrounding the city with *Das Reich* to the west, *LAH* to the north and *Totenkopf* to the east.

Opposite: 'Manstein's miracle', the recapture of Kharkov in March. The victory, won in a fast-moving and imaginative action, stabilized the front, redeemed the reputation of the Waffen-SS *and gave the Nazi propaganda machine good news following the disaster of Stalingrad.*

The troops of General Golikov have captured Kharkov. On Tuesday Soviet artillery, brought from Zhopozhnikov and moved into position around Kharkov, aimed three hours of devastating fire at the German positions....Two German panzer divisions took extremely heavy losses as Russian assault artillery followed hard in the wake of Russian tanks.

Soviet Information Bureau
Moscow, Wednesday 17 February 1943

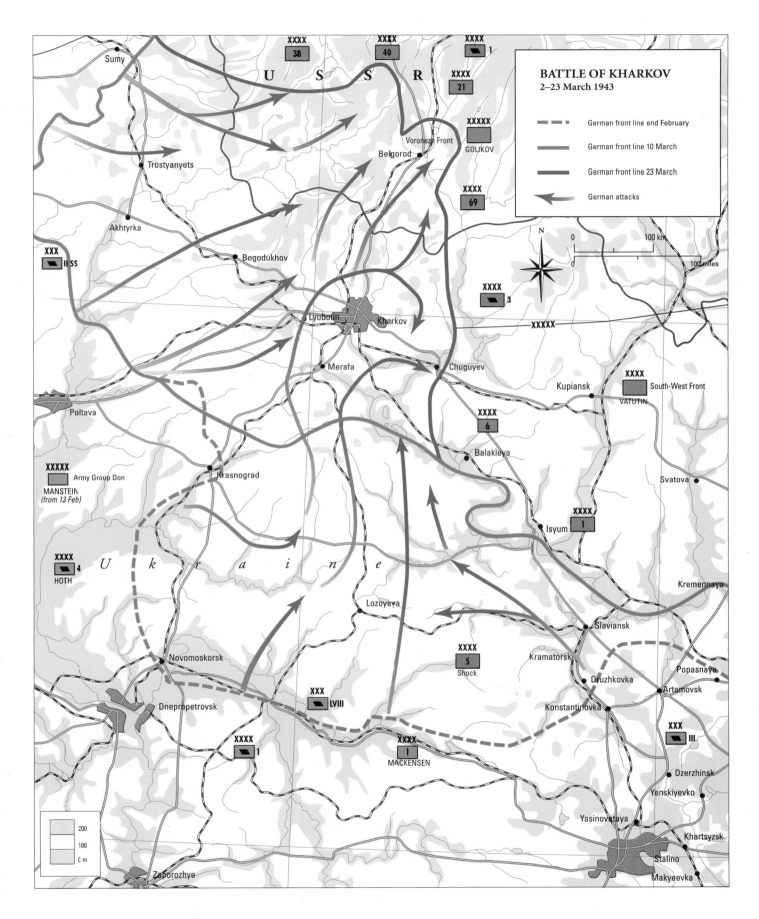

BATTLE OF KHARKOV
2–23 March 1943

German front line end February
German front line 10 March
German front line 23 March
German attacks

Sumy

U S S R

XXXX 38
XXXX 40
XXXX 1

XXXX 21

XXXXX GOLIKOV

Trostyanyets

Voronezh Front
Belgorod

XXXX 69

Akhtyrka

XXX II SS

Bogodukhov

0   100 km
0   100 miles

N

Lyubotin   Kharkov

XXXX 3

Poltava

Merafa

Chuguyev

Kupiansk

XXXX
South-West Front
VATUTIN

XXXXX Army Group Don
MANSTEIN
(from 13 Feb)

Krasnograd

XXXX 6

Balakleya

Svatova

XXXX 4
HOTH

U   k   r   a   i   n   e

XXXX 1

Isyum

Kremennaya

Lozovaya

Slaviansk

Novomoskorsk

XXXX 5
Shock

Kramatorsk

Popasnaya

Druzhkovka
Artemovsk

Dnepropetrovsk

XXX LVIII

Konstantinovka

XXX III

XXXX 1

XXXX 1
MACKENSEN

Dzerzhinsk

Yenskiyevko

Yasinovataya

200
100
0 m

Zaporozhye

Khartsyzsk

Stalino

Makyeevka

Manstein's original order was to stay out of the city. Hausser was initially ordered to surround the city and not to get involved in it, but on 9 March was told to take it, if possible, by a *coup de main*. At 04:00 on 11 March, the *LAH* launched two regimental groups in four different columns leading into the city from the north.

The *LAH* attack started off north of the city. *SS-Standartenfuhrer* Teddy Wisch's 2nd *Panzergrenadier* Regiment sent Sandig's 2nd *Panzergrenadier* Battalion and Hugo Kraas' 1st *Panzergrenadier* Battalion respectively west and east of the main railway line to Belgorod. Both ran into stiff opposition. The main attack by units of the 1st *Panzergrenadier* Regiment down the main road to Belgorod reached the Cemetery, the City Park and the Zoo. In the heart of the city, they cleared the vast Dzerzhinsky Square. Joachim 'Jochen' Peiper's 3rd Battalion moved southeast from the square at 10:30 on 12 March and captured a bridge across the Kharkov River. Even further to the east, the *LAH* reconnaissance battalion under Kurt 'Panzer' Meyer (not in the order of battle) had reached the junction to the Chuguev exit road, fighting a desperate action all day.

Peiper's two *Panzergrenadier* regiments had been slowly fighting their way through the Soviet perimeter on the northern edge of Dzerzhinsky Square but were not able to make contact with Meyer's battalion, which by that time was fighting for its very existence. In response to the critical situation, Wisch ordered Peiper's battalion of half-tracks to break through to Meyer. By that time, one of Meyer's companies was encircled in a cemetery and another was pinned down in the upper floors of a school building. A third company was out of contact with Meyer and its precarious situation was unclear.

Before dawn on 13 March, Peiper smashed through the Soviet defences in the centre of the city and reached Meyer's beleaguered battalion. The rest of Wisch's regiment followed in the wake of Peiper's thrust and began the fight for the southern half of Kharkov. Witt's battalions cleared the Square, secured the surrounding area and made contact with Wisch's battalions. The *Panzergrenadier* battalions linked up and drove forward in a coordinated attack. Battle groups methodically blasted the Soviet troops out of their defensive positions, supported by point-blank fire from howitzers, tanks and assault guns. The troops that survived were forced into the southeastern quadrant of the city.

By now, *Das Reich*, which had been fighting in the west of the city, passed through *LAH* to assist *Totenkopf* to pursue the fleeing Soviets in the northeast. By the evening, two-thirds of Kharkov was in German hands, but it took further furious fighting by *LAH* to clear the last enemy pockets in the factory area by 15 March. Hitler was delighted at the recapture of Kharkov. He awarded a swathe of decorations to the men of the SS divisions but, rather spitefully, left Hausser out. He had not forgotten his act of disobedience. In the light of *LAH*'s role in each phase of Manstein's Kharkov counterattack, it is clear why its men, after suffering heavy losses to retake the city's blood-stained streets and ruined buildings, renamed the enormous Dzerzhinsky Square '*Platz der Leibstandarte*'.

THEODOR EICKE

Over 11,000 *Waffen-SS* soldiers and over 40,000 Soviets were killed or wounded during the battle of Kharkov from 30 January to 20 March 1943. Among those killed was the commanding officer of *SS-Panzer Division Totenkopf*, *SS-Obergruppenführer* Theodor Eicke. Flying in a Fiesler Storch liaison aircraft, he decided to land near a *Totenkopf* panzer regiment at a village called Michailovka. Soviet troops, who were dug in less than 800m (875 yards) away, opened fire as the aircraft dropped to 100m (328ft). It crashed and caught fire and only at nightfall was the general's burned and mutilated body recovered.

Eicke remains a controversial figure in the history of the *Waffen-SS*. He had served with the Imperial German Army during World War I and won the Iron Cross. After 1918, he was active in the *Freikorps*, a paramilitary rightwing organization, before becoming an inspector in the Thuringian police force. In 1928, he joined the National Socialist German Workers Party (NSDAP), which would become the Nazi Party, and two years later took command of a *Schutzstaffel* (SS) formation of the Rhine-Palatinate.

In 1932, he was suspected of carrying out bomb attacks on political opponents, and was advised by Himmler to go and live in Italy. A year later, when Hitler came to power, Eicke returned to Germany and was appointed as commandant of the newly established concentration camp at Dachau near Munich. In May 1934, Eicke was given responsibility of reorganizing Germany's concentration camp system. One of his recommendations was that guards should be warned that they would be punished if they showed prisoners any signs of humanity. During the Night of the Long Knives, Eicke was given the task of killing the head of the *Sturmabteilung* (SA),

Opposite: During the spring of 1943, Field Marshal von Manstein makes a frontline reconnaissance in the Kharkov area. He is accompanied by a Hungarian officer, as well as a member of his staff (background, saluting).

Opposite: A Leibstandarte Adolf Hitler MG 42 crew scans the streets of Kharkov. They are wearing a mixture of Waffen-SS winter warfare clothing and the reversible white and field grey quilted uniforms that were developed following the winter of 1941–42. The NCO with the binoculars has leather and felt boots.

Ernst Roehm, and other leaders. Three days after the purge, Eicke was appointed Inspector of Concentration Camps.

On the outbreak of World War II, Eicke was placed in command of the *Totenkopf* Division, which drew into its ranks some men who had previously served in concentration camps. In 1940, the division executed over 100 British prisoners of war in the 2nd Royal Norfolk Regiment at Le Paradis in France. *Totenkopf* fought with distinction in Russia and under Eicke held the Demyansk Pocket surrounded by Soviet forces in the winter of 1941. For several months, they were resupplied by the *Luftwaffe*. Eicke ate the same rations as his men and exercised strong personal leadership. The Demyansk pocket would be seen as the model for the Stalingrad pocket a year later.

For Eicke, there was only one crime that he would hold against the men under his command – that of cowardice. *Totenkopf* was almost his personal fiefdom and the men who succeeded him reflected his values.

THE KURSK SALIENT

Now in the winter of 1943, the battle of Kharkov would be part of a counterattack on the southern flank of the two Soviet Fronts, which inflicted heavy losses, forcing them back behind the river Donets. To the south, Operation 'Leap' had overextended itself and it ended on 18 February, when the First *Panzerarmee* demolished Vatutin's mobile group. Part of the reason for Manstein's triumph may have been his close tactical control of the fast-moving battle; there were no long, encoded Enigma signals back to Hitler's HQ at Rastenburg in East Prussia. It was signals like these that were frequently the undoing of German plans since these were intercepted and decoded as part of the ULTRA operation at Bletchley Park in the United Kingdom.

On 1 March, Army Group Centre began an operation codenamed 'Buffalo', a phased withdrawal from the Rzhev salient opposite Moscow – even Hitler agreed that it was no longer a credible threat to the Soviet capital. By 23 March, the Germans halted on a line from Velizh to Kirov; they had cut their frontage by nearly 400km (249 miles) and freed enough troops to keep Rokossovsky's Central Front in check. Despite the huge German losses following the surrender at Stalingrad, Hitler remained optimistic. He had 3.07 million soldiers in Russia, slightly more than in June 1941, and new weapons and equipment were reaching them in the front line. Operation 'Buffalo' had yielded an extra army, the Ninth, which under the vigorous command of the monocled General Walther Model had for 14 months held the toughest part of the Eastern Front, the line around Rzhev.

In April 1943, German soldiers discovered a mass grave in the Katyn forest near Smolensk in western Russia. The grave held the bodies of between 4000 and 5000 Polish army officers. Hoping to drive a wedge between the Soviet Union and its Western allies, Nazi officials publicized their find and accused the Soviet Union of the massacre. Moscow denied the charge and claimed the Germans were attempting to cover up their own atrocity. Despite evidence that the

SS-OBERGRUPPENFÜHRER UND GENERAL DER WAFFEN-SS PAUL HAUSSER

Born in Brandenburg on 7 October 1880, Paul Hausser served with distinction in World War I, winning the Iron Cross 1st and 2nd Class. After the war, he served with the *Reichswehr*, reaching the rank of Lieutenant-General before he retired in 1932. He joined the *SS-Verfügungstruppe* (SS-VT), the forerunners of the *Waffen-SS*, and became inspector of the *SS-Junkerschule*. In 1939, he was an observer with the joint Army/SS Panzer Division 'Kempf' in Poland. The SS-VT was formed into a division, with Hausser in command, and he led it through battles in the West and Barbarossa. During his command of *Das Reich* in Russia, Hausser was awarded the Knight's Cross on 8 August 1941. He was severely wounded and lost an eye in the East. After he had recovered, he commanded the II *SS-Panzerkorps* in the fighting at Kharkov in 1943. He led this formation at Kursk in the summer of 1943 and he received Oakleaves to his Knight's Cross on 28 July 1943. The corps, now composed of the 9th and 10th SS Panzer Divisions, were then stationed in the West and fought at Normandy in 1944. Hausser remained with the Corps, when it was encircled at Falaise, to ensure that as many men as possible escaped from the pocket. Swords were added to his Knight's Cross on 26 August 1944. He ended the war on the staff of Field Marshal Albert Kesselring. Hausser died on 21 December 1972 at Ludwigsburg.

Left: SS-Obergruppenführer und General der Waffen-SS *Paul Hausser, the highly respected commander of* II SS-Panzerkorps. *Hausser, who had served in the German Army in World War I, was a shrewd tactician and also a frontline commander, losing an eye in fighting on the Eastern Front.*

years later, the Soviet government handed over to Polish President Lech Walesa previously secret documents revealing that Soviet leader Joseph Stalin had directly ordered the killing of the Polish army officers. Most of the victims in the Katyn forest were Polish army reservists – lawyers, doctors, scientists and businessmen – who had been called up for active service following the Nazi invasion of Poland in 1939. Instead of fighting the Germans, however, about 15,000 Polish officers found themselves prisoners of the Red Army, which had occupied eastern Poland under the terms of a secret Moscow-Berlin treaty. In the spring of 1940, about 4500 of these officers were taken by their Soviet captors to the Katyn forest. Most were then gagged, bound, shot once in the head and buried on the spot. The other Polish POWs were taken to other locations, where many of them were also executed. The denial by Britain and the United States of an investigation of the Katyn massacre was one of the less honourable episodes of World War II, where political expediency – the need to maintain allies in the fight against Nazi Germany – took precedence over the search for truth.

Kremlin was indeed behind the massacre, Britain and the United States chose to look the other way. The British Prime Minister, Winston Churchill, opposed a call by the Polish government-in-exile for an investigation by the International Red Cross into the discoveries. Following the war, at the Nuremberg war crime tribunals, the issue of Katyn was included on the list of crimes attributed to the Nazis. But it was later dropped, apparently to avoid any embarrassment for the Soviet Union.

Only in 1990 did Soviet President Mikhail Gorbachev admit Soviet involvement in the Katyn forest massacre. Two

Fighting in Soviet Russia had now taken on a pattern: it normally slowed down with the spring thaw, which halted movement as the roads turned to soft mud. After the victory at Kharkov, the front line stabilized into a huge Soviet salient 190km (118 miles) wide and 120km (74.5 miles) deep, which had the railway city of Kursk at its centre. On one of the tracks running northwards to Kursk was the little station of

Prokhorovka. The salient was an open plain broken by dry gullies (or *balkas)*, copses, villages, farms and marshy rivers. Standing crops made visibility difficult and the ground rose to the north, which favoured the defenders. The maximum rainfall in June-July was 60–85mm (2.3–3.3in) per month, falling as light rain on 13–14 days a month, with downpours on a couple of days in June and July. The summer heat could trigger between five and 20 thunderstorms in these months, and these storms were followed by squally winds. During downpours, and especially during the lingering rains, unpaved roads became difficult to traverse for wheeled traffic. Unpaved airfields at that time were almost inoperative. With these factors in mind, there were two approaches to the planned German summer offensive of 1943.

ZITADELLE

The realistic option had considerable support, including that of General Heinz Guderian, Inspector-General of Armoured Troops, and Manstein – two of the best German field commanders – and its goal was modest. It suggested compensating for the large Soviet numerical advantage by fully utilizing the superiority of the German commanders and soldiers in tactics and command, and by fighting a strategy of dynamic mobile defence that would cause great losses to the Soviets in a series of local clashes. In short, the realistic goal was simply to stop and delay the Soviets, recognizing that a decisive victory was no longer achievable. The optimistic option, proposed by General Kurt Zeitzler, Chief of the OKH, suggested

concentrating almost all German tanks and other forces in a major decisive battle against a large portion of the Soviet armour, in order to destroy them and, in so doing, to hopefully regain the initiative.

The most suitable place for such a battle, as Zeitzler proposed, was the Kursk salient. The idea was to pinch out the Kursk bulge, with attacks from the north by Army Group Centre under Field Marshal Günther Hans von Kluge and the south by Army Group South under Field Marshal Erich von

Right: The bodies of some of the 4500 Polish officers who were captured by Soviet troops in 1939 and, on Stalin's orders, shot in the woods at Katyn in the Ukraine. Many of these officers were reservists and included in their ranks lawyers, doctors and scientists – the intellectual 'enemies' of the Soviet Union.

Manstein. The attacks would be codenamed Unternehmen Zitadelle – Operation 'Citadel'; the attack would encircle and destroy the Soviet Central and Voronezh Fronts in a huge pocket. It was obvious that the Soviets would keep a large tank force there, and the plan was to repeat the successes of 1941 and 1942 and encircle them in a classic blitzkrieg-style pincer movement of German tanks from north and south, and destroy them.

When Hitler discussed the two options with his generals on 4 May, exactly two months before the German attack began, it became clear that each of the two options had a major problem. The major problem with Zeitzler's plan, to attack the Kursk salient, was that aerial photos clearly revealed that the Soviets were building dense and deep

Below: Dressed in their sheepskin-lined field grey parkas, Waffen-SS soldiers roll into Kharkov. The man seated on the right of the StuG III has an MG42 and his squad are not only enjoying a ride but are also in position to give local defence for the assault gun.

fortifications there in order to counter such an attack, and that many Soviet tanks had moved deeper behind the front line. Instead of an open battlefield *blitzkrieg*, it was going to be a direct charge at dense antitank defences. General von Mellenthin warned that such a direct attack would be a '*Totenritt*', a 'death ride', for the German tanks. The major problem with Guderian's option was that it lacked the optimistic hope of a major change in the war, which still appeared possible in Zeitzler's plan. So the optimist Hitler decided in favour of Zeitzler, and calmed his worries by ordering the attack to be delayed for a while to give time to incorporate more of the new advanced German aircraft, tanks and tank destroyers into the plan. The date was set at 4 July 1943.

DISPOSITIONS

Once the order was given, the Germans prepared as best as they could. The entire region was photographed from the air, the German commanders visited the front line to observe

Above: In a training exercise, a Goliath *remote-control demolition vehicle is steered towards a captured Soviet assault gun. Like a number of German weapons, the* Goliath *with its 60kg (132lb) charge was a great idea in theory but proved less effective used in action at Kursk.*

GOLIATH E

The tiny *Goliath E (elektrisch)* battery-powered, remote-controlled tracked demolition vehicle would have its combat debut at Kursk. The first version, designed and built by the Hansa-Lloyd-Goliath Werke Carl F.W. Borgward, was powered by two converted electric starter motors. It carried 60kg (132lb) of TNT and was directed towards its target by its operator through signals transmitted along a cable. The targets were often bunkers or fixed emplacements. It was 1.5m (4.9ft) long, 56cm (1.8ft) high, 85cm (2.7ft) wide and weighed 375kg (826.7lb). It had a road range of 1.5km (0.93 miles) and maximum speed of 10km/h (6.2mph). The *Goliath V (vergasermotor)* was a more effective petrol-powered version developed later.

their intended routes, and the Germans concentrated all available forces in two armies, north and south of the Kursk salient, leaving minimal forces along the rest of the long Russian front. The German force included a total of 50 divisions, including 17 armoured and mechanized divisions. These included the most powerful and best equipped German divisions, such as *Großdeutschland* and the *Waffen-SS* Panzer Divisions *Leibstandarte-SS Adolf Hitler, Totenkopf* and *Das Reich.* The Germans concentrated all their new armour and all available air units and artillery, and despite the problems inherent in the German plan, it was a formidable concentrated mobile armour force with great offensive potential.

FIELD MARSHAL GÜNTHER HANS VON KLUGE: 'CLEVER HANS'

Hans von Kluge was born in Poznan, Germany, on 30 October 1882. He joined the Imperial German Army and served in the field artillery during World War I. Von Kluge remained in the army and by 1933 had reached the rank of major general. The following year, he was placed in charge of the Westphalian military district. In 1938, von Kluge objected to the aggressive foreign policy adopted by Adolf Hitler and as a result was dismissed from office. However, on the outbreak of World War II, von Kluge was recalled and placed in charge of the Fourth Army in the invasion of Poland. He also led it in the invasion of France in the summer of 1940, and was rewarded with promotion to the rank of Field Marshal on 19 July 1940.

Von Kluge also took part in Operation *Barbarossa*. His Fourth Army took Smolensk in July 1941, before being sent into the Ukraine. The soldiers under his command, punning on his name, nicknamed him *'Klug Hans'* – 'Clever Hans'. Three months later, he was ordered to attack Moscow. However, following a counterattack by the Red Army, the operation came to a halt in December 1941. Von Kluge

replaced Fedor von Bock as commander of Army Group Centre at the beginning of 1942. He immediately clashed with Heinz Guderian and, with the support of Adolf Hitler, removed him as commander of the Second *Panzerarmee*.

On 27 October 1943, von Kluge was badly injured when his car overturned on the Minsk-Smolensk road. He was unable to return to duty until July 1944. Kluge soon discovered that many of the leading generals were arguing for peace negotiations with the Allies. He shared these views, but Hitler was unwilling to accept that he was on the verge of defeat. Von Kluge was now approached by Henning von Tresckow to join in the plot to overthrow Hitler. He refused, but was kept informed about the conspiracy.

After the failed July Plot, the Gestapo informed Hitler of their suspicions that Kluge was now unreliable. On 16 August 1944, Hitler sent a letter to von Kluge in France, suggesting that he came back to Germany for a rest. On his way back to Germany, he ordered his driver to divert to the site of the Franco-Prussian battlefield of Metz, where he committed suicide on 18 August.

Army Group Centre under von Kluge consisted of the Ninth Army under *Generaloberst* Model. Model commanded three Panzer Corps, the XLI (General of *Panzertruppen* Harpe), XLVI (General of Infantry Zorn), and XLVII (General of *Panzertruppen* Lemeisen). There were two Army Corps, the XX (General of Infantry von Roman) and XXIII (General of Infantry Freissner). The Army Group was supported by *Luftflotte* VI under Colonel-General Greim, made up of the 1st Air Division commanded by Lieutenant-General Deichmann.

Army Group South under Field Marshal von Manstein consisted of Army Detachment Kempf, which was commanded by General of *Panzertruppen* Kempf, and the Fourth *Panzerarmee* under *Generalleutnant* Hoth. The Kempf group was made up of the III Panzer Corps (General of *Panzertruppen* Breith), the XI Army Corps (General of *Panzertruppen* Raus) and the XLII Army Corps (General of Infantry Mattenklott). The Fourth *Panzerarmee* had the

Opposite: Field Marshals von Kluge (left) and Model confer. Both veterans of World War I have the wound badge and Iron Cross from that conflict. Though a good soldier, Kluge was also a realist and realized by 1943 that Germany was doomed to lose the war.

powerful II *SS-Panzerkorps* (*SS-Obergruppenführer* Hausser), the XLVIII Panzer Corps (General of *Panzertruppen* von Knobelsdorff) and the LII Army Corps (General of Infantry Ott). *Luftflotte* IV under General Dessioch was assigned to support the Army Group.

The *Leibstandarte Adolf Hitler*, commanded by *SS-Brigadeführer* Wisch, was again part of the II *SS-Panzerkorps* and assigned the right flank while the elite *Wehrmacht* Panzer division *Großdeutschland* commanded by Lieutenant-General Hoernlein was part of the XLVIII Panzer Corps. The *schwere Panzerkompanie* of the *LAH* had 12 Tigers ready for the assault, which, coupled with all the other Tiger tanks in Fourth *Panzerarmee*, made for 100 Tiger E models in the area. The total number of tanks for the *SS-Panzerkorps* was 425, with 110 assault guns.

Leibstandarte strength was 12 Tigers, 72 PzKpfw IV, 16 PzKpfw III and II and 31 assault guns. As part of the Fourth *Panzerarmee*, Hoth had the heavy tank unit s.Pz.Abt. 503, which had been brought up to full strength with 45 Tigers ready for the attack. Among its ranks was the 21-year-old Kurt Knispel, gunner of a Tiger commanded by *Unteroffizier* Rippl. With a total of 162 kills, he would become one of the top German tank soldiers of World War II.

Above: Overheating problems dogged the German Panther Ausf D when it went into action at Kursk, and many were lost due to mechanical failures. It was a good design and once the defects had been resolved, the tank proved to be one of the best of the war.

Opposite: Waffen-SS soldiers scan the windows of the apartment blocks near Red Square in Kharkov in March 1943. As the fighting at Stalingrad in 1942 had demonstrated, some buildings could be turned into natural fortresses with extensive cellars and strong walls.

The plan drafted by Zeitzler was not as ambitious as *Barbarossa* and 'Case Blue', the big offensives of 1941 and 1942. Hitler saw it as an operation that would give Germany psychological leverage after Stalingrad, and would 'light a bonfire' to impress the world and also possibly intimidate the Soviet high command. It received a mixed reception from those senior officers who would be closely involved with its implementation. Guderian feared that the new Panther tanks

were not ready for operational deployment and that a major tank battle would deplete carefully husbanded tanks and armoured vehicles. He felt that they should be held back in anticipation of a major landing by the Allies in the west. Both Field Marshal Manstein and Colonel-General Model felt that an attack on the Kursk salient was too obvious a move and would have been anticipated by the Soviets. Field Marshal von Kluge, however, was in favour of launching *Zitadelle*.

Below: The Tiger with its tough armour and powerful gun was a real threat to the Soviet T-34/76. It could engage them at long range. The Tiger crews were carefully selected and well trained and consequently produced several Panzer aces in the East.

On 19 April, Hitler issued Operational Order Nr. 6 from 4/15 (Nr. 430246/43). It read: 'I have decided, as soon as the weather allows, to conduct Operation "Citadel" as the first strike of this year. This attack has decisive significance. It must be executed quickly. It must seize the initiative for us this spring and summer. Therefore, all preparations must be conducted with great circumspection and energy. The best formations, the best weapons, the best commanders, large amounts of ammunition must be committed on the main effort…The victory of Kursk must be a beacon to the world.'

ULTRA AND 'LUCY'

One of the great triumphs of Bletchley Park, where German Enigma messages were decoded, was the interception of the coded radio signals about the plans for *Zitadelle*. These were passed to the Soviet Union through the 'Lucy' spy ring in Switzerland. The spy ring was operated by a Hungarian named Sandor Rado, who was assisted by Rudolf Rössler, a Bavarian journalist with strong Protestant convictions. As

Opposite: Field Marshal Model (left) confers with a tank commander who has been awarded the Knight's Cross. Model believed in leading from the front and was an expert in juggling limited resources to fight withdrawals in both the Eastern and Western Fronts.

early as the late 1930s, Rössler had been cultivating a cadre of young officers, mostly from aristocratic backgrounds, in the *Abwehr* (the German Armed Forces counterintelligence department), who were to have unrestricted access to Hitler's top-secret plans for his invasion of the Soviet Union. Under cover of his work as a rare book and documents dealer in Lucerne, Switzerland, he transmitted reams of intelligence received from Berlin prior to and throughout the war. (With his Swiss radio operator, he transmitted from a moving van to avoid detection.) Had Stalin not initially rejected Rössler's reams of infallible intelligence on Hitler's *blitzkrieg* plans for the USSR (he distrusted and disdained spies who did not demand money), the German invasion could have turned out disastrously for Hitler long before Stalingrad.

FIELD MARSHAL WALTHER MODEL

Walther Model, the son of a musician, was born in Genthin, Germany, on 24 January 1891. He joined the Imperial German Army and during World War I won both classes of the Iron Cross. After the war, Model remained in the army and in 1930 was appointed head of the War Ministry's technical warfare section. As a young officer, he made a name for himself when he published a book on the Prussian General von Gneisenau. A great supporter of mechanized warfare, Model was placed in charge of the department responsible for creating new and improved weapons.

Model was sympathetic to the policies of Adolf Hitler and the Nazi Party and he was accused of favouring officers who shared his political beliefs. In 1939, Model took part in the invasion of Poland and he served under Ernst Busch in the Sixteenth Army in the Western Offensive during 1940. The following year, he served under Heinz Guderian during Operation *Barbarossa* and in October 1941, Model was promoted to commander of XLI Panzer Corps.

On 14 January 1942, Model was transferred to the Ninth Army. Under attack from Soviet partisans, Model asked Hitler for a panzer corps to help protect his troops. Hitler's refusal led to a heated argument and Model told him that a commander at the front was in a better position to develop strategy than people in the rear studying maps. Hitler, who

respected Model as a soldier, eventually gave in and gave him the troops he demanded.

Despite such disagreements, Model was promoted to general in February 1942. While retreating from the Soviet Union in 1943, he gave orders for the systematic destruction of towns and their populations, thus earning the label of war criminal. In March 1944, he replaced Erich von Manstein as Commander in Chief in the Soviet Union. With his distinctive monocle and cap worn at a rakish angle, he developed a reputation as a skilled defensive fighter, earning the nickname 'the Führer's Fireman'. As a result, he was posted to France in 1944 to halt the Allied breakout from Normandy. However, after 18 days, Hitler had second thoughts and Model lost his command to Gerd von Rundstedt.

Model was sent to command Army Group B in Holland and Belgium, where he managed to halt the Allied advance. In October 1944, he joined Hasso von Manteuffel in the Ardennes Offensive. In 1945, Model and what was left of his troops had to defend the Ruhr. Once again, he clashed with Adolf Hitler, who refused to let him retreat to the Rhine. Aware that he would be tried as a war criminal if he surrendered, and trapped with 325,000 German troops in the Ruhr pocket, he shot himself in a wood near Duisburg on 21 April 1945.

The detailed high-grade material on the proposed Kursk offensive came through the 'Lucy' ring from the ULTRA team at Bletchley Park. The spy ring was a convenient way of filtering this information to the Soviet Union, which was not privy to the code-breaking operation in Britain. Until details of the ULTRA operation became public in the 1970s, the 'Lucy' ring was assumed to have had contacts with senior officers deep inside the OKW. Unknown to the British and Americans, however, the Soviet Union had their own direct line to Bletchley Park and, in John Cairncross, a man inside the top-secret establishment itself. The ULTRA information would give the Red Army a massive advantage.

NEW GERMAN TANKS

For *Zitadelle*, the Germans brought up a total of 900,000 men and 2700 tanks and armoured vehicles, including Tigers and Panthers, to the northern and southern shoulders of the salient. They were supported by some 1700 *Luftwaffe* fighters and bombers in the IV and VI *Luftflotten*. The attack on the left flank would be supported by 700 aircraft and that from the south by 1000.

Kursk would be the operational debut of the Panther tank. The PzKpfw V Ausf D Panther had been rushed into action from the production lines of Maschinenfabrik Augsburg-Nurnburg (MAN) and many suffered from mechanical

breakdowns and problems with their tracks. Very much the brainchild of General Guderian, the Panther was designed to combat the T-34 that had outclassed the PzKpfw IV in Russia. MAN completed the first Panthers in September 1942. In all, 5508 Panthers were built, but initial production rates were very slow, only 12 being produced each week. The Panther was 8.86m (29ft) long, had a crew of five and was armed with a 7.5cm (2.9in) KwK42 gun and one co-axial 7.92mm (0.312in) machine gun. Later marks of the Panther had a hull machine gun and one on an AA mount by the commander's hatch.

Armour was between 30mm and 110mm (1.2–4.3in) and weighed 43.69 tons (48.2 tonnes). The Maybach HI230 P30 700hp petrol engine produced a top road speed of 55km/h (34.1mph) and range of 177km (110 miles). In after-action analysis at the end of the war, the US Army estimated that it took five M4 Shermans or nine T-34s to knock out a single Panther. After Kursk, the Soviet Army equipped whole regiments with captured Panthers, and after World War II these tanks were also used by the French Army.

The *Panzerjäger* Tiger (P) *Elefant* – 'Elephant' – SP antitank gun would also go into action at Kursk for the first time. It had been the loser in the competition to design the Tiger, so the chassis that had been built were converted into huge self-propelled antitank guns. It was armed with the

Below: The Sturmpanzer IV Brummbär *had been developed in the light of experience at Stalingrad. It put the short barrelled 15cm (6in)* Sturmhaubitze *in a fully armoured compartment, which protected the crew from air bursts and small arms' fire – a major threat in open-topped SP guns.*

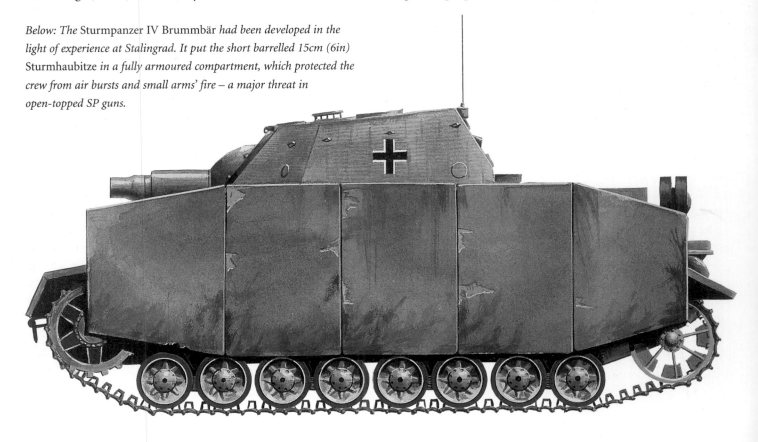

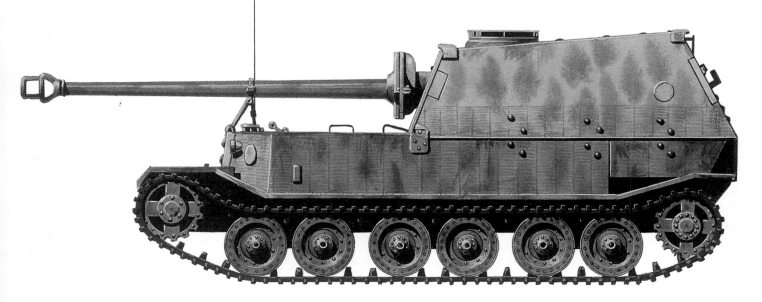

powerful 8.8cm (3.1in) Pak 43/2/L/71 gun, but had no hull machine gun and so was incredibly vulnerable to Soviet infantry. The vehicle was known as the 'Ferdinand' after its designer Ferdinand Porsche. Some *Elefants* were later fitted with a hull machine gun and used in a semi-static role in Italy. Armour protection for the crew of five was between 25mm and 100mm (1–3.94in) and it weighed 63.9 tons (70.4 tonnes). The slab-sided hull stood 2.99m (9ft 10in) high and was 8.12m (26ft 8in) long. The Two Maybach HL 120 TRM 12-cylinder petrol engines produced 530hp and a road speed of 20.1km/h (12.5mph) and range of 153km (95 miles). As with Tiger tanks, the Ferdinand heavy tank destroyers were assigned to a separate regiment, comprising two battalions. *Jagdpanzer Regiment* 656 had *PzJagAbt.* 653, commanded by Major Steinwachs, and *PzJagAbt.* 654, under Major Noak. The vehicles were all dark yellow with heavy sprayed lines of olive green, and carried three-digit numbers in white to denote the battery, section and vehicle.

The Ferdinands of *PzJagAbt.* 654 also displayed a white N on the front left mudguard, denoting their battalion commander. During Operation *Zitadelle*, the Ferdinands were to be used as break-through tanks, a role for which they were completely unsuited. Several *Panzergrenadierere* were carried with each vehicle for protection against Soviet tank-killer infantry, but they were fully exposed and often unable to fight effectively from moving vehicles. Furthermore, the chassis was very vulnerable to mines, as the loss of even one set of wheels rendered the *Elefant* immobile, and many damaged vehicles had to be abandoned.

The fighting in Stalingrad had identified the need for a powerful armoured, close support vehicle to destroy enemy

Above: Designed by engineer Ferdinand Porsche, the Ferdinand, or Elefant, was his ideal fighting vehicle – a big gun that had plenty of armour. It was, in fact, very vulnerable to attack at close range by infantry since it lacked a machine gun.

bunkers and fortifications. To meet this requirement, the Vomag factory at Plauen produced between 1943 and 1944 some 313 StuPz 43, or *Sturmpanzer IV Brummbär* – 'Brown Bear' – or *Sturmhaubitze 43 L/12 auf Fgst PzKpfw IV (Sf) SdKfz 166*. This was a distinctively different vehicle with a high silhouette and a boxlike fighting compartment for the crew of five. The main armament, the 15cm (6in) *Sturmhaubitze L/12*, was in a ball mounting and the vehicle carried 38 rounds. It used the PzKpfw IV F, G, H and J chassis. The sides were protected by *Schürzen* – armoured 'skirts'. The vehicle armour arrangement changed in later models, consisting of two plates at the front instead of one.

The *Hummel*, or 'Bumble Bee', SP gun was a hybrid of PzKpfw III and PzKpfw IV hulls. It was part of the organic artillery support for formations like the 20th Panzer Division. Well over 600 were built between 1942 and 1944 and the 7.17m (23ft 6in) long self-propelled gun with its 15cm (6in) sFH 18 howitzer, was popular with its six- or seven-man crews, having plenty of room and 18 rounds of ready-use ammunition. Some 150 were converted as ammunition carriers since wheeled vehicles could not keep pace with the tracked SP guns. The Maybach V-12 petrol engine developed 265hp, giving a road speed of 42km/h (26mph) and a range of 215km (134 miles).

The *Panzergrenadiere* would ride into battle in the superb *mittlerer Schützen-Panzerwagen Typ HL SdKfz 251* half-track.

The design work for the superb SdKfz 251 began in 1935 and by the time the Ausf D model had been introduced in 1943, a total of 2650 had been built by Borgward and Hanomag. It was a popular and versatile vehicle, though access to the engines was difficult. It was used as a platform for support weapons, as well as a command vehicle and ambulance, with 22 special-purpose variants being built. It was the inspiration for the American M3 half-track. With a crew of two and a ten-man infantry squad, the armament for the half-track consisted of one or two 7.92mm (0.3in) machine guns. Armour protection ranged from 8mm to 12mm (0.31–0.47in) and the 5.8m (19ft) long vehicle weighed 7.93 tons (8.74 tonnes). The Maybach HL42 TUKRM 120bhp petrol engine produced a top road speed of 53km/h (33mph) and a range of 300km (185 miles).

SOVIET DEFENCES

The attack at Kursk was first scheduled to begin on 4 May 1943 but was then rescheduled for 4 July. Even Hitler was starting to suffer from 'cold feet' and confessed that he was worried that the operation would not achieve the same level of surprise enjoyed in offensives in previous years.

Manstein had urged that the operation be launched in May since he anticipated that there would be a shift to the strategic balance in the West. Writing about Hitler's decision, Manstein noted that by June the *Führer* 'hoped our armoured divisions would be stronger still after being fitted out with new tanks. He stuck to his decision even after it was pointed out to him that unfavourable developments in Tunisia could mean that if "Citadel" were put off any longer, there would be a danger of its coinciding with an enemy landing on the Continent. Nor would he recognize that the longer one waited, the more armour the Soviets would have – particularly as their tank output undoubtedly exceeded that of Germany'.

Hitler was wrong to delay and right to be worried. To counter the anticipated attack, STAVKA, the Soviet High Command, planned to reinforce the two Fronts holding the salient, and had deployed 13,000 guns, 6000 antitank guns, 1000 *Katyusha* multiple rocket-launchers, 3300 tanks, 2560 aircraft and 1,337,000 troops. These were built into a sophisticated defensive system that would become a steel breakwater against the wave of Panzers.

Right: During the short-lived liberation of Kharkov in March 1943, Soviet T-34/76Ds drive through Dzerzhinsky Square. Soldiers on the rear deck are enjoying the warmth from the engine as well as providing local protection. The turret is fitted with grab rails for these tank riders.

Above: Junkers Ju 87D-3 Stukas move into formation to launch an attack. By 1943, the slow-moving bombers were vulnerable to Soviet fighters and AA fire; however, where the Luftwaffe *achieved local air superiority they could provide superb support to ground troops.*

As early as 8 April, Marshal Zhukov and the STAVKA Chief of Staff Marshal Aleksandr Vasilevsky had drafted plans to fight a defensive battle to break the impetus of the anticipated German summer attack. It took four days to convince Stalin that a defensive action would be the most effective strategy. The Soviet Fronts would then launch Operations *Kutuzov* and *Rumyantsev*, massive counterattacks to the north and south, using men and tanks held in reserve. Opposing the German forces were the Soviet Central Front, led by General Konstantin K. Rokossovsky, and the Voronezh Front, led by General Nikolai F. Vatutin. The Central Front, with the right wing strengthened by Lieutenant-General Nikolai P. Pukhov's Thirteenth Army and Lieutenant-

General I.V. Galinin's Seventeenth Army, was to defend the northern sector.

To the south, the Voronezh Front faced the German Army Group South with three armies and two in reserve. The Sixth Guards Army, led by Lieutenant-General Mikhail N. Chistyakov, and the Seventh Guards Army, led by Lieutenant-General M. S. Shumilov, held the centre and left wing. East of Kursk, Colonel-General Ivan S. Konev's Steppe Military District (renamed Steppe Front on 10 July 1943) was to hold any German breakthroughs and then mount the counteroffensive.

ORGANIZATION

Soviet tactical defences at Kursk included a series of defensive positions and belts occupied by rifle companies, battalions, regiments, divisions and corps that were linked together by engineer measures and tied in with the supporting fires of antitank and anti-aircraft artillery; and tactically employed armoured battalions, regiments and brigades, backed up by infantry and armoured operational reserves. Engineer measures glueing the entire defensive structure together had been mandated by April 1943 Instructions on the Construction of Field Defences, issued by the General Staff on the basis of analysis of war experiences. The instructions required the creation of battalion defensive regions, linked together by elaborate trench systems and laced with antitank defences, as the basis for each defensive belt. The tactical defence zone contained two defensive belts. The first (main) defensive belt consisted of three defensive positions, cutoff positions (switch lines), and artillery firing positions occupied by the rifle corps' first-echelon rifle division. The battalion defensive region, with a 2km (1.25 mile) frontage and a depth of 1.5–2km (0.93–1.25 miles), provided the basis for the three defensive positions. In turn, the battalion region was subdivided into company and platoon strongpoints.

The first defensive position, designated to engage the enemy in front of the defences and to absorb the first enemy blows, involved the most thorough engineer preparation. It consisted of two to three trench lines and communication trenches, interspersed with engineer obstacles, and was occupied by the two first-echelon rifle battalions of first-echelon rifle regiments. Infantry and heavy weapons in the second and third trenches, located 150–250m (104–271 yards) and 1–1.5km (0.62–0.93 miles) from the first trench respectively, provided covering fires for trenches to their front and gave depth to the battalion defensive region.

The second-echelon rifle battalion of the first-echelon rifle regiment occupied the second defensive position that consisted of one or two trenches 2–3km (1.25–1.86 miles) from the forward edge of the battlefield. Deployed in company strongpoints or in battalion defensive regions, troops of the second defensive position covered those in the first position, contained supporting artillery and tanks, and provided a base from which to launch local counterattacks. Second-echelon rifle regiments of first-echelon rifle divisions manned the third defensive position that was composed of one or two trenches 4–6km (2.5–3.7 miles) from the forward edge of the battlefield. The division reserve formed in the third defensive position or nearby.

The third position, although less fortified than the first two, provided a basis for new defence lines against penetrating enemy forces, contained additional fire support and provided a region from which to launch counterattacks. Cutoff positions, normally running diagonally or perpendicularly to the front, consisted of one or two trenches and served as interior defensive lines or routes for redeployment of forces between sectors. They also covered the flanks of defending units and threatened the flanks of penetrating enemy units.

The second defensive belt was less well prepared by the engineers than the first, and was located 10–15km (6.3–9.3 miles) from the first belt. The second-echelon rifle divisions of the rifle corps occupied the second defensive belt and were tasked with preventing enemy units that had penetrated the first belt from advancing into the operational rear of the defence. In addition, the second defensive belt covered the manoeuvre into combat of forces from the rear and provided another base from which to launch

THE FOURTH MAN

John Cairncross, born on 25 July 1913, was a British intelligence officer during World War II who, along with four other men (Kim Philby, Donald Maclean, Guy Burgess and Anthony Blunt), passed secrets to the Soviet Union during the war. This group became known as the Cambridge Five.

Cairncross was educated at Glasgow University and Trinity College, Cambridge, where he studied modern languages. After graduating, he worked in the Foreign Office. Like many men of his generation, he was an anti-Fascist idealist and in 1937 he joined the Communist party. In 1942, he worked on ciphers at Bletchley Park and MI6. During this time, he passed documents to the USSR through a KGB officer at the Soviet Embassy in London. Since Cairncross worked in the hut in Bletchley that intercepted *Luftwaffe* signals, he was able to provide the complete *Luftwaffe* order of battle and plans for Kursk.

Cairncross admitted to spying in 1951 after the British counter-intelligence service MI5 found incriminating papers in his possession. He was never prosecuted, however, which later led to charges that the government engaged in a conspiracy to cover up his role. Indeed, the identity of the infamous 'fifth man' in the Cambridge Five remained a mystery until 1990, when KGB defectors Yuri Modin and Oleg Gordievsky fingered Cairncross.

After his confession, Cairncross moved to Rome, where he worked for the United Nations Food and Agricultural Organization until he retired to the south of France. He insisted that the ULTRA intelligence passed by him to the USSR did not harm the UK and that by passing it directly he helped to save lives and hasten the end of the war. He died on 8 October 1995.

Above: In a rather staged photograph, Soviet T-34s with supporting infantry emerge from a wood. The soldiers in this picture have been identified as NKVD troops tasked with policing the rear areas and ensuring that they were clear of hostile partisans and deserters.

counterattacks. The depth of the second defensive belt forced the enemy, after overcoming the first belt, to regroup its forces and disperse its artillery prior to engaging the defenders of the second defensive belt.

MINES

The elaborate trench system provided increased security to rifle forces, improved the durability of the defence and provided for freer manoeuvre of forces during combat. Engineer preparation of the battlefield also inhibited movement of the enemy – in particular, the armoured units. Antitank obstacles reinforced the natural barriers available, and liberal use of mines further threatened enemy personnel and tanks alike. A July 1943 STAVKA order prescribed the laying of mines to the depth of the defence integrated with defensive fires of the infantry and artillery, with emphasis on main attack avenues into defensive positions. Specifically, the

order required that mines be employed in groups of over 100 mines, sown 6–10m (20–30ft) apart in unequal rows. The rows themselves were to be 15–40m (50–130ft) apart but not parallel. Accordingly, the minefields at Kursk achieved densities of 1700 anti-personnel mines and 1500 antitank mines per kilometre (0.6 miles) of front, four times that at Moscow, and two to five times the amount used at Stalingrad. The highest density of mines was forward of and within the first defensive position.

Thus at Kursk, each battalion defensive region of the 25th Guards Rifle Corps (of Seventh Guards Army) had an average 1.6km (1 mile) of barbed wire covering its position, and 1000 antitank mines emplaced per kilometre (0.6 miles) of their defensive frontage. On Thirteenth Army's 81st Rifle Division's front, the 1000 antitank mines laid accounted for the destruction or disabling of 17 of the 40 enemy tanks that took part in the initial German assault. The minefields were designed to channel the German tanks towards the antitank guns, and if they broke through one layer of defences, there was another behind it. However, Soviet antitank mines were not as sophisticated or mechanically reliable as the German *Tellermine*.

The *Tellermine* – literally 'plate mine' because of its flat cylindrical appearance – was also known as the T-Mine and was the standard German antitank mine. During the war, four versions were produced, the *Tellermine 43 (Pilz)* – 'Mushroom', the *Tellermine 1942*, the *Tellermine 35* and the *Tellermine 29*. They weighed 8.6kg (19lb) of which 5kg (11lb) was the TNT filling. T-Mines operated under a pressure of 108.9–181kg (240–400lbs). The casing had threaded slots to take anti-handling pull switches like the *Zugzünder 35*, which operated on a pull of between 4kg and 5.8kg (9–13lbs) and would detonate the mine if lifted by hand. The *Entlastungszünder 44* pressure-release device, containing 226g (8oz) of TNT-PETN, could be positioned beneath the mine. It required a weight of 4.5kg (10lbs) to hold it safely in the armed position. Soviet sappers would often dig up and re-bury these mines for use against their original owners. The less reliable Soviet mines included the metal TM/39, which weighed 5.1kg (11.25lbs) and contained 3.6kg (8lbs)

Above: A lightly camouflaged 76.2mm (0.3in) gun is brought into action. The Soviet soldier on the left has the M1936 helmet based on a Swiss design while the other crew members have the M1940 helmet. All are armed with the rugged PPSh submachine gun.

of TNT, and was 220mm (8.6in) long and wide, and 80mm (3.1in) high. The wooden T-IV weighed 4.2kg (9lbs) with a filling of Amatol or Dynamon. It was 215mm (8.5in) long and wide and 100mm (4in) deep. The firing pressure for both mines was between 200kg and 700kg (441–1544lbs).

Some anti-personnel mines consisted of a demolition charge in a waterproof box with a simple mechanism like a VPF pull or MV-5 pressure switch. The pull or load that would operate these switches could be very small and consequently they might be set off by a man. The Soviet philosophy was that if a mine virtually vaporized a soldier this would be bad for enemy morale – however, it made laying mines particularly hazardous for Soviet sappers.

Above: General I. Konev (right) confers with General P. Rotmistrov, commander of the 5th Guards Tank Army. The camouflaged command post dug in close to the front line was typical of the style of forward command favoured by both Soviet and German commanders.

The mines would prove an effective obstacle. In July 1943, the commander of *sPzAbt.* 505, *Hauptmann* Graf Kageneck, reported the problems with mines and poor tactical handling that his scattered unit encountered:

'III.Panzer Korps reported the loss of 13 Tigers in one Kompanie that had started out with 14 Tigers on the morning of 5 July 1943. Nine Tigers fell out due to mine damage. It would take two or three days to repair each one of them. The reason for this extraordinarily high loss rate from mines was: From the start, there wasn't a single map available showing the location of mines that had been laid by the German units in front of the bridgehead. Two completely contradictory mine plans were available, and both were incorrect. Therefore, two Tigers ran onto our own mines directly after setting off. Another two Tigers hit mines during further advances across terrain that was shown on the map to be free of mines.

'Mine clearing was sloppily conducted, so that three additional Tigers fell out due to mines after being shown supposedly mine-free gaps. After this, 120 mines were lifted from an area shown on the map to be free of mines.

'The eighth Tiger drove onto mines when it attempted to move into position against an enemy tank attack reported on the left flank. Eight Tigers fell out for two or three days as a result of carelessness or tactically incorrect employment. Therefore, during the period they were not available for their actual purpose, fighting enemy tanks and heavy weapons.'

SOVIET ARTILLERY

Artillery of all types and calibres made the defence resilient and produced the necessary attrition in enemy forces. Prior to Kursk, the Soviets lacked large quantities of artillery. This, when combined with a lack of skill in properly integrating artillery into defences and employing it when under assault, was a major factor for the German success in penetrating Soviet defences. By July 1943, however, new regulations, derived from the analysis of war experiences, and the improved skill of Soviet commanders produced a more effective use of artillery. The principal heavy weapons now available were the 122mm (4.8in) M 1939 and the 152mm (5.9in) M1937 howitzer.

The M1939 howitzer had a crew of eight, and fired a 21.8kg (48lb) HE shell to a maximum range of 11,800m (7.3 miles.) An experienced full-strength crew could fire five to six rounds a minute. The M1937 howitzer weighed 7.1 tons (7.8 tonnes) in action and fired a 43.6kg (96lb) shell to a maximum range of 17.265km (10.7 miles). A trained crew could keep up a rate of fire of four rounds a minute. From 1943 onwards, the gun was also mounted on the JSU-152 heavy assault gun and used against tanks and reinforced concrete emplacements.

In addition to artillery, the Soviet forces had US supplied 6 x 4 Studebaker 2-ton trucks fitted with BM-13 *Katyusha* – 'Little Katy' – 16-rail rocket launchers.

An idea of the effect of a massed bombardment is given in a description by the Soviet war correspondent Yvgeny

Below: With F-1 fragmentation and RG-42 blast grenades ready by their trench, two Soviet soldiers use the grass and crops of the Ukraine for camouflage. Small groups like this were hard to spot from a closed-down tank and were a serious threat to German AFVs.

Right: The crew of a Soviet 203mm Gaubitsa obr. 1931 prepare ammunition for use. The gun weighed 17.7 tons (19.5 tonnes) and fired a 100kg (220lb) shell to a maximum range of 18.025km (11.2 miles). A well trained crew could fire a round every four minutes.

Vorobyev: 'The air shook from the guns firing in salvos. All kept their mouths open looking like stunned fish landed on shore. And all were stunned indeed, because by its nature the human ear cannot endure so much infernal din, roar and clang…. In the south, the horizon disappeared behind a screen of smoke and earth. Kicked up by shell bursts, the black mass of earth remained hanging in mid-air in defiance of the law of gravity. Before the particles of earth thrown up from shell craters could settle, they were propelled upwards by new blasts and lumps of kicked-up earth'.

Indirect artillery fire, under control of unit commanders at each echelon, was co-ordinated with the operations of infantry and armour. Rifle corps commanders designated artillery missions and the location of corps and division

MARSHAL IVAN KONEV

Born in 1897, Ivan Stepanovich Konev, or Koniev, joined the Imperial Russian Army as a 15-year-old private. In 1918, he joined the Bolshevik Party. In the Civil War, he served as a Commissar and then joined the officer corps in 1924. Konev graduated from the Frunze Military Academy in 1926. In August 1941, he served in the Smolensk sector and then from October 1941 to 1942 Konev was Commander of the Kalinin Front, resisting the German advance on Moscow. In 1943, after Kursk, his troops recaptured Orel, Belgorod and Poltava. In 1943–44, he commanded the Steppe Front, which became the 2nd Ukrainian Front. He cut off 10 German divisions at Korsun-Shevchenko, trapping about 20,000 German troops. Konev then led the 1st Ukrainian Front that took Lvov. He advanced from the Vistula to the Oder with Marshal Zhukov and occupied Berlin. He reached the Elbe and made contact with the US forces at Torgau on 25 April 1945. His forces also liberated Prague. During the Soviet attack on Japanese forces in Manchuria in 1945, he was named commander of Soviet forces in the Far East Theatre. After the war, he was high commissioner for Austria and then succeeded Zhukov as Commander-in-Chief of Soviet ground forces and became Minister for Defence in 1955. He died in 1973.

Above: The Soviet T-34 with its well sloped armour, Christie suspension and 76mm (3in) gun combined the defining principles of a tank – protection, mobility and fire-power in exact proportions, making it an almost perfect tank. The Germans even modified captured tanks and used them on the Eastern Front.

antitank regions. The rifle division commander organized the fires of divisional weapons covering the areas immediately forward of the forward defence, the depth of the division's defences, the division's flanks, and in the gaps between units. Regimental commanders controlled regimental artillery support group fires and directed battalion fires covering the gaps in regimental defences. Battalion commanders co-ordinated the fires of organic artillery and that of subordinate rifle companies. In addition, divisional artillery participated in the artillery preparation or the counterpreparation fired under army control.

ANTITANK GUNS

Effective use of antitank guns was critical for a successful defence against *blitzkrieg* tactics. Before July 1943, Soviet antitank fire had taken a toll of enemy armour but had never halted a major offensive spearhead. The Soviets used the experiences gathered from numerous failures to build a thorough antitank defence at Kursk and thereafter. The antitank defence was based on the use of deeply echeloned antitank forces integrated into every level of command: antitank guns, mines and infantry bunkers were grouped in armour-killing grounds called *Pakfronts*. The majority of antitank units and weapons performed an active role in the defence by occupying antitank regions or strongpoints

scattered throughout the defence and massed on likely tank approaches into the defence. Other large antitank forces, supplemented by mobile obstacle detachments, served as antitank reserves at every level of command.

In their 57mm (2.24in) M1941 antitank gun, Soviet gunners had a very powerful weapon. Developed by the Soviet Main Artillery Directorate and General Grabin's design bureau, it put a new barrel for the ZiS-3 76mm divisional gun just going into service. The new barrel, 57mm (2.24in) in bore and very long at over 4m (13ft), produced high muzzle velocities and very high penetration levels for the time. Eventually, the weapon, which used tungsten-cored 'arrow' projectiles, generated a muzzle velocity of 1020m/s (3346ft/s). which could penetrate 140mm (5.5in) of armour at 500m (546 yards). It also fired a useful HE-FRAG round, and after the war, it remained in production. Over 10,000 were built, and have been encountered worldwide until recently.

Captain Nikolai Kanischev, who fought at Kursk, described in his diary the terrifying dynamics of a tank and antitank gun action. 'There is a specific point about the performance of an antitank gun which we learned from personal experience. Once it engages tanks, it cannot quit, it can only win or perish. A foot soldier or a tank may withdraw from action at practically any stage. But not the antitank gun. When the first enemy tanks appeared, we all started counting them. I personally tried several times but lost count. I began again and gave up. I remember the last time I got to something like 30. But more and more came lumbering out of the wood … were there 36 of them, or more, or less? … it no longer made much difference to us. Only when the distance between us and the tanks was 450–500 metres

[437–547 yards] did we open fire. One after another the tanks went out of commission. The enemy, apparently, never dreamed that one gun dared to engage 36 tanks and an infantry assault. No doubt they thought they had run into considerable forces. When the tanks started going out of commission, they must have been confirmed in that belief.'

THE PARTISANS

Behind the German lines, partisan groups had expanded, made up of Soviet Army soldiers who had evaded capture, local men and women, and political and military leaders who had been parachuted in. Ideally, partisans required a friendly, or at least passive, local population who would provide intelligence and food. Parachute drops at night would bring supplies of weapons and ammunition and more would be captured in ambushes and by theft. Dense woods, swamps or mountains were essential to provide safe areas in which the partisans could hide, train or nurse wounded. Successful operations were undertaken around the cities of Yelnia and Dorogobuzh east of Smolensk, where it was mostly conducted by Soviet Army stragglers.

Near the end of 1942, surviving elements of the Political Administration of the Soviet Army (PURKKA) brought the Army groups under central control. NKVD officers and Komsomol members were parachuted into occupied areas to assist PURKKA. Stalin demanded that the partisans should not become a force independent of Moscow. In 1943, the partisans began to take the war to their occupiers, concentrating on attacking road and rail links. Railways were cut and roads mined, and if the German repair teams were inadequately protected, they could also be ambushed. Farid Fazliahmetov, a partisan who became expert in minelaying and demolitions, recalled the attacks on the railways.

'To combat partisan harassment on the railways, the Germans built fortifications, laid mines around crossings, stations and bridges, and chopped down trees on both sides of the tracks. Guards mowed down people who appeared on the tracks or anywhere near them. We often watched German sappers with mine detectors and dogs moving down railway tracks, preceded by guards on both sides who also had dogs with them sometimes. What we did was lay our mines after the guards had passed. Fooling the bloodhounds was more difficult. They had been trained to nose out tolite [a compound of TNT], so they found the mines. Then we started to divert their attention by dropping little bits of melted tolite here and there. The dogs would mistake these for mines. They would then be punished for that, and start ignoring the real mines. The Germans remarked wryly: "The partisans have recruited our dogs."'

Below: Armoured warfare seen from the cockpit of a Luftwaffe Fieseler Fi 156 Storch *liaison and observation aircraft. The tanks are spread out to make them less vulnerable to air attack or artillery fire, although the open terrain allows commanders to maintain visual control.*

Above: While one man keeps guard on the bridge, a Soviet partisan prepares it for demolition. The attacks behind the German lines disrupted movement of men and supplies and caused tension and insecurity. Troops and resources were diverted from the front to protect railways and roads.

After the victory at Stalingrad, the partisans began to penetrate the Briansk region and were strong around the fringes of the Pripet marshes. Other groups infiltrated the woods and swamps towards the River Dneiper and the wooded areas of the northern Ukraine.

FINAL PREPARATIONS

The original date for the offensive to take place had been 4 May 1943, but Hitler wanted to wait for the new Panther and *Elefant* tanks to be ready, so a series of postponements followed. The next scheduled date was 12 June, but the collapse of the African front in Tunisia also delayed the start of the offensive for a further three weeks until July. On the night of 3 July, German Army sappers cleared and taped paths through some of the minefields, an extremely

dangerous business, as the ground was full of metal and the readings on detectors went into a frenzy.

This meant that the mines had to be prodded with a bayonet and lifted out and made safe by hand. Testimony to the expertise of the *Großdeutschland* engineers was the fact that 10 men of the 2nd Engineer Company on the night of 3 July lifted and made safe a total of 2700 mines, which worked out at a rate of a mine a minute by each man. On the same night, the Red Army captured a sapper of the 6th Infantry Division, Private Fermello, and he informed the Soviets of the start time of the offensive which was to be at 03:00 on 5 July. In the Belgorod sector, a Slovene sapper deserted and also told the Soviets of the date and start time of the offensive, confirming what they already knew. Igor Balabanov, quoted in *In the Heat of the Kursk Battle*, described the last hours before *Zitadelle* exploded across the steppe. 'The men did not sleep on the eve of a battle, and did all kinds of chores. They were in that tranquil frame of mind that people usually experience before a major event in their lives. They mended their clothing, made their boots fit so their feet would be comfortable, examined their weapons and shaved one another. One of the soldiers wanted to change into new underwear, but the others stopped him, saying: "What's the matter, you getting set to die?! Wait a while, there's still a lot of fighting ahead. Plenty of time for that." The old timers said to him, "Keep that underwear till victory day. You'll need it when you get home.'"

So detailed was the Soviet knowledge of the German plan for the attack at Kursk that they launched an artillery bombardment just before the German assault was due to go in and before the Germans had opened fire. In the air,

however, they enjoyed less success. At the HQ of General Hans Seidemann, who was in overall command of the two *Luftflotte* assigned to *Zitadelle*, radio monitoring units began to report a surge in air traffic, indicating that large numbers of Soviet aircraft were airborne. The German Freya 125 MHz early warning radar at Kharkov then detected the Red Air Force formations en route to attack. There was a mad scramble to get the fighters of JG 52 at Mikoyanovka got airborne. At Kharkov, the fighters of JG 53 'Udet' actually taxied through the ranks of bombers that had their engines

WAR OF THE RAILS

The high point in the partisan war against Germany consisted of two operations carried out in 1943. By that time, order had been introduced into the partisan movement; it had been 'purged' and brought under rigid central control. As a result of work by NKVD teams, the partisan movement had been taught the latest methods of warfare and the most advanced techniques of sabotage. The operation, known as the 'War of the Rails', was carried out over six weeks from August to September 1943. It was a very fortunate time to have chosen. This was the moment when the Soviet forces, which had exhausted the German army in defensive battles at Kursk, then went over to the offensive. To support the advance, a huge operation was undertaken in the rear of the enemy with the object of paralyzing his supply routes, preventing him from bringing up ammunition and fuel for the troops, and making it impossible for him to move his reserves around. The operation involved the participation of 167 partisan units with a total strength of 100,000 men. More than 150 tons (165 tonnes) of explosives, more than 150km (90 miles) of cable and over half a million detonators were transported to the partisan units by air.

The NKVD teams were instructed to maintain strict control to ensure that missions were completed. Most of them operated independently in the most dangerous and important places, and they also appointed men from their units to instruct the partisan units in the use of explosives. The 'War of the Rails' was carried out simultaneously in a territory with a front more than 1000km (620 miles) wide and more than 500km (310 miles) in depth. On the first night of the operation, 42,000 explosions took place on the railway lines, and the partisan activity increased with every night that passed. The *Ostheer* (German Army in the East) committed strong forces to defend their lines of communication. Every

night, along with the thump of explosions as bridges and railway lines were blown up, there were also the sounds of battle with the German forces as the partisans fought their way to or from their targets. According to Soviet sources, partisans in the Bryansk area alone attacked more than 400 locomotives, thousands of railway cars, seven armoured trains and nearly 1000 troop trains. They also destroyed 42 railway bridges and more than 300km (186 miles) of track. The largest partisan operation was the destruction of the strategic railway bridge near Vygonichi. In the course of the operation, a total of 836 complete trains, 184 rail and 556 road bridges were blown up. A vast quantity of enemy equipment and ammunition was also destroyed. Having won the enormous battle at Kursk, the Red Army sped towards the river Dnieper and crossed it in several places.

A second large-scale operation in support of the advancing troops was carried out in the enemy's rear under the name of 'Concert', which was in concept and spirit a continuation of the 'War of the Rails'. Operation 'Concert' began on 19 September 1943. That night, 19,903 cuts were blown in the railways in Belorussia alone. On the night of 25 September, a further 15,809 attacks were launched. All the KGB units and 193 partisan units took part in the operation 'Concert'. The total number of participants in the operation exceeded 120,000. In the course of the whole operation, which went on until the end of October, 148,557 cuts in tracks were made with explosives, several hundred trains with troops, weapons and ammunition were derailed, and hundreds of bridges were blown up.

Despite a shortage of explosives and other material needed for such work, on the eve of the operation only 80 tons (88 tonnes) of explosives could be sent to the partisans. Nevertheless 'Concert' was a tremendous success.

running, ready for take-off. 'It was a rare spectacle,' wrote Seidemann. 'Everywhere planes were burning and crashing. In no time at all, some 120 Soviet aircraft were downed. Our own losses were so small as to represent total victory, for the consequence was complete German air control in the VIII Air Corps sector'.

In the first moments of the battle, the Soviets lost 120 aircraft. By the end of the day, this had risen to 432, and twenty-four hours later it stood at 637. In this way, the Germans achieved local air superiority during the initial stages of the battle. This gave them a tactical advantage at Kursk, but the *Luftwaffe* had lost the strategic battle with the Soviet Air Force. As with tanks, once a good design had been established, factories went all out to mass-produce it. So when in the closing months of the Stalingrad campaign the newly introduced Yakovlev Yak-9 showed that it was a tough

Below: A PzKpfw VI Tiger Ausf H in a wooded concentration area behind the front lines. The tank had a 8.8cm (3.5in) gun with 92 rounds of mixed HE and APCBC ammunition. The two 7.92mm (0.3in) machine guns had 5700 rounds in 38 belts of 150 rounds.

and versatile airframe, the huge Factory No 153 in the Urals began to build it in quantity. By the close of the war, it had built 15,000 of the 30,000 Yak-9s.

ONE MAN'S WAR

The fighting at Kursk produced its quota of heroes whose careers are well documented. Less well known is the story of the *Landsers*, the German 'Squaddies' or 'Grunts', the ordinary soldiers who fought and died in this major action. Drawing on the information recorded in his *Wehrpass*, or paybook, G. Tankard has pieced together the story of a 19-year-old *Gefreiter* (Corporal) named Heinz Klostermeyer. The son of a lathe operator, he was born in Lerbach, near Hildesheim, on 12 January 1924 and trained as a machine fitter. With the armaments industry now working under increasing pressure, he was probably in a secure civilian job, but he apparently volunteered for the army in October 1942. Although the *Wehrpass* states he was initially called up, he joined the replacement unit of *Panzergrenadier-Division Großdeutschland (GD)*, which was strictly an all-volunteer formation. He remained with 4.*(M.G.)/ Inf. Ers. Regt. GD*

THE SOVIET SOLDIER

Major-General Friedrich von Mellenthin, who served during the war in Europe, North Africa and the Soviet Union, provides a trenchant analysis of the fighting at Kursk and the performance of the Soviet troops who fought there. There is a certain national arrogance in the comments written in the mid-1950s at the height of the Cold War.

'Experience shows that the Russian soldier has an almost incredible ability to stand up to the heaviest artillery fire and air-bombardment, while the Russian Command remains unmoved by the bloodiest losses caused by shelling and bombs, and ruthlessly adheres to its pre-conceived plans. Russian lack of reaction to even the heaviest shelling was proved though not explained during Operation *Zitadelle*...

The stoicism of the majority of Russian soldiers and their mental sluggishness make them quite insensible to losses. The Russian soldier values his own life no more than those of his comrades...without so much as twinkling an eyelid, he stolidly continues the attack or stays put in the position he has been told to defend. Life is not precious to him. He is immune to the most incredible hardships, and does not appear to notice them; he seems equally indifferent to bombs and shells...

Russian indifference to bombardment is not new; it was apparent during the First World War and Caulaincourt comments on it in his description of the battle of Borodino in 1812...

Regarding Russian officers in command, it is as well to know that:

a) in almost every situation and every case, they strictly and rigidly adhere to orders or to previous decisions. They disregard changes in the situation, the reactions of the enemy, and losses of their own troops. Naturally this attitude has serious drawbacks, but it brings certain compensations.

b) they have at their disposal almost inexhaustible resources of human material to replace casualties. The Russian Command can afford high losses and ignores them.'

A Russian soldier confided his observations of his comrades and their characteristics to his diary during the war.

'First state: soldier with no chiefs around. He is a grumbler. He threatens and shows off. He is keen to pocket something or grab someone in a stupid argument. One can see from this irritability that the soldier's life is hard for him.

Second state: soldier in the presence of chiefs: submissive and inarticulate. Readily agrees with what he is told. Easily believes promises. Blossoms when praised and is eager to admire the strictness of officers whom he makes fun of behind their backs.

Third state: working together or in battle: here he is a hero. He won't leave his comrade in danger. He dies quietly, as if it is still part of his work.'

until the beginning of February 1943, when he left for Russia. He arrived at *Großdeutschland* at the end of February and was assigned to 2./ *Gren. Regt. GD*, part of the half-track equipped 1st Battalion. This battalion was commanded by Major Otto Remer, an ardent Nazi, who would later win the Knights Cross with Oak Leaves and who commanded the GD unit in Berlin that foiled the plot to overthrow Hitler in 1944.

The division was in the Ukraine as part of *Korps Raus*, Army Detachment Kempf. It had recently seen extremely heavy fighting in halting the Soviet drive to the west of Kharkov. Just as Klostermeyer arrived, the division was being pulled out of the line and was moving to Poltava, where it was to be rested and replenished. Klostermeyer was obviously part of the reinforcements sent from Germany to make up for the recent losses. After just over a week of rest, *Großdeutschland* moved back into the line in preparation for the German counteroffensive to recapture Kharkov. In this

sector, the offensive began on 5 March 1943 at 05:00. Klostermeyer's battalion was to play an important part in the coming offensive.

As it was the only half-track mounted battalion in the division, it was the only infantry formation able to keep pace with the division's armour across the snowy terrain. The division easily brushed aside the Soviet forces and quickly advanced to the north east of Kharkov. Whilst the *Waffen-SS* panzer divisions recaptured Kharkov itself, *Großdeutschland* pushed on past the city towards Tomarovka. Here the counteroffensive was halted by 23 March, more by mud and exhaustion than Soviet resistance. In less than two weeks, the Soviet forces around Kharkov had been thrown back or destroyed and the city recaptured. German infantry divisions arrived and relieved *Großdeutschland* in its defensive positions. The division was then withdrawn to the Akhtyrka area for a well-earned rest and refit.

BM-13 *KATYUSHA*

The BM-13, which began development in 1933, was a 16-rail 132mm (5.19in) multiple rocket launcher. The use of rockets in a surface-to-surface role had been examined by a team of engineers led by Petropavlovsk at the Leningrad Gas Dynamics Laboratory. He died in 1935, but the research continued under A. Kostikov, and the weapon initially known as Kostikov's Gun, or the BM-13, was mounted on a Zis-5 truck and first test-fired in March 1941. The results were so impressive that an order was signed in June for mass production to start.

The BM-13 mounting was soon switched to the Zis-6 truck because of the added stability offered by the dual rear wheels. Later variants were mounted on Lend-Lease US-built 6 x 4 2?-ton Studebaker trucks (BM-13N). They were also mounted on old T-60 hulls. The first successful combat use occurred at Orsa, near Smolensk, on 7 July 1941, where their salvos caused great panic among the Germans troops.

Soviet soldiers called it *Katyusha* –'Little Katy' – after 'Katerina', a popular song composed by Isakovskiy. The BM-13 could deliver a terrifying punch and operated with a distinctive howl – a metallic sound generated at launch as the rockets left their rails, which earned it the nickname 'Stalin's Organ' among German soldiers.

The rails for the M13 launcher were 487.7cm (192in) long and could be elevated to 45° and traversed 10° or 20° according to the chassis. The standard Soviet MP41 mortar dial sight was used for aiming. They were aimed by aligning the vehicle in the direction of fire and then adjusting the rocket rack up or down with the hydraulic ram for range.

Initially the rockets were armed with high explosive (HE) warheads, but armour-piercing, illumination, incendiary and signalling rockets were introduced later. The rockets had an 18.5kg (41lb) warhead and, travelling at 355m/s (1165ft/s), had a maximum range of 8500m (5.28 miles). The 7.08kg (15.6lb) of propellant was probably solventless cordite, but there are also references to Soviet munitions factories using black powder.

For the next three months, while Operation *Zitadelle* was being planned and organized, the division remained in the same area, preparing itself for its role in the offensive. At the beginning of July, the division moved into its jump-off positions to the west of Belgorod, where it formed part of XLVIII Panzer Corps, Fourth *Panzerarmee*. In order to capture a series of ridges in front of the main Soviet defences, Fourth *Panzerarmee* launched a series of a reconnaissance-in-force operations at 16:00 on 4 July, the day before the actual offensive began.

In *Großdeutschland*'s sector, this was undertaken by a number of its infantry battalions. After several hours of fighting, the Soviet battalion-sized outposts were eliminated and the main force of *Großdeutschland* then moved up in preparation for the next day. At 05:00, advancing on a frontage of only 3km (1.9 miles), Klostermeyer's division attacked towards the fortified village of Cherkasskoe, defended by 67th Guards Rifle Division. The tanks supporting the attack ran into concealed minefields and massed antitank fire in front of the village and, unsupported, *Grenadier-Regiment GD*'s sister infantry regiment, *Füsilier-Regiment GD*, suffered heavy casualties as it attempted to press home their attack on the right flank of the village.

Grenadier-Regiment GD, Klostermeyer's regiment, fared better. After expelling a Soviet battalion from Butovo, a village on the road to Cherkasskoe, they broke into the trench systems directly in front of Cherkasskoe and, in extremely heavy fighting, cleared them by 09:15. They then advanced into the village itself and throughout the rest of the day were engaged in fierce fighting for it. By late afternoon, the village was almost entirely in German hands. With the fall of Cherkasskoe, the Soviet first line of defence had been breached and the Germans prepared for a renewal of the offensive on 6 July.

In order to allow themselves time to reorganize, the German attack did not begin until mid-morning. After a 90-minute artillery bombardment, XLVIII Panzer Corps moved forward and quickly routed what remained of the defenders of the first defensive belt. *Großdeutschland* advanced to the northeast through open country to engage the second Soviet defensive line. Klostermeyer's battalion, riding in its armoured half tracks, formed the vanguard together with the tanks of *Panzer-Regiment GD*. The Soviet defences consisted of deep bunkers, dug-in T34s, minefields, flame-throwers and trench systems.

They were also excellently camouflaged. Throughout the afternoon, the men of I./ *Grenadier-Regiment GD* fought their way through the Soviet defences, trying to clear a path for the tanks, which had suffered heavy losses. By early evening, they had captured Hill 247.2 near Dubrova. Here, in the midst of the Soviet defences, together with the tanks, they took up all-round defence in a 'hedgehog' defensive position. Other units of *Großdeutschland* closed up during the night in preparation for a renewal of the attack the next day.

On the morning of 7 July, *Großdeutschland* struck out northwest towards Sirtsev, with *Grenadier-Regiment GD* accompanied by the tanks. Once again, however, an undetected minefield halted the tanks and the half-tracks of Klostermeyer's battalion. While paths were cleared through the minefields, the troops were subjected to very heavy fire.

This delay meant that it was not until 11:30 that Klostermeyer's battalion, accompanied by II./ *Panzer-Regiment GD*, swung to the south of Sirtsev. The force of this, combined with attacks by other GD units from the north, meant that the Soviet hold on Sirtsev was untenable. Late in the afternoon, after fierce close-quarter fighting, the Soviets withdrew to the northwest in the direction of Sirtsevo. The Germans then prepared to assault the Soviet positions around Sirtsevo. By the evening, an armoured task force consisting of Klostermeyer's battalion, *Aufklärungs-Abteilung GD* and *Sturmgeschütz-Abteilung GD*, had succeeded in wresting control of Hill 230.1 from the Soviet defenders, who had been strongly supported by tanks. The hill gave the Germans excellent jumping-off positions for an attack on Sirtsevo the next day.

It was during this fighting, south of Sirtsevo, that Klostermeyer was killed in action. His grave is probably lost in the huge, anonymous rolling wheat fields of the Ukraine while his documents record that he received no decorations.

Below: Loading a BM-13 Katyushka. *Known originally as 'Kostikov's gun' after its designer, the multiple rocket launcher was nicknamed Little Katy, or* Katyushka, *by* frontoviks *(frontline troops). To the Germans, it was Stalin's Organ because of the shriek of the rockets as they travelled up the launch rails.*

CHAPTER TWO

UNTERNEHMEN ZITADELLE – THE NORTH

The first day of the attack, 5 July 1943, was a hot sultry day. To the north, the German Ninth Army, under Model, had 900 tanks in three *Panzerkorps*, two Army Corps and supporting infantry, but it achieved only minor successes against a determined Soviet defence. They had as their objective the village of Olkhovatka, about a third of the way to Kursk.

PREPARATIONS FOR THE attack included drawing rations for 10 days for 266,000 men – 5320 tons (5864 tonnes) of food. Ammunition deliveries stood at 12,300 tons (13558 tonnes), fodder for the 50,000 horses at 6000 tons (6614 tonnnes) and fuel for tanks and trucks occupied 11,182m³ (14,626 cu yds).

MODEL'S PLAN
Model had tasked *Luftflotte* VI, commanded by *Generaloberst* Ritter von Greim, with three missions:
1. To disrupt the enemy's command and control in the Kursk area.
2. To disrupt and paralyze enemy movement.
3. To support the main effort near Kursk.

Left: A German motorcycle combination is dwarfed by the smoke and dust of a tank action on the horizon. Though the fighting at Kursk took place in the summer, localized rain storms turned dirt tracks that were officially 'roads' into muddy sloughs that halted even tracked vehicles.

Born in 1896, Rokossovsky held commands during the Spanish Civil War. During the Purges of 1938, he was imprisoned but was later reinstated. He commanded the southern section of the Siberian Army during the defence of Moscow in 1941. He was then sent to Stalingrad and in December 1942 led the decisive breakthrough, cutting off the German Sixth Army. In June 1944, after Kursk, he commanded the 1st Belorussian Front against the German centre and took Lublin and Brest-Litovsk, but in July 1944 his advance stopped for six months just outside the Polish capital Warsaw. In August that year, Polish patriots launched an uprising in the city, but the Soviets did nothing to help, Rokossovsky claiming that he had insufficient supplies and was faced by strong German armoured formations. In January 1945, the Fronts were regrouped and he led the 2nd Belorussian Front, which finally captured the ruined city of Warsaw. He then pushed through northern Poland, reaching the Gulf of Danzig on 26 January, trapping the German armies in East Prussia. On 5 May 1945, Rokossovsky's forces linked up with the British at Lübeck. After the war, he became Chief of Soviet Armed Forces in Poland. He died in 1968.

The *Luftflotte* had, in fact, been undertaking operations prior to 4 July in preparation for *Zitadelle*. In May, Stukas hit the Kostornoe–Kursk and Arkhangesk–Yelets railway lines. A heavy attack by 168 aircraft was made on 5 May against the Gorki tank plant – this important AFV repair and rebuilding facility was hit again a day later and then again on 14 May and 22 May. Railway stations at Ryasan, Stalinogorsk and Tula were also attacked. On the first day of the attack, the *Luftflotte* would fly 2088 sorties and shoot down 163 aircraft from the Soviet Sixteenth Air Army for the loss of only seven of their own aircraft.

Model's plan for the attack on the left flank was in three phases and was surprisingly conventional.

1. To break through the enemy positions with infantry only.
2. Three panzer divisions to follow in the second echelon as the main effort group.
3. Two panzer and one armoured infantry division to follow in the third echelon and attack into the open [operational] area.

Among the ground forces available to Model were the Ferdinand antitank vehicles grouped in *Panzerjäger*

Battalions 653 and 654, commanded by *Oberstleutnant* von Jungenfeldt. The German staff was aware that the Ferdinand was vulnerable to close-range attack, so infantry accompanied them riding on a sled attached by a cable to the rear of the hull. Some of the crews of *Panzerjäger* Battalion 654, commanded by Major Noak, had taken MG34 machine guns aboard their vehicles and attempted close-range defence by opening the breech of their 8.8cm (3.4in) guns and firing the machine gun down the barrel.

Summer rain, as well as mines and antitank guns, reduced mobility, while Model's traditional use of infantry to achieve penetration for an armoured breakthrough slowed down the attacks. These had been disrupted from the outset when just before dawn 600 Soviet batteries from General Konstantin Rokossovsky's Central Front opened fire on the soldiers and vehicles of the Ninth Army grouped in their assembly areas. Though a huge German bombardment soon followed, the Soviet artillery fire had caused casualties, imposed delay and rattled the men of the Ninth Army.

THE FIRST DAY

As the German infantry advanced, they came under heavy small arms and artillery fire. When they tried to find cover, the 'dead ground' had been sown with anti-personnel mines and pre-registered by the artillery batteries of the Central Front. The German 258th Infantry Division had been tasked with breaking through to the Kursk–Orel highway, but the stubborn defence meant that it ground to a halt after a day of fighting; the same situation faced the 7th Infantry Division.

Infantry divisions that attacked with tank support, however, enjoyed greater success. The 20th Panzer Division, supporting a thrust on a 16km (10 mile) section of the front, had breached the first Soviet trench lines between Gnilets and Bobrik by 09:00. However, pioneers had to work ahead of the division's PzKpfw III and IV tanks, clearing mines. Prisoner interrogation suggested that Bobrik was less heavily defended, so General von Kessel ordered an attack on the village. Preceded by a heavy artillery barrage, the 20th Panzer Division rolled up the front of the Soviet 321st Rifle Regiment. The capture of Bobrik cracked the defensive positions of the 15th Rifle Division.

On the right of the 20th Panzer Division, the 6th Infantry Division went into action at 06:20, attacking along the valley

Opposite: Marshal Rokossovsky in a command post at the close of the war. He was a survivor of Stalin's purges before World War II, going on to lead with distinction at Moscow, Stalingrad and Kursk before the assault on Germany in 1945.

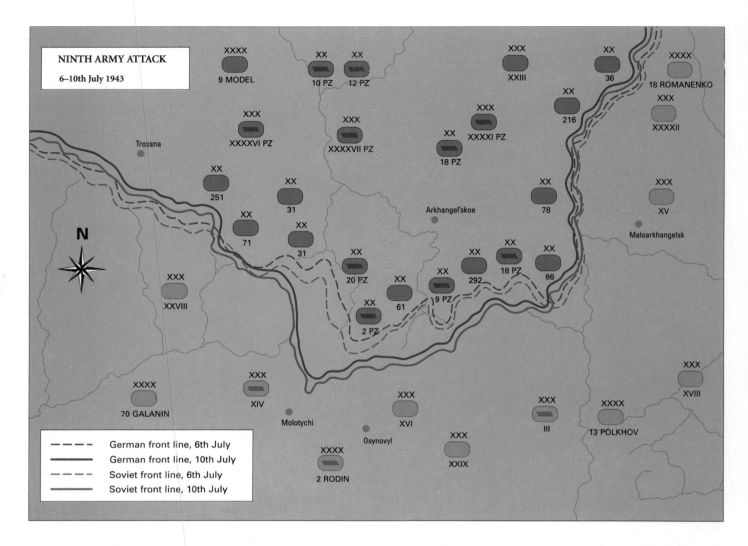

NINTH ARMY ATTACK
6–10th July 1943

German front line, 6th July
German front line, 10th July
Soviet front line, 6th July
Soviet front line, 10th July

Above: The lines of fortifications and determined Soviet resistance made the attack in the north by the German Ninth Army a slow and very costly process. Once it had lost the impetus of the assault, the battle of attrition moved in favour of the Central Front.

of the Oka. Three hours later, the 1st and 2nd Companies of the *sPzAbt.* 505 with Tiger 1s, attached to the 6th Infantry Division, moved forward. The two Tiger units destroyed a defensive screen of T-34s and antitank guns before hitting the open flank of the 676th Rifle Regiment. By midday, Major Sauvant's Tigers had taken the village of Butyrki and were threatening to unhinge the left flank of the 81st Rifle Division, which was already under pressure from the 292nd Division of General Harpe's XLI Panzer Corps. This Soviet division had been fighting a savage battle throughout the morning. Penetrations of Soviet positions in this sector of Thirteenth Army had been achieved by the Ferdinands of *Jagdpanzer Abteilung 653*. While the detachment of Ferdinands operating with 292nd Infantry Division

succeeded in driving straight through the defence lines of 81st Rifle Division to Alexsandrovka, Soviet infantry emerged from bunkers to seal the breach. This forced the German infantry without armour support to fight metre by metre.

During the day, as pressure built up on the Thirteenth Army, Soviet sappers laid a further 6000 mines that channelled the attacks by the German armour and led to the destruction of at least 100 armoured vehicles. In the standing crops of rye and wheat, some of the antitank mines could simply be placed on the ground, where they would be invisible to the driver of a buttoned-up tank.

In the late afternoon, troops of the German 86th Infantry Division had reached the outskirts of Ponyri. On the eastern flank of the main German thrust, the 216th and 78th Infantry Divisions of General Freissner's XXIII Corps launched a heavy attack against the heavily defended road junction town of Maloarkhangelsk. They deployed Ferdinands and also Goliath demolition vehicles. The

Germans penetrated the outer defensive belt, but the Soviet 129th Armoured Brigade launched a counterattack.

By the end of the day, the XLVII and XLI Panzer Corps had penetrated between 6.4km and 9.6km (4–6 miles) into the Soviet defensive belt. This was only the first line of defences and had been achieved at high cost, but Model had been prepared for a tough fight to break through the Soviet positions and by the end of the day was still essentially satisfied with the outcome of the fighting.

THE SOVIET RESPONSE

German commanders tended to characterize their Soviet opponents as unimaginative and strict adherents to pre-planned operations, but in reality many were shrewd tacticians who could read the battle. This was certainly true of Rokossovsky. He deduced that Model would deploy the bulk of his armour in the Butyrki and Bobrik area, where the Soviet 15th Rifle Division had been under heavy fire. An attack here would place the main weight of the Ninth Army on a line towards Olkhovatka and, anticipating this, Rokossovsky shifted reinforcements to cover this axis.

By dawn on 6 July, the Soviet troops were ready. The 18th Guards Rifle Division had been deployed to beef up the defences at Maloarkhangelsk and the III Tank Corps had moved into position south of Ponyri. The XVII Guards Rifle Corps had been moved to reinforce the Thirteenth Army's defences. The XIX Tank Corps was positioned west of the XVI Tank Corps to cover the possible enemy thrust towards Olkhovatka.

The fighting exploded in the early morning, when some 100 T-34 and T-70 tanks of the XVI Tank Corps rumbled

Below: Laden with ammunition boxes and other equipment, German infantry pass a StuG III. Here a farmhouse and trees offer cover, but in the open cornfields the infantry and armour were very exposed to artillery and air attack even before they closed with the Soviet defences.

into action. They succeeded in driving the Germans back 3.2km (2 miles), but there, in turn, they were counterattacked by the 2nd Panzer Division, which fielded PzKpfw IV tanks and the Tigers of *sPzAbt.* 505. Backed by heavy supporting fire from artillery and *Nebelwerfer* batteries, the Germans advanced through Soviet artillery fire in the direction of Hill 274 and the village of Olkhovatka. The chain of hills of which Hill 274 was part were the middle section of the central Soviet-held ridge between Orel and Belgorod. From the summit, there was a clear view as far as Kursk. Model was convinced that a breakthough at this point would allow his armoured and mechanized forces to drive into the Soviet rear areas in a classic *blitzkrieg* attack and reach the objective of Kursk.

Below: The 14.5mm (5.7in) Degtyarev-PTRD antitank rifle was becoming obsolescent by 1943. Soviet tank hunting crews waited in ambush until a tank was closer than 500m (1640ft), which gave them a good chance of knocking out the vehicle with shots to sides or back.

The heat increased during the day as the *Nebelwerfer* crews fired ripples of rockets into the enemy positions, but the Soviets used *Katyusha* rocket launchers to fire counter-battery missions.

Rokossovsky appreciated that Olkhovatka was the key to his defences, and it had been turned into a huge fortress constructed from field fortifications and bunkers. The Tigers with their heavy armour were able to push ahead and reach the village of Soborovka. As the fighting appeared to be moving in their favour, the Germans committed more armour and by 12:00 they had about 1000 armoured vehicles in action on a 9.6 km (6 mile) front between the two villages. It was here that the defence in depth with the trench lines and *Pakfronts* began to take its toll. Soviet infantry, armed with the cumbersome 14.5mm (0.57in) Degtyarev-PTRD antitank rifle, waited in close-range ambush positions. The single-shot weapon, firing a very powerful steel- or tungsten-cored bullet that could penetrate 25mm (1in) of armour at 500m (457 yards), had a semi-automatic action and could

Above: Model, as a Generaloberst, *talks to* Oberleutnant Ernst-Georg Buchterkirch (left), *a tank platoon commander of Panzer Regiment 6, 3 Panzerdivision. Buchterkirch, who had fought in Poland, won the Knight's Cross on June 29, 1940 in France, and the Oakleaves in 1944.*

fire between eight and 10 rounds per minute. It was 1.96m (78.74in) long, weighed 17.44kg (38lb) and had a muzzle velocity of 1010m/s (3320ft/s). Other soldiers attacked with petrol bombs, 'Molotov Cocktails', or the powerful VPGS 1940 rifle-launched hollow charge grenade. Mines like the TM-41 antitank mine stopped other tanks. The supporting German infantry, who were supposed to remove many of these threats, were themselves cut down by cunningly sited machine guns.

In a succession of attacks and counterattacks, the tanks of the 2nd and 9th Panzer Divisions were ground down. By the evening, the two Tiger units that had provided the cutting edge were seriously depleted. The German XXIII Corps had also failed to take Maloarkhangelsk. It had turned into a battle of attrition and not the *blitzkrieg* punch through the Soviet lines that Model had hoped for.

THE BATTLE FOR PONYRI

On 7 and 8 July, Model widened the front and switched the weight of his attack from the Orel-Kursk road towards Ponyri village to the east. Here for three days the Ninth Army would pound away without result, even though they were supported by *Luftflotte* IV, which had been reassigned from the southern

Above: German armour moving along a road as an axis of advance. The rolling Ukrainian wheat fields often lacked any obvious landmarks and consequently a clear point of reference was vital for tank crews, particularly if they were closed down for action.

part of the salient to support them. Rokossovsky pulled in troops from the relatively quiet sectors of the line covered by the Sixtieth and Sixty-Fifth Armies. With remarkable flexibility, the Sixtieth moved a complete division to support the Thirteenth Army while the Sixty-Fifth provided two tank regiments. The tank crews were ordered to dig in so that their hull-down positions gave both concealment and cover from the powerful 8.8cm (3.5in) guns of the Tigers.

At Ponyri, fighting had degenerated into bitter hand-to-hand combat. The railway embankment and the northern edge of the linear settlement had been captured, but the water tower, school, collective farm tractor distribution centre and railway station became the focus for the fighting. The village would later be dubbed 'The Stalingrad of Kursk' by Soviet propagandists. On 9 July, the German 508th Grenadier Regiment, attacking from the cover of woods and supported by the fire of Ferdinands, captured Hill 253.3 to the east of the village. On the night of 10/11 July, Model committed his last reserves to the fighting in Ponyri ,but by now the 292nd Infantry Division was exhausted and had been fought to a standstill. The weather was foul with grey skies and driving rain.

It was a battle in which self-sacrifice became commonplace: the commander of the Soviet 1st Battalion of the 1032nd Rifle Regiment was killed leading a counterattack at Ponyri, running forward at the head of his soldiers. His opposite number, *Hauptmann* Mundstock, in command of the 3rd Battalion of the 508th Grenadier Regiment, died on the same day during fighting for the school.

The Soviet propaganda machine was keen to provide its soldiers with role models. Konstantin Blinov, a tank commander at Ponyri and a former member of the *Komsomol,* or Young Communists League, became a posthumous Hero of the Soviet Union and the subject of a leaflet circulated among Soviet tank crews.

'Comrade soldiers, non-commissioned officers and officers, The best of our comrades, Senior Lieutenant Konstantin Blinov, Hero of the Soviet Union, died in the hospital today of a severe wound. In all the battles, Blinov has been, to all of us, a model of combat skill, fortitude and heroism. At Ponyri, Blinov did not leave the battlefield for three days. An expert soldier, he was sent to the most crucial points in our defences. Wherever Blinov came with his tank, the enemy was sure to sustain a defeat. In those heavy battles, Blinov destroyed six enemy tanks, eight antitank guns and nine weapon emplacements; with machine gun fire and the treads of his tank, he killed 380 Germans. Swear that you will make the enemy pay dearly for the death of Hero of the Soviet Union, K. Blinov!'

After the war, a street in Kursk was named after Blinov.

OPERATION *KUTUZOV*

On 12 July, the whole balance of fighting changed. In Operation *Kutuzov,* the Soviet Sixty-Third Army and Third Guards Tank Army attacked towards Orel from the east, supported by the First Air Army, while the Eleventh Guards Army struck deep into the Second *Panzerarmee* from the north, actually attacking through its own barrage rather than after it and with air support from the Fifteenth Air Army.

On 14 July, Model issued orders to the soldiers in the Orel salient. 'The Red Army…is attacking on the entire front of the Orel salient. We are facing a battle that will decide everything. In these hours, which will require all our efforts and strength, I have taken command of the combat-tested Second Panzer Army.'

Now in command of both the Second *Panzerarmee* and the hugely depleted Ninth Army, which by now had lost 50,000 men, 400 tanks and 500 aircraft, Model was forced into a fighting withdrawal, evacuating the Orel salient. Hitler, who continued to advocate a policy of no withdrawal, was faced by his commanders with the prospect of a second Stalingrad if the salient was not evacuated. Consequently, Model's forces fell back to the Hagen Line, a partially-completed belt of fortifications in front of Bryansk.

NEBELWERFER

'*Nebelwerfer*' means 'smoke launcher' and was a name adopted to confuse enemy intelligence. However, it has probably caused more confusion since the war. When the development started in the early 1930s, the programme was top secret and intended to give Germany rocket-based artillery. To disguise that, the designation '*Nebelwerfer*' was used, although the smokescreen role of the weapon was secondary.

The first attempt to develop rocket artillery was not successful, the *Do-Gerät* 38 being inaccurate and dangerous to its crew. By contrast the next one, the NbW 451, was very effective and became synonymous with '*Nebelwerfer*'.

The 15cm (6in) NbW 451 six-barrelled rocket launchers weighed 540kg (1188lb) in action, elevated from –5.5° to +45°, traversed through 24°, had a range of 6.7km (4.16 miles) and a 2.5kg (5.51lb) warhead that produced a massive blast effect.

The NbW 451 *Nebelwerfer* was mounted on a modified version of the split-trail 3.7cm (1.4in) Pak 35/36 carriage.

The tubes had to be fired one at a time, taking ten seconds to complete a full salvo, to prevent the weapon from overturning. Though inaccurate, it could be reloaded in 90 seconds and was very manoeuvrable. The rockets were of unusual design, with the solid fuel motor mounted at the front and venting through a ring of 26 angled venturi positioned about two-thirds from the nose of the projectile.

The heavier 28/32 *Nebelwerfer* 41 was a trailer with launch rails for six 28cm (11in) or 32cm (12.5in) rockets. The 32cm (12.5in) rocket had an incendiary warhead and the 28cm (11in) had 50kg (110lb) of TNT or amatol. A 30cm (11.8in) rocket, the *Wurfkörper 42 Spreng* had a 45kg (33.2lb) HE warhead and range of 6000m (6564 yards). This rocket was popular with the crews of the six-rail *Nebelwerfer* 42 since it produced very little smoke, which meant that there was no 'signature' when it was fired.

By the end of World War II ,the Germans had 150 *Werferregimenter*, in part because the rounds were much more cost effective than 10.5cm (4.1in) leFH 18 shells – rockets came in at RM 3350 and shells at RM 16,400.

CHAPTER THREE

UNTERNEHMEN ZITADELLE – THE SOUTH

To the south, the attack by the men of Army Group South made better headway. They had 1500 tanks and AFVs, including 94 Tigers and 200 Panthers, backed by 2500 guns and mortars. It was a formidable force made up of the Fourth *Panzerarmee* with Hausser's II *SS-Panzerkorps* and Knobelsdorff's XLVIII Panzer Corps and, to the southeast, Army Detachment Kempf under the command of Lieutenant-General Werner Kempf.

HAUSSER'S CORPS WAS made up of three *Waffen-SS* panzer divisions, the *Leibstandarte Adolf Hitler* (*LAH*), *Das Reich* and *Totenkopf*. Although all three were technically Panzer Grenadier divisions, each had more than 100 tanks when *Zitadelle* began. Knobelsdorff's corps was composed of the 167th and 332nd Infantry Divisions, the 3rd and 11th Panzer Divisions, Panzer Grenadier Division *Grossdeutschland* and Panther Brigade Decker.

Opposite them, Lieutenant-General Chistyakov of the Sixth Guards Army urged his subordinate commanders on

Left: The build up to Operation Citadel saw German armour concentrating on both flanks of the Kursk salient. This formidable column of Tiger tanks would become the sharp end of the armoured wedge formations, with lighter tanks on the flanks to punch into Soviet defences.

Opposite: Changing an engine of a PzKpfw III in the field. German tank formations also fielded captured T-34s that had been modified and upgraded with parts taken from battle-damaged German tanks. With their new crews, these vehicles proved very effective against their former owners.

the evening of 4 July to be particularly vigilant. 'In front of you stand Hitler's Guards formations. We must expect the main effort of the German offensive on this sector'.

For some men of the *Waffen-SS,* the battle of Kursk would be over in hours. *Unterscharführer* Erwin Bartmann with the *LAH* recalled his experiences on the second day of the fighting.

'As we attacked, we had to pass through a wood, where I was wounded by a shell splinter. We had been lying in shell scrapes, and the shells were exploding in the trees above us. There was so much shrapnel and wood splinters flying around that every second man was hit. I was hit by shrapnel in the left shoulder, which went through into my lung, missed my heart by just a few millimetres and lodged between my ribs. I partly lost my eyesight and could only vaguely distinguish between light and dark. Another lightly wounded comrade led me back to the dressing station'.

GERMAN ARMOUR

On the grand tactical scale, far from the personal battle for survival that Bartmann was now fighting, Generals Kempf and Hoth, unlike the more conservative Model, had instructed their tank commanders to adopt the formation known as a *Panzerkeil* – an armoured wedge. At the tip of the wedge were the heavily armoured Tiger tanks and, on the flanks, Panthers and PzKpfw IV tanks. Behind the tanks, the *Panzergrenadiere* rode into battle in SdKfz 251 half-tracks and to the rear, the mortars, rocket launchers and artillery followed up. Though this was a more aggressive tactic, it had one fatal flaw: the heavy armour and 8.8cm (3.4in) gun of the Tiger meant it was better equipped to stand off from Soviet T-34s and destroy them at long range rather than to close to shorter ranges, where it was more vulnerable.

Though the PzKpfw VI Tiger had none of the sloping armour of the Panther or later Tiger II, it made up for some of these design flaws by its sheer strength. The armour was

Below: Framed by the 7.5cm (3in) KwK 40 gun of a PzKpfw IV, tanks and SdKfz 251 half-tracks move in loose formation across the exposed wheat fields of the Ukraine. While this type of terrain offered little cover to defenders, it also left attacking tanks and infantry exposed.

25–100mm (1–3.94in) thick. Armament consisted of one 8.8cm (3.5in) KwK 36 gun and two 7.92mm (0.3in) MG 34. It weighed 54.1 tons (59.6 tonnes) and the Maybach HL 230 P45 12-cylinder petrol engine developed 700hp, giving a road speed of 38km/h (24mph) and range of 100km (62 miles) The Tiger entered production in August 1942, and a total of 1350 were built before production ceased in August 1944, when it was replaced by the Tiger II. Part of its success was down to its carefully selected and highly trained crew of five. The Tiger was an excellent tank but was mechanically complex and the overlapping wheels designed to spread the weight tended to clog in snow and mud.

In action, there were four formations authorized for the Tiger platoon. Line abreast (*Linie*), with the platoon leader (*zugführer*) on the extreme right and the section leader two vehicles away, was used for assembly. Row (*Reihe*), with the platoon leader at the head and the section leader in the third vehicle, was used both for assembly and marching, the former with 10m (33ft) between vehicles, the latter at 25m (84ft) intervals. Double row (*Doppelreihe*), which for a platoon was actually a box formation, was used for approach marches over open country and in the attack, with the platoon leader at the head of the right hand row and the section leader alongside him. In combat, the rows were to be 150m (165 yards) apart and the lines 100m (110 yards) apart. The wedge (*Keil*), was the attack formation most often used, with the platoon leader and the section leader level and separated by 100m (110 yards), and the second tank in each section 100m (110 yards) behind and the same distance to right and left, respectively. Therefore, when combat started, the platoon leader was to move to a position within the formation from where he could make the best use possible of both terrain and situation, and the chances of either double row or wedge staying intact for very long seemed slight.

There were five authorized formations for the Tiger company. The column (*Kolonne*), used for assembly, was essentially three platoon rows side by side, with the company commander and his alternate vehicle at the head of the centre row. For marches, an extended row was adopted. The company commander took the lead, followed by the second company HQ vehicle, with the three platoons strung out behind. For approach marches, a company double row was adopted, with the third platoon alongside the first. The company wedge was essentially a wedge of wedges, with the company headquarters vehicles in the centre of the formation, in echelon behind the rearmost tanks of the first platoon and ahead of the lead tanks of the second and third platoons; as an alternative, the second and third platoons

could form a row or double row behind the company headquarters vehicles. The broad wedge (*Breitkeil*) was the company wedge in reverse, with two platoons up and one back, and the company headquarters vehicles in the centre of the formation, in echelon ahead of the two lead tanks of the third platoon. Where the company found itself on an open flank, the third platoon would deploy in an echelon to the open side. In either company wedge or broad wedge formation, the company occupied an area some 700m (765 yards) across and 400m (440 yards) deep.

Where Tigers operated independently, with less capable medium tanks in support, the wedge formation was favoured, with a single heavy tank at its point and medium tanks (and later PzKpfw V Panthers) making the tail. This was modified as early as July 1943, into a 'bell' or *Panzerglocke*. This was essentially a right arc or rounded wedge of medium tanks with a Tiger in its centre, where a bell would have its clapper. Major General von Mellenthin in *Panzer Battles* states that the *Panzerglocke* was a sufficiently adaptable formation that it allowed tanks to operate at night. Night operations hampered enemy antitank guns, but to be effective 'well trained officers and experienced tank drivers were indispensable.'

Evidently, the tactical directives were modified in light of experience, and particularly when it became clear that far from being 'especially suitable for pursuit', the Tiger was actually at its best in an ambush position, picking off incoming enemy tanks at long range with its superior gun. However, when they came within range of the Soviet T-34s and more powerful ISU-152 assault guns, even the Tigers were vulnerable.

SOVIET ARMOUR

The formidable 9.80m (32ft 1in) long, five-man ISU-152 assault gun, that used the chassis of the KV1 heavy tank, entered service just in time for the fighting at Kursk. Its main armament was the powerful 152mm (5.9in) M1937 gun-howitzer, with its distinctive multi-baffle muzzle brake, which fired a 48.8kg (107.6lb) high explosive armour piercing shell that could penetrate 124mm (4.8in) of armour at 1000m (1100 yards); with an HE round, it could reach out to 17.3km (10.7 miles). The vehicle weighed 45.5 tons (50.1 tonnes) and armour protection was between 35mm and 100mm (1.38–3.94in). The V-12 diesel engine, developing 520 bhp, produced a road speed of 37km/h (23mph) and a range of 180km (112 miles)

The T-34/76 tank that would bear the weight of the armoured action had a crew of four and was armed with a

76.2mm (3in) gun and two 7.62mm (0.3in) DT machine guns. Armour protection was between 21–70mm (0.8–2.75in). It weighed 30.9 tons (34 tonnes), and the V-2-34 12-cylinder water-cooled diesel engine developed 500 hp giving a road speed of 55km/h 34mph) and range of 365km (226.8 miles). The T-34 was produced in six main variants, all with a four-man crew and armed with a 76.2mm (3in) gun and two or three machine guns designated as T-34/76, produced in following variants: A (model 1940), B (model 1941), C (model 1942), D (model 1943), E (model 1943) and F (model 1943). From 1940 to 1944, some 35,119 T-34/76 tanks were produced.

When they first encountered the T-34/76 during the opening phases of Operation *Barbarossa* in June 1941, the German commanders were both impressed and concerned: 'Very worrying' said General Guderian when he was Commander of the Second *Panzerarmee*; 'We had nothing comparable' reported von Mellenthin, then Chief of Staff of XLVIII Panzer Corps. Field Marshal Ewald von Kleist, of First

Above: A Soviet rifleman with a VPGS antitank grenade ready for use. Fired from a rifle using a powerful blank cartridge the grenade had a range of about 59.4 metres (65 yards) and its 326-gram (11.5 oz) shaped charge warhead could penetrate 30mm (1.2in) of armour.

Panzerarmee simply called it 'The finest tank in the world' while the more sober General G. Blumentritt reported that 'This tank adversely affected the morale of the German infantry'.

Waffen-SS units also did not hesitate to use captured T-34/76 tanks and *Das Reich* and *Totenkopf* pressed significant number into service. The T-34/76 tanks used by '*Das Reich*' are of particular interest. When in March 1943 the *SS-Panzerkorps* recaptured Kharkov, some 50 T-34/76 tanks of various models were captured. All of those were being repaired in a local tractor (tank) factory that had been overrun and was now designated as *SS-Panzerwerk* (SS Tank Workshop). These were repaired and also modified to bring them up to German standards, and were repainted and given

Above: Each side was now bringing reinforcements forward. Here Soviet infantry cling to the hull and turret of a camouflaged T-34. Normally Soviet troops maintained a very high level of camouflage discipline that was known as 'masking'.

German markings. Modifications included installation of commander's cupola (from damaged PzKpfw III and IV tanks), *schürzen* (armoured skirts covering the running gear) and other equipment such as Notek night-driving lights, stowage bins, tools, radio equipment and antenna. Twenty-five of them entered service with the newly created 3rd SS Panzer Battalion of the 2nd SS Panzer Regiment of *Das Reich*. *SS-Hauptscharführer* Emil Seibold from 3rd SS Panzer Battalion scored some 69 kills during his career, including those in his *Panzerkampfwagen* T-34 747(r) in July and August of 1943, during the Battle of Kursk. Seibold received the Knight's Cross during the last ever decoration ceremony on 6 May 1945. On 4 July 1943, *Das Reich* had 18 operational T-34 tanks and 9 in repair. *Totenkopf* also pressed number into service but had none at Kursk. Overall, there were some 22 T-34/76 tanks in active service with *Waffen-SS* Panzer Divisions during the battle of Kursk.

The Soviet tanks were not as well-made as German or Allied vehicles, the welded finish looked crude and the interiors were not as comfortable. They were however reliable, rugged and capable of being mass produced. Early in the war, the Soviet munitions industry had been evacuated from the western borders and moved thousands of miles to the east. At a chain of factories in cities beyond the Ural Mountains at Nizhni Tagill, Sverdlovsk, Omsk and the huge 'Tankograd' plant at Chelyabinsk men and women worked in grim conditions to produce tanks by the thousand.

Second only to the T-34 in numbers produced was the SU76M tank destroyer. With its open top and rear, the 10.6 ton (11.7 tonnes), 4.88m (16ft) long vehicle was not popular with its four-man crews. Though its armour was only 25mm (1in), it was fast, mobile and its ZIS-3 76mm (2.9in) gun was effective. Powered by two GAZ six-cylinder petrol engines each developing 70hp, it had a road speed of 45km/h (28mph) and range of 450km (280 miles). The Soviet crews, however, nicknamed it 'Sucha' ('Bitch') because of its spartan interior and as a pun on its designation. The massed tanks were backed by the formidable Soviet artillery,

Opposite: Field Marshal von Kluge in his Mercedes-Benz 4 x 4 Type 1500A staff car with a Tiger tank formation on July 3, 1943. Kluge was an ambitious and experienced panzer commander who had fought in Poland, France and the USSR.

which was not only powerful, but was also used in mass. Huge barrages would crash down on enemy assembly areas, advancing forces and precede the Soviet counterattacks.

OPENING MOVES

The power of Soviet artillery was demonstrated at 10:30 on 4 July 1943 when, as Hoth's Fourth *Panzerarmee* was moving into its starting positions, artillery of the Sixth and Seventh Guards Armies delivered a crushing barrage. This disrupted the German deployment, but it quickly regrouped and at 14:45, backed by the *Luftwaffe*, it delivered a savage counter-bombardment. As the Sixth Guards Army reeled under a weight of shells that was reported to be greater than that fired in the campaigns in 1939 and 1940 in Poland and France, the Fourth *Panzerarmee* moved forward under cover of the barrage. On the left flank, *Grossdeutschland* advanced between Ssyrew and Luchanino while the 3rd and 11th Panzer Divisions attacked on the left and right flanks. By the evening, the XLVIII Panzer Corps had secured the important hills around Butovo. Probes by Ott's LII Army Corps and Knobelsdorff's Panzer Corps directly to the south of Oboyan pushed back General Chistyakov's Sixth Guards Army. Rain and heavy Soviet artillery fire slowed down the attacks.

In the hours before the attack, an officer with the *LAH* had written home.

'For reasons of security, we have not been allowed to move about during the daytime and you can understand how hard this is, but now the waiting is over…it is coal black outside the Command bunker. Black clouds cover the sky and the rain is streaming down. We are rested and refreshed…the mud might slow us down but it cannot stop us. Nothing will. The barrage has just begun. I can feel its force even down here deep in the earth.'

At 15:00, the Berlin and Brandenburg Regiments of *Grossdeutschland*, together with *Kampfgruppe* Pape, had moved off for a preliminary attack against the Belgorod–Gotnya railway line and the village of Gertsovka, to secure the area for the armoured attack. They achieved this by nightfall and the division was able to move the 2nd Battalion, 6th Panzer Regiment onto its start line. Earlier that same day, Father Ruzek, the Division's Viennese Catholic Chaplain, earned the lasting respect of the men of *Grossdeutschland*. After soldiers were trapped in a minefield,

Opposite: Loading a 15cm (6in) Nebelwerfer 41 rocket launcher with the 34.15 kg Wurfgranate 41 Spreng HE rockets. The NbW 41 had a maximum range of 6900 metres (7545 yards) and could fire six rockets in ten seconds or three salvos of six rockets in five seconds.

some of them wounded and dying, Ruzek did not wait for pioneers to clear a path but with the words 'I can't keep the Lord waiting' walked out to the men. Among the dying were three seriously wounded soldiers, who clearly had a chance of survival if they received prompt attention. Ruzek made six journeys in and out of the minefield, carrying the wounded, and miraculously he did not trigger a mine.

More conventional bravery was demonstrated by *SS-Hauptsturmführer* Georg Karck commanding 9th Company, 2nd Panzer Grenadier Regiment *LAH*. With his thinning hair and pipe, the 32-year-old Karck, who was the father of three boys, must have looked like an old man to the young frontline soldiers of the *LAH*. However, he was a seasoned veteran and had fought with the *LAH* in France and Greece and throughout the war on the Eastern Front, including Kharkov. On 4 July, his regiment was given the mission of capturing a feature known as Hill 228.6, northwest of Jachostoff, to prepare the start line for the main attack. On the night of 4/5 July, Karck led his men in a spirited attack that took them into the complex of trenches and bunkers on the hill. As they fought towards the summit, Karck received a head wound, but nonetheless continued fighting and personally accounted for five enemy bunkers. An immediate counterattack by the Soviets saw bitter hand-to-hand fighting that lasted for two hours.

Neither of these brave men or any of the German soldiers massed for the attacks at Kursk would have taken comfort from the assessment that had been produced on 4 July by *Fremde Heere Ost* – Foreign Armies East – the German army department responsible for evaluating all military intelligence from the Soviet Union:

'From the point of view of the general war situation, there is not one ground that could justify launching Operation "Citadel" at the present juncture. The prerequisites for victory in the offensive were twofold – numerical superiority and the advantage of surprise. At the time originally planned for the launching of the offensive, both conditions were met. But now, from what we see of the enemy situation, neither is met. For weeks, the Russians have been waiting for our attack, in the very sector that we have picked for the offensive, and with their customary energy they have done everything in their power to halt our offensive as soon as it begins. Thus there is little likelihood that the German offensive will achieve a strategic breakthrough.

'Taking into account the total reserves available to the Russians, we are not even entitled to assume that "Citadel" will cost them so dear that they will later be incapable of carrying out their general plan at the time they choose. On the German side, the reserves which will become so desperately necessary as the war situation develops (particularly in the Mediterranean!) will be tied down and thrown away uselessly. I consider the operation that has been planned a particularly grave error, for which we shall suffer later.'

The author of this report was the head of *Fremde Heere Ost*, the shadowy and controversial Reinhard Gehlen. A career soldier, Gehlen had been promoted through a series of staff posts in the first years of the war. In the winter of 1941–2, he was visited by *Oberst* Henning von Tresckow. They discussed the war and agreed that Hitler must be removed. Although not an active member of the conspiracy, Gehlen would develop close ties with Tresckow and fellow conspirators Generals Helmuth Stieff and Adolf Heusinger, as well as the young colonels Claus von Stauffenberg, Wessel

Below: German soldiers in training for close combat with tanks lie prone as an AFV passes over them. After the war, these techniques were introduced to the French Foreign Legion by former German soldiers running recruit training at the depot at Sidi bel Abbés in Algeria.

von Loringhoven and Alexis von Roenne. Heusinger brought Gehlen into the plot while Stieff and Gehlen discussed the 'actual tactics' of the planned *coup d'etat*. In 1942, Gehlen was promoted to colonel and appointed head of *Fremde Heere Ost*. He was horrified at atrocities committed against Soviet prisoners of war and civilians. His organization recruited over 100,000 former Soviet prisoners of war into the Russian Liberation Army (ROA). On 17 July 1944, von Loringhoven informed Gehlen that Stauffenberg planned to assassinate Hitler at the next scheduled *Führer* briefing. Gehlen successfully eluded the Nazi regime's suspicion throughout the witch hunt that followed the abortive 20 July uprising. In December 1944, he was promoted to General, but after falling out with Hitler in April 1945 he was dismissed from *Fremde Heere Ost*. After the war, Gehlen continued his work in intelligence for both the US and West German governments.

THE ATTACK BEGINS

At 05:00 on 5 July, the main attack of the operation that Gehlen had warned against was launched in the south by the Fourth *Panzerarmee* and Army Detachment Kempf. In what

seemed almost a vindication of Gehlen's fears, the Soviet Sixth and Seventh Guards Armies had fired a pre-emptive barrage, but the Germans fired a counter-battery mission soon afterwards. Heavy rain was, however, proving as much an obstacle as Soviet defences and the small streams in front of German forces had degenerated into a morass.

Großdeutschland, commanded by Lieutenant-General Hoernlein, struggled through mud and shellfire. Engineers had been clearing mines during the night and then at 04:00 a heavy barrage hit Soviet positions. The 10th Panzer Brigade, with Panther tanks and with *Großdeutschland* in support, moved off into the attack. It then encountered new minefields near Butovo, where 36 of the new Panther tanks were immobilized. The main attack by *Großdeutschland* went in at 05:00. After hours of ferocious fighting, they secured the village of Cherkosskoye by 09:15 but at a heavy cost. Major-General Chistyakov, commanding the Sixth Guards Army, attempted to reinforce the 67th Guards Rifle Division, which had been holding the village with two regiments of antitank

guns – but to no avail. The 3rd Panzer Division on the left flank was unable to break into Savidovka despite launching repeated attacks.

In fighting for Hill 220, south of Korovino, men of the 2nd Company, 3rd Panzer Grenadier Regiment of *Großdeutschland* had an unforeseen encounter. As the section commanded by *Hauptmann* Mogel was working its way through the Soviet trench system, they heard German voices. Moving cautiously forward, they encountered a dozen unarmed German soldiers. It quickly emerged that they were PoWs, who had been used to construct defences in the salient and who had evaded their captors once the attack began and then taken cover in an abandoned bunker. The story had an added twist: as the patrol and liberated prisoners talked,

Below: Waffen-SS Panzergrenadiere *use the side of a Soviet antitank ditch for temporary cover, their simple positions protecting from direct and indirect fire. The Grenadiers' Kar 98k rifles are close by but propped up to keep them out of the dirt.*

Mogel realized that the elderly NCO in the group was his uncle.

To the east, *Obergruppenführer* Hausser watched the attack from the command post of the *Deutschland* Panzer Grenadier Regiment. Hans Harmel, the commander of the regiment, reported that the attack was going well. The spearhead was formed of the 3rd Battalion commanded by Günther-Eberhard Wisliceny. His 10th Company, commanded by *SS-Hauptsturmführer* Helmuth Schreider, had reached the first antitank ditch and dug in, seeing off furious Soviet counterattacks.

On 5 July SS-Panzer-Grenadier Regiment 2, *Leibstandarte Adolf Hitler,* supported by the Tiger-*Kompanie* and *Sturmgeschutz Abteilung Leibstandarte Adolf Hitler,* moved forward toward the day's objective, the village of Bykovka. It

Below: Fatigue lines the faces of men of Das Reich *as they ride forward in their SdKfz 251, supported by StuG III assault guns. The half-track is stacked with extra ammunition for the MG42 and the soldiers' rifles since resupply would be unreliable in a fast-moving action.*

was their job to clear a string of small towns along the Vorskla River of enemy forces and to prevent the Soviets from outflanking them from the west bank of the Vorskla. Once again, Karck was in the vanguard of the attack. Taking a small hand-picked group, he worked his way through a minefield and drove the Soviet defenders off their fortified hill. On 23 July, Karck's regimental commander, *SS-Obersturmbannführer* Hugo Krass, recommended him for the Knight's Cross. He survived until the night of 3 July 1944, when his Kubelwagen was in collision with an ammunition truck and he died in an inferno of fire and explosions.

On 5 July, an officer in the *LAH* remembered how he '…saw our leading Tiger sections roar away and vanish almost completely in the peculiar silver-grey grass which is a feature of the area. Our mine-lifting teams mark the position of Ivan's mines by lying down alongside them, thus using their bodies to mark a gap in the field. There are thousands of mines all over the area…' Moving north, the first Soviet defensive position of Hill 220.5 was soon encountered. This strongpoint was riddled with mines, covered with barbed

wire, and dotted with well-fortified bunkers and trench systems. This Soviet field position had been developed into an elaborate, deeply echeloned fortification system. The crack 52nd Guards Rifle Division occupied the trenches and earth bunkers, reinforced by artillery regiments, antitank artillery, battalions of antitank riflemen, tank companies, mortar regiments, and other formations resisting stubbornly and refusing to give ground. The SS *Kriegsberichter* (war correspondent) Martin Schwaebe, attached to the *Waffen-SS* regiment *Deutschland*, described his view of the attack:

'The morning of 5 July dawned pale. For two hours, the pioneer assault troops cleared the frontline trenches. They took the Soviet outposts by surprise while it was still dark. Now it was our turn, the time for the *Panzergrenadiere*. The Soviets established bunkers, field defensive positions and antitank ditches 30 kilometres [18.6 miles] deep. This had to be overcome! By the evening, the bunkers of the last line of defence had to be captured. The 3rd Battalion of *Deutschland* was on the main axis. Its mission: to overcome the positions in front of the tank ditches, conquer the town, and break into the large antitank ditches! The ammunition trains were to be quickly moved forward. All hell broke loose: suddenly, Soviet barrage fire fell all around! The attack bogged down 400 metres [437 yards] in front of the antitank ditches. The "Tigers" and assault guns did not arrive as planned. The thunderstorms of the previous night made the heavy vehicles impossible to move.'

Above: The vulnerable fuel drums attached to the rear hull of the T-34 can be seen in this picture. The fuel in the drums extended the range of the tank, but German tank crews realized that a hit on them could destroy or immobilize a T-34.

The fire was *kontrpodgotovka* – counter-preparation – and the decision by Soviet commanders to fire these heavy barrages was not taken lightly. It used up large stocks of ammunition, and they knew that if their calculations were wrong, 'he' – Stalin – would hold them personally responsible. Zhukov, writing nearly 30 years after the battle and long after Stalin's death, commenting on the *kontrpodgotovka*, says:

'There is no denying of course that the counter-preparation fire inflicted heavy losses upon the enemy and disorganized control over the offensive, but we had expected more from it. Watching the battle and questioning German prisoners, I came to the conclusion that the Central and Voronezh fronts started that fire too early, when the Germans were still sleeping in trenches, dug outs and ravines and armoured units were concealed in the waiting areas. The enemy armour and manpower losses would have been bigger still if the counter-preparation fire had been opened later. It should have been opened at the earliest half-an-hour before the enemy went into the offensive.'

Von Mellenthin with *Großdeutschland* noted that 'On the second day of the attack we met our first setback, and in spite

Above: Panzer IIIs of the Totenkopf *division advance towards smoke plumes rising on the horizon in the opening phase of Operation Zitadelle. Tank formations found infantry support essential in mopping up any opposing infantry with antitank weapons.*

of every effort of the troops were unable to penetrate the Russian line.' The division was bunched up against a swampy area when it came under heavy Soviet artillery fire. 'The engineers,' he noted, 'were unable to make suitable crossings and many tanks fell victims to the Red Air Force – during this battle Russian aircraft operated with remarkable dash in spite of German air superiority.' More disturbingly, Soviet troops infiltrated back into areas that were thought to be secure.

INTENSE FIGHTING

But now both sides were fully committed to action and the intensity of the fight for Hill 220.5 and the village of Beresov can be gauged by reading the operations log of the *Großdeutschland* HQ:

'03:00. Friendly artillery preparation.

04:30. Regimental commanders move forward to their armoured reconnaissance vehicles.

04:50. Artillery fire strike

05:00. Own infantry and armour leave the line of departure: Butovo–Gersovka, with assault guns and 4th Company of *Großdeutschland* Armoured Engineer Battalion near the 3rd Battalion under *Hauptmann* Senger.

09:00. Point 237.8, west of Cherkaskoe is reached! – The 12th Company penetrates to the west. – Own tanks have difficulties in front of the antitank ditches at the Gerzovka Valley. – The neighbouring unit of the right – the 11th Panzer Division – is located near Hill 237.8. The neighbour on the

Opposite: A 7.5cm (3in) Pak 40/3 (L/46) auf Pz.Jag 38 (t) Marder self-propelled antitank gun moves past Soviet prisoners used as porters by a German 8cm (3.1in) mortar detachment, who have taken cover with the mortar crew. Both sides used prisoners to carry heavy equipment or ammunition.

left – armoured infantry – has advanced the same distance as we. Strong enemy air activity.

09:15. A direct hit on the regimental command post. Casualties: the regimental adjutant *Hauptmann* Beckendorf, *Leutnant* Hofstetter the 4th Battalion adjutant, *Leutnant* Stein of the antitank battalion, *Großdeutschland* are all dead.

10:00. Orders from the division operations officer to the Panther Brigade: advance on Point 210.7. – The 1st and 2nd Battalions are to link up. – The execution was delayed by the halt at the antitank ditches. – The 2nd Battalion had problems making the connection, because the antitank battalion blocked the way.

11:00. A bridge is constructed across the Gerzovka *balka* – near the centre of the division attack lane.

13:50. The Soviets attack with seven tanks in the direction of Korovino, in the vicinity of our 3rd Battalion.

Below: A Soviet 57mm (2.2in) M1941 antitank gun crew awaits the order to fire. The gun fired a 3.148kg (6.9lb) shell that could penetrate 140mm (5.5in) of armour at 500 metres (546 yards), and as late as 1973 it was still in service with armies of nations allied to the USSR.

13:53. All seven attacking Russian tanks are destroyed by own tanks. From time to time, the enemy renews its air activity.

14:30. The 1st Battalion and the Panther Brigade are at the beginning of the antitank ditches. The 2nd and 4th Battalion lead elements are south of Point 229.8 and in the depression.

15:30. The temporary bridge over the Beresoviy *balka* is destroyed by the crossing of the Panthers.

17:50. The Regimental Command Post is redeployed to the western edge of Yamnoe.

19:00. Bethke's Battalion (2nd) is ordered to attack Cherkaskoe from the direction of Butovo, through Point 237.8. The 11th Panzer Division is northeast of Cherkaskoe. In the early afternoon, elements of the 1st Battalion attacked the northern area of Cherkaskoe with tanks. The 1st Battalion assaulted enemy batteries and entered the northwestern area of Cherkaskoe.

19:55. The 2nd Battalion began its attack on Cherkaskoe – to the southwest. – Freedom of movement in the southwestern area was soon established by the attack of the 2nd Battalion. – Flame-thrower tanks from the 11th Panzer

Division had already worked over the area. – At night, there was heavy enemy air activity.'

The *Totenkopf* Division under *Brigadeführer* Priess occupied a critical position on the extreme flank of Hoth's Fourth *Panzerarmee*. Here the division was expected not only to keep pace with the northerly advance of the *SS-Panzerkorps* but also to screen the Fourth *Panzerarmee* against any possible Soviet penetration from east of the Donets until such time as supporting infantry had moved up to take over their positions. The *Totenkopf* attack crashed into the heavily entrenched Soviet 52nd Guards Division, and by the end of the day its lead elements, working closely with their tanks, had penetrated the second line of defences and captured the fortified village of Yakhontovo, which was the forward command post for the Soviet Sixty-Ninth Army.

Earlier that same day, *Unterscharführer* Herbert Brunnegger of *Totenkopf* had led a patrol out on reconnaissance.

'I took half the group with me. We took with us machine pistols, hand grenades, gas masks and bayonets. Our order – to form a line of infantry, spaced out just so that the man in front was in view…

'I was at the head of the group, trying to make as little noise as possible, when suddenly we were stopped in our tracks by loud shouts from behind us: "Stop, stop, you're standing right in the middle of a minefield!" Christ, this was too much, and we'd only just set off. One false step could mean instant death. I ordered everyone to get down on their haunches without touching the ground with their hands. Then, the last man in the line took the first step back out of the minefield along the path indicated by the engineers. We got out without losses.'

Brunnegger's patrol set off again and in the darkness his sharp nose picked up the smell of Machorka – the powerful and pungent Russian tobacco.

'As we crept further forward, the aroma of Machorka grew stronger. I had our Russian speaker brought up to the head of the line, and instructed him that should we stumble unexpectedly upon the enemy, we should quite brazenly pretend to be Russians…

'A few minutes later, I spotted a dark cluster of people lying just below my feet. As I crouched down, I noticed that it was two Russians sleeping in a hide-hole behind a light machine gun. Karp raised his machine pistol, but I gestured to him to put it away. That's the last thing we needed on a nice summer evening like this. I carefully lifted the machine gun out of the hole and gave the signal to continue.'

AIR SUPREMACY

On the Soviet side, General Chistyakov of the Sixth Guards Army was optimistic that the battle would run according to plan and the German attacks would be halted by the deep defences. Three hours after the start of the attacks, the general was sitting under an apple tree in the garden of a farmhouse that had been set up as his forward HQ. He was enjoying a second breakfast when he received unexpected and unwelcome visitors. General Katukov of the First Tank Army and General Popel, a member of his Military Council, arrived to monitor how the fighting was developing. Chistyakov invited them to join him for breakfast. Popel noted, 'On the table were cold mutton, scrambled eggs, a carafe with chilled vodka to judge by the condensation on the glass, and finely sliced white bread – Chistyakov was doing himself well.' Breakfast was not to be enjoyed, for moments later there were shell bursts and the chief of staff reported 'hastily and nervously' that strong enemy forces had managed to break through.

As Katukov and Popel ran to their vehicles, Chistyakov raced to the house for an update. An artillery commander staggered, wounded, into his HQ: 'My regiment has been in action for an hour, Comrade General, but one-third of its guns are already eliminated. The German aircraft are dropping vast numbers of small bombs which have a colossal high-fragmentation effect. The Stukas are dominating the air space. They are just doing what they like up there. We are helpless.' Chistyakov was not to know at this stage in the battle that the three Soviet Air Armies which should have dominated the battlefield had suffered heavily in their preemptive attacks against the *Luftwaffe* airfields.

On the southern flank of the attack in the 7th Panzer Division, part of Army Detachment Kempf, the Tiger tank of

Below: Waffen-SS MG42 machine gun and 8cm (3.1in) GrW 34 mortar crews pause in the cover of farm buildings. Heat, humidity and the strain of combat – let alone carrying a load like the mortar baseplate or barrel – were punishing for even the toughest soldiers.

Opposite: Though the German attack in the south enjoyed greater success, the strong Soviet defence meant that it was not coordinated and exposed flanks were vulnerable to counterattacks. It was on the right flank of the II SS Panzer Corps that such an attack would fall.

the 1st Company, with Kurt Knispel as its gunner, was delayed at the Donets. The bridge over the river, which had been constructed by army engineers, had been hit by Soviet artillery fire, and it collapsed as tanks were crossing. The vehicles were from *Gruppe* Oppeln, commanded by the Olympic equestrian gold medal winner Colonel Hermann von Oppeln-Bronikowski, and was part of the 11th Panzer Regiment. It now crossed further south, to be placed under command of the 7th Panzer Division. With *Oberst* Adalbert Schulz and Major Dr Franz Bäke, von Oppeln carried out an attack on a broad front. It was the biggest armoured attack he had ever experienced, with 240 tanks breaking through Soviet positions on the Pena river line.

Opposite this force was the fortified village of Krutoy Log, held by an infantry battalion commanded by Captain A. Belgin and part of the Seventh Guards Army. The Germans

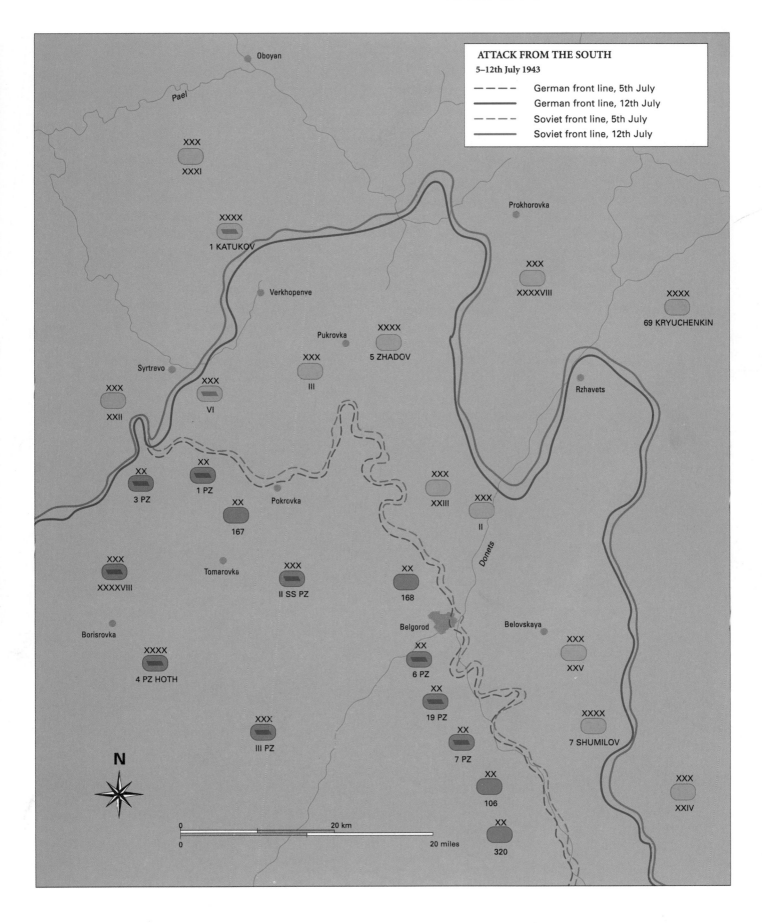

ATTACK FROM THE SOUTH
5–12th July 1943

- – – – German front line, 5th July
- ——— German front line, 12th July
- – – – Soviet front line, 5th July
- ——— Soviet front line, 12th July

Oboyan

Pael

Prokhorovka

XXX
XXXI

XXXX
1 KATUKOV

XXX
XXXXVIII

XXXX
69 KRYUCHENKIN

Verkhopenve

Pukrovka

XXXX
5 ZHADOV

XXX
III

Syrtrevo

XXX
VI

XXX
XXII

Rzhavets

XXX
XXIII

XXX
II

XX
3 PZ

XX
1 PZ

Pokrovka

XX
167

XXX
XXXXVIII

Tomarovka

XXX
II SS PZ

XX
168

Donets

Belgorod

Belovskaya

Borisrovka

XXXX
4 PZ HOTH

XX
6 PZ

XXX
XXV

XXX
III PZ

XX
19 PZ

XXXX
7 SHUMILOV

XX
7 PZ

XX
106

XXX
XXIV

XX
320

N

0   20 km

0   20 miles

initially committed 12 tanks supported by a regiment of infantry. Waiting until their targets were within range, the antitank guns in the Soviet garrison concentrated on the tanks while machine gunners raked the advancing infantry. Belgin was wounded in the fighting but knocked out a German tank.

It was the first of 11 attacks that lasted for 12 hours. According to the Soviet historian Boris Solovyov, the *Pakfront* position destroyed 14 tanks and killed up to 600 enemy soldiers. Belgin, who would die during the fighting, Captain I. Oliyasov and Sergeant S. Zorin were awarded the title of Hero of the Soviet Union.

By 19:30 on 5 July, *Leibstandarte Adolf Hitler* was within 500m (546 yards) of the southern edge of Jakovleva, a village

Below: A PzKpfw III and a PzKpfw II tank – battered, blazing and abandoned. Kursk was not fought exclusively by Tigers and Panther:, many of the German tanks were obsolescent and had only remained in service with modifications like stand-off armoured plates and enhanced armament.

Opposite: A German army machine gun crew wait in a captured Soviet communications trench. The trench is deep enough for a man to crawl under cover and the summer vegetation has camouflaged it very effectively. It is a good example of the well-designed defences at Kursk.

within the second defensive line. However, the Germans had also suffered. *LAH* alone had 97 killed and 522 wounded. By nightfall, both the XLVIII Army Corps and II *SS-Panzerkorps* appeared to be through the Soviet defences, but as their lines were breached the Soviet forces fell back to pre-prepared positions. The night was marked by continuous fighting between German and Soviet infantry, the Germans taking out bunkers and fortified positions by attacking them with flame-throwers.

Manstein and Hoth realized that they would not achieve a link-up with the Ninth Army attacking north towards Oboyan, and assessed that the Soviet forces would attempt a counterattack from the direction of Prokhorovka. They planned to halt this attack before driving north again. Now that German generals were thinking on their feet and not

NIKITA KHRUSHCHEV

The grandson of a serf and the son of a coal miner, Nikita Khrushchev was born in Kalinovka, Kursk Province, Ukraine on 5 April 1894. After a brief formal education, he found work as a pipe fitter in Yuzovka. During World War I, he became involved in trade union activities, and after the Bolshevik Revolution in 1917 he fought in the Red Army. He rose in the party organization to a position in the Politburo. During World War II, Khrushchev served as a political officer with the equivalent rank of Lieutenant-General.

In the months following the German invasion in 1941, Khrushchev came into conflict with Stalin over the conduct of the war in the Ukraine, where Khrushchev was the local party leader. He considered Stalin's unwillingness to accept retreat as a military option to be wasteful in the face of the overwhelming force the soldiers were facing.

He was a political commissar at the Battle of Stalingrad and was the senior political officer in the south of the Soviet Union throughout the war – at Kursk, entering Kiev on liberation, and in the suppression of the Bandera nationalists of the UNO (who had earlier allied with the Nazis before fighting them in the Western Ukraine).

After Stalin's death in March 1953, there was a power struggle between different factions within the party. Khrushchev prevailed, becoming party leader on 7 September, and his main rival, NKVD chief Lavrenty Beria, was executed in December. Khrushchev's leadership marked a crucial transition for the Soviet Union. He pursued a course of reform and shocked delegates to the 20th Party Congress on 23 February 1956 by making his famous Secret Speech denouncing the 'cult of personality' that surrounded Stalin, and accusing Stalin of the crimes committed during the Great Purges. This effectively alienated Khrushchev from the more conservative elements of the Party, but he managed to defeat what he termed the Anti-Party Group after they failed in a bid to oust him from the party leadership in 1957.

Under his leadership, the USSR would take the lead in space exploration. However, poor economic policies and the perceived climbdown over the Cuban Missile crisis in 1962 led to his removal from office on 14 October 1964 by the Central Committee. He lived in retirement in Moscow, where he wrote his memoirs, *Khrushchev Remembers* (1971). Nikita Khrushchev died on 11 September 1971.

working a plan that was known to STAVKA, events were beginning to run in their favour.

Dusk was beginning to fall as the 394th Panzer Grenadier Regiment stormed the village of Korovino. The village was a *Pakfront* position and formed the western anchor of the first line of Soviet defences. *Oberst* Pape, the regimental commander, an officer who always led from the front, mounted a skilful attack, but a short way into the village he was wounded. His place was taken by Major Peschke, who drove the defenders out of the village.

Leutnant von Veltheim, as commander of the light platoon of the 2nd Battalion, 6th Panzer Regiment, now saw his opening. He followed up hard behind the withdrawing Soviet troops and in the light of a blazing windmill drove into the village of Krasny Pochinok, the last bulwark of the Soviet defences in front of the River Pena. As von Veltheim stood by the river, he realized that the 3rd Panzer Division had reached its objective for the first day. It was now 9.6km (6 miles) into the Soviet defences. During the short summer night, the 255th Infantry Division worked its way forward to take up a position to the left of the 3rd Panzer Division next to the 332nd Infantry Division from Silesia.

THE SECOND DAY

On 6 July, the Fourth *Panzerarmee*, with the XLVIII Panzer Corps and II *SS-Panzerkorps*, continued its thrusts towards Oboyan. However, they were now encountering Lieutenant-General M.Y. Katukov's First Tank Army, which was dug in behind the Sixth Guards Army. The General had with him a formidable political officer in Nikita Khrushchev. An experienced senior political officer, Khrushchev had already provided the backbone to the hard-pressed Sixty-Second Army at Stalingrad.

According to some Soviet histories, the fact that Katukov's tanks were dug in and had not been committed to an attack in the open was the result of heated discussions during the night. Vatutin had proposed that the 640 tanks of the II and V Guards Tank Corps, which made up the First Tank Army, should be used in a counterattack against the Fourth *Panzerarmee*. Katukov pointed out that too many tanks had been destroyed at long range by the guns of the Tigers and Panthers and that it would be a needless sacrifice by his T-34s and few KV-1s. In hull-down positions, the Soviet tanks dug in, covering the approaches to Oboyan. As with so much of the history of Kursk, these moves have been given a strong political slant by Soviet historians. Following Stalin's death, Khrushchev was portrayed as a military genius who had sided with Vatutin and Vasilevsky, and in an attempt to discredit the popular Zhukov, the marshal's name was linked to Stalin and the potentially disastrous proposal to launch a counterattack. The incident is made more curious still by the fact that *Luftwaffe* air photographs had apparently disclosed that 82 Soviet tanks had been dug in on the Fourth *Panzerarmee* sector *before* 4 July.

Beith's III Panzer Corps fought its way slowly northeast of Belgorod. The 19th Panzer Division, supported by the 168th Infantry Division, was embroiled in fighting that would last for three days. The 7th Panzer Division advanced, leaving the 106th and 320th Infantry Divisions of the XI Corps to cover its flank. The Soviet Volchansk Group attacked the XI Corps, but were unable to break these German defences.

By noon on 6 July, *Leibstandarte Adolf Hitler* and the remainder of the II *SS-Panzerkorps* were 32km (20 miles) deep into the Soviets defence zone. A huge gap had been torn into the Soviet's Sixth Guards Army around Luchki by a *coup de main* of the *Der Führer* Regiment of *Das Reich,* and the front line lay wide open. In the vicinity of Yakovlevo, *LAH* clashed with tanks of the First Tank Army. A veteran of *LAH* recalled the action.

> The third day of the German-Fascist large-scale offensive whose dimensions are steadily increasing with the influx of fresh reserves, has once again resulted in only minor territorial gains by the German forces, which are out of proportion to the heavy losses they sustained to make them.
>
> *Soviet Information Bureau,*
> *Moscow, 8 July 1943*

'On separate slopes, some 1000 metres [1094 yards] apart, the forces faced one another like figures on a chess board, trying to influence fate, move by move, in their own favour. All the Tigers fired. The combat escalated into an ecstasy of roaring engines. The humans who directed and serviced them had to be calm; very calm, they aimed rapidly, they loaded rapidly, they gave orders quickly. They rolled ahead a few metres, pulled left, pulled right, manoeuvred to escape

Below: General Vatutin stands in a forward command post with Nikita Khrushchev, the senior political officer with the Voronezh Front. Khrushchev, who is scanning the area through binoculars, would lead the Communist Party after Stalin's death, and in 1956 he exposed many of Stalin's crimes.

Opposite: A young Unteroffizier *scans the horizon. He has an MP38 submachine gun slung from his shoulder and his 6 x 30* Dienstglas *prismatic binoculars to hand. A shaded flashlight is buttoned to his right epaulette. Men like this were the core of the German infantry.*

the enemy crosshairs and bring the enemy into their own fire. We counted the torches of the enemy tanks which would never again fire on German soldiers. After one hour, 12 T-34s were in flames. The other 30 curved wildly back and forth, firing as rapidly as their barrels would deliver. They aimed well but our armour was very strong. We no longer twitched when a steely finger knocked on our walls. We wiped the flakes of interior paint from our faces, loaded again, aimed, fired.'

Lieutenant-General Nikolai Popel, the Member of the Military Council with the First Tank Army, would later recall, using the language of that Russian obsession, chess:

'I suppose that neither I nor any of our other officers had ever seen so many enemy tanks at once. Colonel-General Hoth had staked everything on a knight's move. Against every one of our companies of 10 tanks were 30 or 40 German tanks. Hoth well knew that if he could break through to Kursk, no losses would be too great and no sacrifices in vain.'

With a crisis building, STAVKA had moved strong tank forces of Fifth Guards Tank Army from the northeast into an area just east of the Donets River. They would arrive at the village of Prokhorovka after a few days' march. Meanwhile, II/Panzer Grenadier Regiment 2 *Leibstandarte Adolf Hitler* received orders to immediately set out for a village identified as Luchki II, where it was to provide cover for the march route to the west and northwest.

During the day and night, the XXXI Armoured Corps of Katukov's First Guards Tank Army had been engaged in ferocious fighting as German infantry, backed by tanks and assault guns, fought in conditions as bad as those at the Western Front in World War I. Rain squalls had turned the area into mud and trenches had become small streams.

The Soviet 183rd Rifle Division's War diary gives an indication of the growing intensity of the fighting.

'At 17:00 July 6 the enemy's forces of up to 120 tanks and up to two rifle companies have reached the Teterevino, Yasnaya Poliana line.

The 10 tanks pushing through the northern suburbs of Teterevino broke through the main defensive position of the 285th Rifle Regiment toward Sovkhoz Komsomolets. Two tanks had been knocked out, the others returned to their initial positions.

At 02:00 the enemy was carrying out an intensive reconnaissance trying to get a prisoner.

At 04:00 July 7 there was heard a sound of engines. According to the reconnaissance on 20:00 July 6, it has marked a large concentration of infantry in Luchki, Nechayevo and up to 150 tanks together with a motorized rifle regiment 3km [1.8 miles] southwest from Luchki.

The enemy's aviation Ju-87, Ju-88 showed high activity from 19.00 July 6 and during the night and the first half of July 7. They intensely bombed the positions of the 51st and 52nd Guards Rifle Division, as well as other units and also the locations of Prokhorovka, Teterevino, Belenikhino, Yasnaya Poliana, Ivanovskiye Vyselki, Sovkhoz Stalinskoye Otdeleniye. Division positioning was not changed.'

II SS PANZER CORPS ADVANCE

Hauser's II *SS-Panzerkorps* had by now advanced 40km (25 miles) into Chistakov's front. The *Waffen-SS* troops kept up the pressure and in the mist-shrouded dawn of 7 July the situation began to look critical for Vatutin's Voronezh Front. However, the Soviet forces had the benefit of interior lines, and once the threat in the north had been neutralized, they were able to transfer more artillery and General Rotmistrov's Fifth Guards Tank Army and Lieutenant-General A.S. Zhadov's Fifth Guards Army from Konev's Steppe Front.

The Soviet 29th Antitank Brigade heavily engaged the II *SS-Panzerkorps* throughout the afternoon. However, the village of Tetervino fell after heavy fighting, meaning that *LAH* and *Das Reich* were free to push on to Greznoye and also the last Soviet defence line in front of the River Psel. The Soviet brigade had stood its ground, fought and been virtually wiped out. The *Waffen-SS* attack had been well supported by air reconnaissance and then by Henschel and Focke Wulf ground-attack aircraft.

The III Panzer Corps made better progress against the flank of the Seventh Guards Army, which prompted Vatutin's redeployment. At the close of the day, *Totenkopf* had shaken itself free of the Soviet defences and penetrated 32.1km (20 miles), crossing and thereby cutting the Belgorod-Oboyan highway. It halted for the night astride the Belgorod–Kursk railway.

7 JULY 1943

The 52nd Guards Rifle Division, which had been withdrawn from the fighting around Oboyan, now received an order from the XXIII Guards Corps on 7 July. The Corps' Commander was to move from the Dumnoye, Mal, Psinka, Svino-Pogorelovo, Petrovka area to Klyuchi, Hill 226.6,

Polezhaev region, and take a defensive position by the morning of 8 July. Its mission was to stay in the second echelon to prevent the enemy's tank and infantry breakthrough in the north and northeast directions.

During the day, the XLVIII Panzer Corps had taken Dubrova and *Großdeutschland* had broken through the Sixth Guards Army positions on either side of Syrtsevo, forcing them back towards Gremutshy and Sytsevo. As they withdrew, they came under heavy German artillery fire. However, as German forces moved forward, the Panthers of Lauchert's Brigade hit belts of mines and were halted during the afternoon on the outskirts of Syrtsevo, coming under accurate antitank gun fire. *Hauptmann* von Gottberg's 2nd Battalion Panzer Regiment. *Großdeutschland* saved the situation. The tanks gathered up the Panzer Grenadiers, and

Below: A T-34 disappears in a spectacular fiery explosion, possibly the result of a hit in the fuel drums on the rear deck. Given the difficulty of photographing in these conditions, this is probably a set-up picture, taken to boost German domestic morale.

> The next two or three days will be terrible. Either we hold out or the Germans take Kursk. They are staking everything on one card. For them it is a matter of life or death. We must see to it that they break their necks!
> *Nikita Khrushchev, First Tank Army HQ*
> *7 July 1943*

in a bold concerted action the main defensive line of General Krivoshein's Mechanized Corps was torn open. In a small hollow immediately behind the front line, Krivoshein listened to reports from runners as they arrived. 'The 3rd Company of Kunin's battalion has lost all its officers. Sergeant Nogayev is in command.' Or 'Headquarters of 30th Brigade has received a direct hit. Most officers killed. Brigade commander seriously wounded.' Though Soviet tanks launched counterattacks, these were halted by the fire of tanks under the command of Graf von Strachwitz's armoured group. Popel would later observe that 7 July was one of the hardest days in the battle of Kursk.

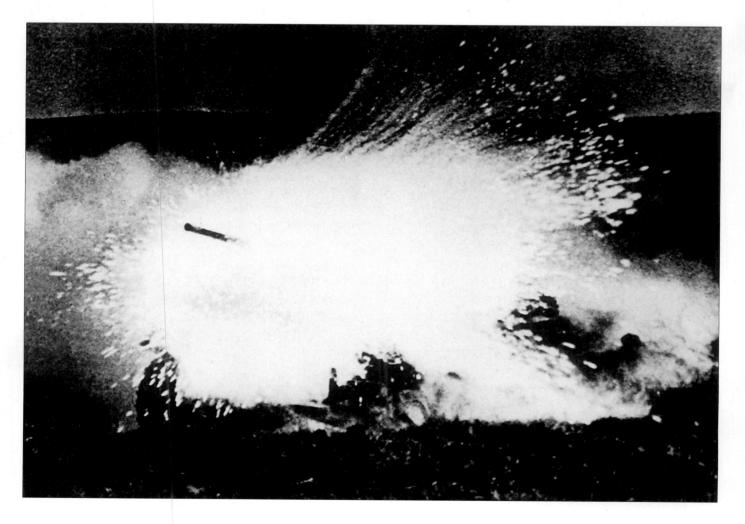

Other elements of *Großdeutschland* penetrated to Verchopenje and north of Gremutshy. On the left flank, the 3rd Panzer Division closed on Beresov. Von Mellenthin recalled: 'On the right wing we seemed to be within reach of a big victory; the grenadier regiment of *Großdeutschland* was reported to have reached Werchopenje. On the right flank of *Großdeutschland*, a battle-group was formed to exploit this success; it consisted of the reconnaissance detachment and the assault-gun detachment and was told to advance as far as Height 260.8 to the south of Nowosselowka. When this battle group reached Gremutshy, they found elements of the grenadier regiment in the village. The grenadiers were under the illusion that they were in Nowosselowka and could not believe that they were only in Gremutshy [14.4km (9 miles) inside the Soviet lines as against 19.3km (12 miles)]. Thus the report of the so-called success of the grenadiers was proved wrong; things like that happened in every war and particularly in Russia'.

A hill north of Gremutshy was, in fact, taken during the evening and the Panzer Regiment shot Soviet tanks off a feature designated Hill 230.1. However, as with all the combatants in Kursk, von Mellenthin noted: 'The troops were already in a state of exhaustion and 3rd Panzer Division had been unable to advance very far, 11th Panzer Division

Above: Smoke pours from a T-34 as Tigers advance along a hedge line. The long range of the 8.8cm (3.5in) gun gave the Tiger crews a serious advantage if they could acquire and engage targets in open ground. It was here that good training paid off.

had reached a line parallel with the forward elements of *Großdeutschland*, whose further advance was badly hampered by fire and counterattacks on the left, where 3rd Panzer was held up.'

Manstein could be pleased with the day's action, as the Fourth *Panzerarmee* was slowly gaining ground on the road to Oboyan. As Soviet prisoners were moved to the rear, it looked as if this part of Operation *Zitadelle* was going to plan – albeit slowly and at greater cost than had been anticipated.

'As they chopped their way forward against tough resistance,' writes Charles W. Sydnor Jr, 'the SS divisions left an immense junkyard of wrecked Soviet armour and heavy weapons; Hausser's field police units herded thousands of dazed and bewildered Soviet prisoners toward the German rear. By the evening of July 7, these previously unmistakable signs of disaster created the impression that the II *SS-Panzerkorps* was poised for a decisive breakthrough which would roll up the southern front of the Kursk salient. Under similar circumstances in the summer of 1941 and 1942, this conclusion might have been valid. In July 1943, however, it bore no relation whatever to the actual situation on the southern sector of the Kursk front. During the night of July 7/8, the SS divisions were only beginning to encounter what proved to be the real Russian opposition.'

At a meeting that evening at the First Tank Army HQ, Vatutin and Nikita Khrushchev issued a categorical order: 'On no account must the Germans break through to Oboyan'.

Major-General Shalin, the chief of staff of the First Tank Army present at the meeting, observed soberly: 'We are confronted by an unprecedented concentration of armour. It is the old tactic. But this time the armoured spearheads are led by Tigers, Panthers and massive assault guns. The cannon

Below: Spread out in open formation, German Panzer IIIs cut a wake through standing crops near Kursk. The crops provided good cover for tank-hunting crews and camouflage for bunkers and trench lines, while the rolling terrain allowed positions to be sited on reverse slopes.

of our T-34s cannot pierce the frontal armour of the fascists' giants.' He also explained that *Luftwaffe* ground-attack aircraft were posing a major threat with their ability to destroy Soviet armour before it had even reached the front line.

At the close of the day, the 6th Panzer Division reported to HQ *Panzerkorps*:

'After a preparatory *Stuka* attack on enemy targets in and around Yastrebovo, *Panzergruppe* Oppeln began to attack out of the 207.9 area and *Kampfgruppe* Unrein out of the Belinska area to the north against the enemy located at Sevryukovo–Yastrebovo. The *Panzergruppe* with the 2/114 Panzergrenadier Regiment, quickly crossed the Rasumnaya, pushed the enemy out of the city, and captured the high ground directly west of the northern edge of Sevryukovo. All bridges leading to the roads on the eastern bank were destroyed. While the bridges on the southern edge of Yasrebovo were repaired in three hours, tank attacks were launched from the north, but they were all repulsed. Combat

equipment was not installed on the bridge to allow tanks to cross the Rasumnaya. *Kampfgruppen* Bieberstein and Unrein did cross over the bridge.

During the occupation of Generalovka and Belinska on 6 July and of Yastrebovo and Sevryukovo on 7 July, the enemy offered tenacious resistance, supported by tanks. The withdrawal, which was also observed from the air, and which was expected to become a retreat, was contrary to the continuous resistance and the contents of an intercepted radio signal, in which they were ordered to hold on. The enemy air force made its presence felt by bombs and aircraft weapons.'

Erwin Bartmann of the *LAH*, wounded early in the fighting, was now in the casualty evacuation chain away from the battle.

'Using a groundsheet as a stretcher, I was carried out of the ambulance and laid on some straw. There I had to wait my turn, as there were many more comrades with worse wounds than mine. I saw many die around me. In the middle of the night, I was taken into the operating tent and laid on the operating table. I was given a rather ineffective anaesthetic, but in any case I wanted to stay conscious. I felt that if I went under I would never reawaken.'

8 JULY 1943

The summer sun had dried out the steppe by 8 July and individual German formations were making slow but effective progress. The Voronezh Front moved its Fortieth Army up to support the flagging Sixth Guards and First Tank Armies. A battlegroup of the XLVIII Panzer Corps pressed ahead of the main body and reached Hill 260.8, from where it wheeled west to push into the rear of the Soviet forces holding up the centre and left of the corps. *Großdeutschland* began to swing west to ease the pressure on the 3rd Panzer Division. Heavy fighting raged around Verchopenje and Hill 243.0, but the German forces failed to make any penetration. 'Height 243.0, immediately to the north of Werchopenje, was held by Russian tanks, which had a magnificent field of fire,' wrote von Mellenthin. 'The attack of panzers and grenadiers broke down in front of this hill; the Russian tanks seemed to be everywhere and singled out the spearhead of *Großdeutschland*, allowing it no rest.'

By midday, Syrtsevo had fallen to *Großdeutschland* and the 3rd Panzer Division, but a counterattack by the Fourth Army kept the XLVIII Panzer Corps busy. In the late morning, some 40 T-34s of General Krivoshhein's III Mechanized Corps had driven out from Syrtsevo in an attempt to halt the German advance. They ran into the guns of the Tiger

company of *Großdeutschland* and 10 Soviet tanks were knocked out before the survivors withdrew. Following the fall of Syrtsevo, Soviet forces pulled back across the River Pena. A rapid German follow-up by the reconnaissance battalion of 3rd Panzer Division, commanded by Major Wätjen, with an assault gun battalion commanded by Major Frantz, took them to Verkhopenye and the tactically important bridge over the Pena. Soviet tanks fought a three-hour battle to hold the town, during which the German assault guns knocked out 35 armoured vehicles.

The German historian Paul Carell described how Major Frantz's youthful radio operator, *Gefreiter* Eberhard, who would become a distinguished academic after the war, transmitted his commanding officer's fire orders.

'Signals in rapid succession thus wove the net in which the Russian attack would be caught. For the young corporal, of course, this was rather like watching an opera with the curtains down. It was his task to translate the major's short, rapid words and orders into numbers from one to twenty-six. And he almost laughed aloud at the ease with which he managed to discharge it. Like rattling off irregular verbs just before the exams, it flashed through his mind.'

As he transmitted the orders, he tried to picture the battle. Along with T-34s, the Soviet forces were using US-supplied M3 medium tanks. [The Soviet tank crews did not care for the 1386 M3 Lee tanks that were sent to the USSR. Its high silhouette of 3.1m (10ft 3in), its archaic configuration with a hull-mounted 75mm (2.9in) gun and turret-mounted 37mm (1.4in) gun, as well as its tendency to catch fire, earned it the grim nickname 'Grave for Seven Comrades'.] Eberhard listened as the detached assault gun troops reported. Suddenly he saw T-34s and an M3 fast approaching their position. The young German NCO was fighting his first battle and watched the highly trained assault gun crews grouped around his vehicle go into action. There were seven attacks. After three hours, 35 tanks were destroyed and five surviving battered T-34s had withdrawn to the cover of a neighbouring wood.

The capture of Verkhopenje by the 6th Panzer Regiment and the motorcyclists of the 3rd Panzer Division was a significant coup. The village stretching along the Pena river was heavily fortified because of its tactically important bridge. The fight for the village had seen duels between antitank guns, PzKpfw IV, Panthers and T-34s. The bridge over the Pena was damaged, but the 2nd Company and bridge-building column of Engineer Battalion 39 repaired it during the night, and by mid-morning they had also constructed a 16-ton (17.6-tonne) capacity bridge. Now

Above: A Soviet 14.5mm (0.6in) Simonov PTRS 1941 antitank rifle crew. The PTRS 1941 was a gas-operated rifle with a five round magazine; it was heavier and more complex than the PTRD but could penetrate 25mm (1in) of armour at 500 metres (546 yards).

tracked vehicles could cross the river.

By now, Hoth's forces had been in action for five days and fuel and ammunition were beginning to run low. They had punched a roughly rectangular salient into the Voronezh Front about 18km (11.2 miles) deep and 30km (18.6 miles) wide. Two days later, however, and after establishing a bridgehead on the River Psel and pushing towards Oboyan, the Fourth *Panzerarmee* was about 40km (24.8 miles) into the Soviet lines. Von Melenthin noted that 'it could no longer be doubted that the back of the German attack had been broken and its momentum had gone.'

To the north of the Kursk salient, Model had now been forced onto the defensive, and this took pressure off STAVKA. Vatutin attempted to attack the right flank and rear of the II *SS-Panzerkorps* at Gostoschevo, using the II Guards Tank Corps. In the late evening, the tanks of the emerging

from wooded cover were spotted by a Henschel Hs 129 of *Luftflotte* IV, commanded by *Hauptmann* Meyer. He immediately alerted the squadron and then, supported by Focke Wulf Fw 190s, attacked in a unique aerial action. Fifty tanks were destroyed and supporting infantry scattered by *Spreng Dickwand* SD-2 anti-personnel fragmentation bombs. The Allies nicknamed them 'Butterfly Bombs', but *Luftwaffe* crews knew them as 'Devil's eggs'. Weighing 2kg (4.4lb), they had a spring-loaded casing that deployed like wings when they were dropped, slowing them down in flight. They could explode on impact or in flight after a time delay and produced a blast radius of 12m (39.37ft). For the first time in history, a tank formation had been destroyed from the air.

SOVIET LOSSES

On 8 July, II *SS-Panzerkorps* HQ reported that 290 Soviet tanks had been destroyed in the three days of fighting. In what can only be called supreme understatement, the situation was judged 'very complex', by Marshal A.M. Vasilevsky, STAVKA's representative. He told the Fifth Guards Army: 'The enemy is moving toward Oboyan. Although our troops have stopped its movement, we can't exclude a possibility that they will attempt to strike towards Prokhorovka with a further turn into the north to enveloping Oboyan from the east'.

As a result, the Voronezh Front's commander had asked Stalin on 7 July to reinforce his front with two armies from the strategic reserve. For 'solid covering of Oboyan's direction and, above all, for supplying an opportune switching of the troops to the counteroffensive in the most favourable moment when it is necessary to start the movement of the troops of General Zhadov to the region: Oboyan, Prokhorovka, Mar'ino and the troops of General Rotmistrov to Prizrachnoye area, immediately'.

Both armies resubordinated to the Voronezh Front had to strengthen their defences on the first stage. First of all, this referred to the Fifth Guards Army. On 8 July, the commander of Steppe Front – I.S. Konev – ordered Lieutenant-General Zhadov: 'On the morning of July 11, reach the Psel river line, take a defensive position and prevent the enemy's movements to the north and north-east'. He also let him know that 'by the end of July 9 the corps of the Fifth Guards

Tank Army of Lt. Gen. Rotmistrov are concentrating to the east from Prokhorovka'.

On 8 July, the X Tank Corps, which had been transferred from the Fifth Guards Army to the Voronezh Front, was beginning to concentrate to the west of Prokhorovka. A battlegroup of the XLVIII Panzer Corps pressed ahead of the main body and reached Hill 260.8, from where it wheeled west to push into the rear of the Soviet forces that had blocked the advance of the centre and left flank of the Corps. *Großdeutschland* began to swing west to take the pressure off the 3rd Panzer Division. There was heavy fighting around Verchopenje and Hill 243.0, but the Soviet defenders could not be ejected. By 12:00, Syrtsevo had fallen to *Großdeutschland* and 3rd Panzer Division, but the Fortieth Army launched an immediate counterattack that kept the XLVIII Panzer Corps busy.

Below: Soviet prisoners captured by Leibstandarte SS Adolf Hitler *huddle against the wall of a building that may have been prepared for defence – the windows have been bricked up. Kursk would be the last time that the Germans captured Red Army soldiers in any numbers.*

However, the OKH War Diary for 8 July reported that the high attrition rate among the new Panther tanks was a cause for concern. Only 40 were operational out of the 200 that had started the battle. 'Some baled-out crews came into our trenches for safety…they do not trust their machines and they say that a hit often causes a fire so that the machines blaze like torches. Some of the crews are very new and inexperienced. For some, this is their first battle…' The Panther had been rushed into service and though some had fallen victim to mines and antitank guns, the Maybach engines had a tendency to overheat, which caused mechanical breakdowns.

At 22:00, Vatutin ordered the Sixty-Ninth Army's commander to move a part of his forces of the left flank of the 183rd Rifle Division from Vinogradovka, Novoselovka,

---

13TH SIBERIANS

The division had fought at Stalingrad, on the slopes of the Mamayev Kurgan, in the Red October Tractor plant and in 'Pavlov's house' (Sergeant Jakob Pavlov was from the Division). Some accounts state that of the 10,000 men of the 13th that crossed the Volga, only between 280 and 320 came out alive.

Following Stalingrad, it was re-built and, alongside the Fifth Guards Tank Army, was held in reserve South of Kursk. The original intention was to use these two formations to counterattack after the German assault had been ground down, but both formations were committed to prevent a possible breakthrough. After three to four days of continuous heavy fighting, including the tank battle at Prokhorovka, they achieved this, grinding the elite *Waffen-SS* formations to a standstill.

Shortly after this, they moved over to the planned counterattack and played a full part in the liberation of their country. They took part in the Kirovograd operation in the Ukraine and were the unit that liberated the historic town of Poltava. By now designated the 13th Guards Rifle Division, it appears to have earned the extra honorific title of '13th Guards Rifle Division, Poltava', indicating that this was not an easy liberation.

In 1945 as part of the 1st Ukrainian Front, they arrived at the southern edge of Berlin and took part in the assault into the heart of the Third Reich. The 13th Guards may even have linked up with the Americans at Torgau, like their parent formation, the Fifth Guards Army.

Shipy towards the railroad to the Sovkhoz Komsomolets, Yasnaya Poliana, Teterevino region.

9 JULY 1943

At 00:35 on 9 July, Vatutin personally ordered the X Tank Corps commander 'to transfer Vasiljevka, Sovkhoz Komsomolets defensive positions to the II Tank Corps and to pass into a subordinate position to the First Tank Army's commander.'

To the west, the 3rd Panzer Division was able to advance on the left of the Rakowo-Kruglik road and prepare for an outflanking attack against Beresovka. During the night of 9/10 July, the tanks entered the fortified village from the west, but the Division's attack to the north was halted by fire from positions in a small forest to the north of the village. On the right flank, however, events were building that would eclipse the action being fought around *Großdeutschland*.

At 01:00, the Fifth Guards Tank Army received its next order and mission details: 'By the end of 9 July reach Bobryshevo, Bol. Psinka, Prelestnoye, Aleksandrovskiy [as the settlement was called at that time; the railway station was called Prokhorovka.] having mission: to be ready to meet fast moving enemy, who have already captured Kochetovka on 8 July.'

The Fifth Guards Tank Army had been born in the battle of Stalingrad. At that time, the formation was called the Sixty-Sixth Army, but it proved itself in eliminating the German forces in the Tractor Plant area and for this it was redesignated the Fifth Guards Tank Army. It was restructured between February–April 1943 according to the decision of the State Defence Committee No. 2761 issued on 21 February. It retained four divisions that had passed through the Stalingrad crucible and also received one rifle and two airborne divisions (all of them Guards), which had received good battle training. After having completed its formation, the army was redeployed at the end of March from Millerovo to Ostrogozhsk. There it entered into the Steppe Military District. On 6 July 1943, it was transferred to the Voronezh Front.

Two corps headquarters were formed according to instructions of the General Staff:

XXXII Guards Rifle Corps – 13th, 66th Guards Rifle

Opposite: During a pause in the fighting at Kursk, a Waffen-SS radio operator with a Torn. Fu. d2 backpack transmitter/receiver sends new target co-ordinates to supporting artillery. The simple, hastily constructed, artillery command post appears to have been dug into the side of a balka.

Divisions, 6th Guards Airborne Division plus corps' units. The hero of Stalingrad, Major-General A.I. Rodimtsev had been appointed the corps commander.

XXXIII Guards Rifle Corps – 95th, 97th Guards Rifle Divisions, 9th Guards Airborne Division plus corps' units. The corps commander was Major-General I.I. Popov.

The 42nd Guards Rifle Division was set as a reserve of the Army Commander.

FIFTH GUARDS TANK ARMY

On 16 May, Fifth Guards Tank Army was a part of the Steppe Military District and had taken up a strategic defensive line: Zaoskol'ie, Aleksandrovka, Rusanovka, Kalinkin, Skorodnoye, Belyi Kolodets. There it was brought up to strength by staff and equipment and training. It received reinforcements, including the 29th Anti-aircraft Division, 308th Guards Mortar Regiment BM-13 ('Katyusha'), 1073rd and 301st antitank Artillery Regiments, 14th Assault

Below: A British-built Churchill tank supplied to the Fifth Guards Tank Army passes an abandoned Sd Kfz 232 armoured car. Some 301 Churchills were sent to the USSR, but they were not popular with their crews because of the tracks system and modest armament.

Engineer Brigade, signals and other standard army units. The X Tank Corps, which had left its positions on July 7, for Prokhorovka was also subordinated to it. Two rifle divisions of the XXXIII Guards Rifle Corps and the 42nd (Reserve) Division took part in the battle.

They were composed of the 95th Guards Rifle Division (8771 men), 9th Guards Rifle Division (9018 men) and 42nd Guards Rifle Division (8046 men). According to the report of the operations of the Fifth Guards Tank Army in July 1943, its strength on the critical day of 12 July was 501 T-34 medium tanks, 261 T-70 light tanks and, interestingly, 31 British-supplied 'Churchill' heavy tanks. The T-70 had entered service in January 1942. It had a crew of two and was armed with a Model 38 45mm (1.7in) gun with 94 rounds and a 7.62mm (0.3in) DT machine gun. The tank, which looked like a cut-down version of the T-34, was made at Zavod Nr 38 and GAZ plants and was powered by two GAZ-202 engines that gave a maximum road speed of 45km/h (27.9mph) and a range of 360km (223.6 miles). Despite its narrow tracks, its weight of 9.96 tons (10.6 tonnes) meant that drivers were able to steer it across firm snow, but the major design defect was the slab-sided one-man turret with its low-calibre main armament. When production ceased in

1943, they had built 8226 vehicles. In addition to these tanks, the Fifth Guards Tank Army had 79 76mm guns (3in), 45 SU-122 SP guns, 330 45mm (1.7in) antitank guns, 1007 antitank rifles, 495 82mm (3.2in) and 120mm (4.7in) mortars and 39 BM-13 'Katyusha' rocket launchers.

On 9 July, the men of the *Waffen-SS* regrouped and pressed on with the assault in the south. *Das Reich* was now placed on the defensive, and *Leibstandarte Adolf Hitler* was to push onwards. 'Exhorted by their commanders to spare nothing in this final heave against the Russian front,' writes Sydnor, 'the weary assault groups of the *Leibstandarte SS Adolf Hitler*, *SS Das Reich* and *Totenkopfdivision* hurled themselves into the maze of antitank positions, machine-gun nests, bunkers and trenches. The sheer fury of the SS assault was enough to overcome even the most stubborn resistance, and on the tenth the Russian defence began crumbling'.

For Herbert Brunnegger with *Totenkopf*, the prospect of fighting through more Soviet defence lines seemed grim.

'Right in front of us was a long line of enemy installations, still completely intact. According to statements from prisoners, there was yet another carefully constructed locking installation beyond this defensive cordon. And, behind this, massed columns of tanks ready to launch a massive Russian breakthrough offensive. I could not help thinking that the enormous mass of hardware assembled on our side was a gigantic drop in the ocean. This would only put paid to the first cordon, which as I saw it, had been left empty or was occupied by only a few men. The second bulwark would bring us to a halt and stop us reaching the core of the enemy installations, the ultimate target of our offensive.'

STAVKA now threw in General Katukov's First Tank Army, which attacked from three sides, and badly hit *Das Reich*, which, however, managed to hold its position and drove off the badly mauled Soviet army. The German attack picked up again. Throughout the days of 9, 10 and 11 July, the *Leibstandarte Adolf Hitler* would fight its way through muddy terrain to the banks of the Psel river, the last obstacle before Kursk. *Leibstandarte* took the lead, and SS-Regiment *Deutschland* protected its right flank.

The 3rd Battalion, 1st Panzer Grenadier Regiment of *Totenkopf*, commanded by *Standartenführer* Karl Ullrich, cleared the last Soviet bunkers in its sector and forded the Psel river. They had established a bridgehead on the northern bank of the Psel, after a frustrating wait for the arrival of heavy bridging equipment. Having been badly mauled by the *SS-Panzerkorps*, the remains of the Sixth Guards Tank Army, First Tank Army and detachments from Fifth Guards Army

THE CHURCHILL TANK AT KURSK

The British Prime Minister Winston Churchill is reported to have said of the heavy infantry tank Mk.IV 'Churchill' 'this tank carrying my name has more drawbacks than me'. It was an obsolete design: to increase room for the tank crew, the design team at Vauxhall Motors mounted some elements of the transmission under the hull so the track was bent around it, as for tanks of World War I. The tank had a 12-cylinder petrol engine of 350hp that gave it a speed of 27km/h (16.7mph). The first models (Churchill I and Churchill II) were armed with a 40mm (1.5in) gun – too weak for a heavy tank. Later versions were armed with either a 76mm (3in) gun or a 57mm (2.2in) gun. The tank had frontal armour 102mm (4.1in) thick, later models having 152mm (5.9in).

The transmission was quite reliable, but the tank had two major disadvantages: first, the tracks were vulnerable from shells and shell fragments because they were too high. And second, the tracks often jammed the tank's turret. However, 5400 vehicles (of all models) were built and this tank served in the British Army until 1952. A total of 301 tanks of both the Churchill Mk. III and IV were sent to the USSR. These two models were very similar and distinguished only by minimal changes in turret design. The USSR probably also received some flame-thrower Churchill Mk VIIs. The Soviet tank crews were not enthusiastic about the Churchill, and after 1942 the UK ceased sending it.

were withdrawn by STAVKA. Both sides were now exhausted and beginning to feel the strain of the intense fighting. Vatutin realized that he had committed the First Tank Army too early.

For the German command, however, the situation had become dangerous because the three *Waffen-SS* divisions had each made deep penetrations separately, and could not establish communication with each other. *Der Führer*'s flank, and the entire *SS-Panzerkorps*'s flank, was left wide open as Kempf's armoured detachment could simply not keep up with the pace of the Waffen-SS divisions. The 13.s.*Kp/SS-Pz.Reg.* 1 engaged the Soviet 181st Tank Regiment, and destroyed the whole unit without suffering a single loss. The main body of Fifth Guards Tank Corps assaulted in a series of uncoordinated strikes with the intention to separate and destroy the divisions separately.

The situation at the end of 9 July was that the Fourth *Panzerarmee* (II *SS-Panzerkorps*, XLVIII Panzer Corps, LII Army Corps) had broken through the second defensive line of the Sixth Guards Army in the Yakovlevo-Teterevino sector, after which it continued pushing towards Oboyan, trying to break the Soviet defences along the highway Belgorod, Oboyan and Kursk. The XLVIII Panzer Corps (11th Panzer Division, *Großdeutschland*, 3rd Panzer Division) had reached Kochetovka, Novoselovka, Verkhopenje and Beresovka. It was within 25.7km (16 miles) of Oboyan. At Beresovka, the 3rd Panzer Division had been checked when it came under fire from Soviet positions in the woods. The 11th Panzer Division struggled to move at all. The delimiting line between it and the II *SS-Panzerkorps* passed along the Solotinka river to the Psel river and then along the Olshanka river. The 332nd Infantry Division of the LII Corps carried out attacks on the left flank, covering the flank of the XLVIII Panzer Corps.

However, by now the Fourth *Panzerarmee* had no operative reserves and was down to 501 effective tanks. The 167th Infantry Division, which had been set as a reserve earlier, began relieving the troops of *Totenkopf* in the Shopino, Visloye area from 18:00 on 8 July. Later it also relieved *Das Reich* troops around Luchki. Correspondingly, *Totenkopf* was ordered to concentrate on the morning of 10 July in the Greznoe area, and *Das Reich* was ordered to concentrate north of Luchki, while its frontline orientation remained to the east.

At the end of 9 July, the Fourth *Panzerarmee*, packing the battle order of the II SS-Panzerkorps, cut its front line almost in half and received a powerful group from three handpicked SS Panzer Divisions in the Krasny Oktiabr, Teterevino and Luchki area. Simultaneously Army Detachment Kempf regrouped the 7th Panzer Division and was concentrating in the Melekhovo vicinity behind the 6th and 19th Panzer Divisions, preparing the offensive against Prokhorovka from the south via Provorot'.

As the thrust in the direction of Oboyan had slowed down by 8 July, the Fourth *Panzerarmee*'s commander transmitted Order No 5. It ordered his troops to continue the offensive on 10 July toward the northeast and simultaneously to envelop the enemy's forces, creating conditions for a further advance toward northeast.

An edited version of the new mission for the German forces reads:

'2. The 167th Infantry Division is to hold its current positions', that it had taken after had taken over from the troops of *Totenkopf*, covering the right flank of the Fourth *Panzerarmee* along the Lipovy Donets western riverside.'

Then the objectives for the Corps were set:

'4. The II *SS-Panzerkorps* is to defeat the enemy southwest of Prokhorovka and force it back toward the east. The Corps is to capture the hills from both sides of Psel river northwest of Prokhorovka.

5. The XLVIII Panzer Corps is to annihilate the VI Guards Tank Corps in front of Oboyan on the Pena's western riverside and continue the envelopment from the Novoselovka region toward the southwest.

6. The 52nd Inf. Corps is to hold its current positions while being ready to cross the Pena river by the army commander's order in the Alekseevka–Zavidovka sector.

7. The Army headquarters are situated in Aleksandrovka railroad station.'

FOURTH *PANZERARMEE* COMMANDER GENERAL HOTH

At 22:00 on 9 July, the II *SS-Panzerkorps*'s commander issued an order which began: '1. The enemy in front of the II *SS-Panzerkorps* on 8 July is strongly defeated. Conducting defensive fights against tanks. Strong enemy tanks south-east of Oboyan, so we need to be ready for an approach of a new enemy tank and motorized reserve in the Prokhorovka area and west from it'. This order testifies to the good knowledge they had of their enemy, thus disproving the statements that the appearance of the Fifth Guards Tank Army 'occurred to be a bolt from the blue to the enemy'. The German command not only had been informed about the appearance of a large Soviet tank group east of Oboyan, but had also accurately predicted its future use.

Soviet historians consider that this order from the II *SS-Panzerkorps* helps to determine the real shape of the battle. First it fixes the date of the beginning of the battle: 'The II *SS-Panzerkorps* is breaking through after regrouping... to the northeast... on 10 July...' Secondly, the corps' objective is specified: to break through 'until Prokhorovka – hill 5km [3.1 miles] east from Kartashevka and annihilate the enemy in this area'. And thirdly, it clearly determines who is to carry out what missions from the beginning of the battle.

The objective of *Leibstandarte Adolf Hitler* was to 'break through from the Teterevino area' to the northeast along the road, 'capture Prokhorovka', in the region: right – 'a forest west to Ivanovskiye Vyselki, Storozhevoye, Leski'; left – 'settlements on the Psel eastern riverside until Verkniaya Olshanka'. *Das Reich* was to remain in its position on the right flank in the current region, having its front line to the east. Moving behind *Leibstandarte Adolf Hitler* in pre-battle order, it had to be covered by one regiment of *Das Reich* the 'right flank' of the latter. 'If the flank of *LAH* meet strong enemy resistance, the *DR* are to take strongpoint positions – or, in other words, to take a defensive position. The main task was to support *LAH* moving forward and carrying out its mission.

The terrain over which these forces would advance and on which one of the world's greatest tank battles would be fought was undulating ground rising from 200–250m (656–820ft) up to 300–350m (984–1145ft). On the Melekhovo axis, *balkas* limited the operations of large tank formations. The watershed between the Don and Dneiper rivers ran along the line Khutor Luchki, Sovkhoz Komsomolets and Oktiabrsky. There were no natural barriers restricting tank and cross-country vehicle operations. The width of this line at its narrowest part – Andreevka–Storozhevoye, a deep ravine overgrown with forest – was about 6km (3.7 miles), and in the Prelestnoye–Yamki area it was 7–8km (4.3–4.9 miles). The Vorskla, Solotinka and Psel rivers from the west and Seversky Donets and Lipovy Donets rivers from the east formed a natural passage.

In 1943 there were two major transport links that allowed the Germans to supply and redeploy units: the Butovo, Yakovlevo, Prokhorovka and Belgorod, Belenikhino, Prokhorovka railways. Scope for camouflage and concealment – or as Soviet doctrine described the technique, 'masking' – was very limited. The most suitable areas were the *balkas*, usually overgrown by bushes, woods and settlements in the lowlands along rivers and by artificial reservoirs. The Psel river was the single water barrier that limited the German operations; they had to cross it and this constricted the attacking front. With a width that did not exceed 10–15m (30–49ft), this was not a serious barrier in a dry period, but after heavy rain the water meadows had a width of up to 100–200m (328–656ft). Gullies and ditches made it necessary to build bridges to carry tanks and other vehicles. The right bank rose to heights of between 20–25m (65–82ft) and was steeply sloping.

This, an area of roughly three square miles (7.7 square kilometres), would be the setting for what has long been described as the greatest tank battle in history.

Below: A PzKpfw IV fitted with stand-off armour around the turret waits rests outside the battle zone. The plates, known as Schürzen – *or 'skirts' – which covered the tracks, may have been lost in action. The tank has traversed its turret to the 6 o'clock position and is using a small farm for cover.*

CHAPTER FOUR

PROKHOROVKA: THE GREAT TANK BATTLE

After receiving Hausser's orders late on 9 July, II *SS-Panzerkorps'* three divisions struggled through the humid darkness of night to fulfil their commander's wishes and reach new concentration areas from which they could launch a vigorous concerted assault on Prokhorovka.

NIGHT MOVEMENT IS ALWAYS difficult, and this case was no exception. By dawn on 10 July, some of the men and vehicles of *Leibstandarte* were still moving up to the Teterevino region and it was clear the corps could not meet Hausser's ambitious timetable. Therefore, it launched the assault on Prokhorovka with only the forces it had at hand. The piecemeal attack immediately encountered difficulties and, once again, was forced off schedule.

Just before dawn, *Totenkopf's* SS-Panzergrenadier Regiment Eicke attacked across the Psel River and attempted to seize Hill 226.6, the key high ground just east of the small fortified village of Kliuchi. However, this attack failed in the face of stout resistance by defending elements of the Soviet 52nd Guards Rifle Division and 11th Motorized Rifle Brigade. Failure to capture Hill 226.6 meant that *Totenkopf*

Left: A Waffen-SS sniper with a Kar 98k ZF, a standard rifle fitted with the Zielfernrohr 42W (ZF 42W), a commercial x 4 telescopic sight adopted by the Wehrmacht. The sights were made by Ziel, Dialyt and Ajax and snipers carried them in metal or leather cases.

was unable to continue its critical drive northeast along the Psel and forced Hausser to delay his companion attack south of the river. Declaring, 'The bridgehead not established, postpone start of the attack,' Hausser ordered his corps to attack at 10:00. However, the heavy rain had produced appallingly bad road conditions and these further complicated necessary artillery regrouping, ultimately delaying the attack for another 45 minutes.

OPENING MOVES

Finally, at 10:45, the corps went into action. *Totenkopf* made up for its early-morning failure when, by noon, its lead elements thrust across the Psel River and managed to secure a foothold on the river's north bank. Heavy fighting raged all

Below: PzKpfw V Panther tanks of Waffen-SS Panzerdivision Das Reich. The commander of the tank has radio communications but is using hand signals to contact one of the tanks in his troop – this may be because the formation is maintaining radio silence.

afternoon for possession of Hill 226.6, but when the fighting subsided at nightfall, *Totenkopf's* Regiment Eicke was in possession of the hill's southern slopes and a small bridgehead east of Kliuchi.

Leibstandarte made even more significant progress against equally heavy resistance. While its 1st *SS-Panzergrenadier* Regiment was regrouping from its previous day's action to the west near Sukho-Solotino, the 2nd *SS-Panzergrenadier* Regiment's battalions, with supporting armour from the division's panzer regiment, advanced straight up the main road toward Prokhorovka. Repelling nearly constant Soviet tank attacks, and under heavy fire from Soviet artillery north of the Psel, the grenadiers had cleared Soviet forces from Komsomolets State Farm by 13:00 and began a bitter struggle for Hill 241.6, the next dominant terrain feature along the road just east of the farm. Fierce Soviet resistance, in particular by dug-in Russian tanks, and scattered heavy thunderstorms in the afternoon hindered *Leibstandarte's* advance until shortly after nightfall, when Hill 241.6 fell into

Above: One of the iconic photographs of the Eastern Front shows a Soviet 45mm (1.8in) Model 1932 L/46 antitank gun crew at the moment when a shell bursts near their gun. However, there is a strong chance that this is a posed picture and the 'shell' a demolition charge.

German hands. The 2nd *SS-Panzergrenadier* Regiment dug into new positions extending from the rail line to Hill 241.6, while the divisional reconnaissance battalion protected the *panzergrenadiers'* lengthening left flank and maintained contact with *Totenkopf* forces south of Mikhailovka. At a cost of 26 killed, 168 wounded, and three missing, *Leibstandarte* had taken 60 Soviet prisoners and 130 deserters and had destroyed 53 Soviet tanks and 23 antitank guns. However, despite this impressive score, the division had failed to secure its day's objective.

Das Reich also made only limited gains on 10 July. Attacking at mid-morning with its *Panzergrenadier* Regiment *Deutschland* and elements of the division's panzer regiment, *Gruppenführer* Kruger's division thrust forward south of the Prokhorovka road from east of Teterevino across the rail line toward Storozhevoe. It, too met, heavy resistance, and after a grinding all-day advance, it seized a portion of Ivanovskii Vyselok, a small village lodged in a long ravine south of the Prokhorovka road and Storozhevoe. Deprived of support

from its *Der Führer* Regiment, which had to defend *Das Reich*'s long right flank from Iasnaia Poliana to near Nechaevka, the best the division could do was to keep abreast of *Leibstandarte*'s forward units.

Hausser was undeterred by his corps' slow progress, and late on 10 July he ordered the attack on Prokhorovka to continue the following day. He had every reason to remain optimistic, for by daybreak *Leibstandarte*'s remaining regiment would be available to join the advance. Meanwhile, he urged both *Totenkopf* and *Das Reich* to shift more forces into the Prokhorovka sector. To facilitate that process, the remaining regiment of the 167th Infantry Division regrouped to the Lipovyi Donets, where it relieved elements of *Das Reich* for use farther north.

During the night of 10 July, *Totenkopf*, which had regrouped from the right to left flanks in the Greznoye area, was tasked with securing the bridgehead on the Psel right riverside, building a bridge for the tanks, then concentrating them to the north of the river. Next it was tasked with

Below: Waffen-SS soldiers with a camouflaged SdKfz 251 half-track mounting a 2cm (0.8in) Flak 30 anti-aircraft gun. During a break in the fighting, the soldiers are displaying a Swastika flag to identify their position to Luftwaffe ground attack aircraft operating in the area.

'breaking through the Psel valley and north of it to northeast and capture Beregovoye and the hills northwest of it'.

Timings for the operation were:

'for *LAH* Division – 06:00.

Totenkopf Division – reports during night about formation of a shock group on the bridgehead.'

DAS REICH ON 10 JULY

Dawn broke at 02:30 on 10 July. The heavy rainstorms had continued and the ground remained muddy. To the west,

after a week of almost uninterrupted fighting, *Großdeutschland* was showing signs of exhaustion and was much reduced in strength. It was ordered to wheel to the south and west and clear out Soviet positions on the left flank. The panzer regiment and reconnaissance detachment with the grenadier regiment were to advance towards Hill 243.0 and then exploit to the north. They were then to seize Hill 247.0 to the south of Kruglik and next move southwards to the small forest north of Beresowka. It was around this woodland that Soviet positions of General Moskalenko's Fortieth Army and Katukov's First Tank Army were holding up the advance of the 3rd Panzer Division.

The heavy fighting and the powerful *Luftwaffe* support for the attack are recorded in the *Großdeutschland* Divisional War Diary:

'The dark of the night slowly passed over to the grey of the rising of 10 July. At about 03.30, the tanks of Panzer Group Strachwitz at Point 1.8 southwest of Novoselovka spotted the enemy tanks they had heard during the night in the water-filled valley before them. Soon afterward, the first armour-piercing shells began falling: a battle between steel giants began this day of fighting on the southern front of the Kursk bulge. By 04:00, the first enemy tanks could be seen burning on the battlefield; but painful gaps had also been smashed in our own ranks. One of 11 Battalion's command tanks took a direct hit in the turret, which killed *Unteroffizier* König. The rest of the crew, some of them wounded, were able to escape from the tank. *Oberst* Graf von Strachwitz was also injured, by the recoil of the breech, while destroying an enemy tank and had to hand command of the Panzer Regiment GD to *Hauptmann* von Wietersheim….With admiration, we watch the *Stukas* attacking the Russian tanks uninterruptedly and with wonderful precision. Squadron after squadron of *Stukas* come over to drop their deadly eggs on the Russian armour. Dazzling white flames indicate that another enemy tank has "brewed up". This happens again and again.'

The attack by *Großdeutschland* went well. Hills 243.0 and 247.0 were taken and Soviet armour and infantry withdrew to cover in the woods north of Beresowka. They were now trapped between *Großdeutschland* and 3rd Panzer. Von Mellenthin now assumed that the enemy defences had been eliminated and that the advance to the north could resume.

Major Franz, the commander of *Großdeutschland*'s assault gun battalion, described the ferocious combat, relating how the desperate Soviets again employed their *Katyusha* multiple rocket launchers in direct fire:

'Widely separated, the assault guns of the two batteries drove at full speed toward the village [Kruglik]. At first, there was no defence at all. At 300m [328 yards] from the village, I already had the impression that the enemy had left the field. I suddenly saw fiery arrows coming toward us from the outskirts of Kruglik. Before I could figure out what they were, there were explosions directly in front of the mass of advancing assault guns. The vehicle next to me, I believe it was *Wachtmeister* Brauner of 1st Battery, began to stream smoke. Thank God it turned out to be one of the smoke candles that every assault gun carried. The vehicle had taken a direct hit in the bow plates but suffered no damage. The explosion and the effect of the projectile revealed that we were under direct fire from a Stalin Organ, the first time we experienced something like this in the campaign. Darkness slowly settled over the battlefield while the assault guns destroyed the Stalin Organ and the nests of resistance which repeatedly flared up at the outskirts of the village. The planned surprise attack misfired, nevertheless we – the armoured reconnaissance battalion and the assault gun battalion together – had once again achieved more than was expected of us.'

FIRST TANK ARMY

The bigger picture was that on the night of 9/10 July, General Katukov's hard-pressed First Tank Army tried to reorganize its defences from the Psel River to the Oboyan road and southward along the Pena River in accordance with Vatutin's instructions. General Getman's VI Tank Corps, with Colonel Chernov's weakened 90th Guards Rifle Division and the remnants of the III Mechanized Corps' 1st and 10th Mechanized Brigades, defended along the Pena River on the First Tank Army's right flank, with Getman's forces facing east and south. Although German forces had already penetrated menacingly westward into his defensive front just north of Verkhopen'e, Katukov took comfort from the fact that his defences were now backed up by the fresh 184th and 204th Rifle Divisions, which were dug-in to his rear. In addition, his corps, which had been reduced to a combined strength of roughly 100 tanks, was now backed up by the reinforcing armour of the X Tank Corps, also positioned to his rear (with about 120 tanks and self-propelled guns).

In Katukov's centre, General Krivoshein's shattered III Mechanized Corps now defended along the Oboyan road, backed up by elements of Colonel D.F. Dremin's fresh 309th Rifle Division, the newly redeployed armour of General Kravehenko's V Guards Tank Corps, survivors of the 67th Guards Rifle Division, and heavy antitank support provided by Vatutin. On the First Tank Army's left flank, General Chernienko's XXXI Tank Corps clung grimly to defences

Above: A 7.5cm (3in) Pak 40/2 auf Sfl II Marder II Sdkfz 131 self-propelled antitank gun. Mounted on a PzKpfw II chassis, the gun had a maximum range of 1.8km (1.1 miles); firing AP40 shot from 500m (546yds), it could penetrate 115mm (0.5in) of armour at 30 degrees.

eastward to the banks of the Psel River, also backed up by riflemen of the 309th Division and remnants of the 51st Guards Rifle Division. Soviet armour in the sector from the Oboyan road to the banks of the Psel River numbered no more than 300 tanks and self-propelled guns. By the evening of 9 July, Vatutin transferred control of the V Guards Tank Corps, X Tank Corps and 204th Rifle Division from the Voronezh Front reserve to the First Tank Army. The stage was set for the bitter fighting that would follow.

General von Knobelsdorff of the XLVIII Panzer Corps had detected the weak junction between the Soviet VI Tank and III Mechanized Corps, and during the night he concentrated his forces to exploit this weakness. His aim was to destroy the

Soviet force along his flank while continuing his northward drive along the Oboyan road. He assigned the flank task to the *Großdeutschland* and 3rd Panzer Divisions and the Oboyan thrust to 11th Panzer. What von Knobelsdorff did not know, however, was that his forces could not do both. The combined armour strength of his corps had eroded to 173 tanks and assault guns (including 30 Panthers) and the *Großdeutschland* Division and its attached 10th Panzer Brigade had fallen to 87 'runners'.

GROSSDEUTSCHLAND

Beginning at 03:30 on 10 July, *Großdeutschland* fought a bitter battle through the groves and ravines northwest of Verkhopen'e. The attack smashed the defences of the Soviet 200th Tank Brigade and forced General Getman to shift his forces quickly to his threatened left flank. In rapid succession, he moved elements of his 112th Tank and 6th Motorized Rifle Brigades and 60th Heavy Tank Regiment into the threatened sector, and they were immediately sucked into the vortex of a confused meeting engagement with *Großdeutschland*'s advancing armour.

Großdeutschland's reconnaissance battalion, with supporting assault gun and half-track battalions, lunged on through the gloom of dawn and seized Hill 247 along the Kruglik–Berezovka road. This severed Getman's communications with the rear and the supporting X Tank Corps, threatening the viability of his entire force. At the same time, the armour spearhead of *Großdeutschland* – Panzer Group Strachwitz, supported by the division's Fusilier Regiment – captured Hill 243 after a vicious three-hour battle. However, intense Soviet flanking fire meant that the Germans took heavy losses, including *Oberst* Graf von Strachwitz, who was wounded.

In his frantic efforts to halt the German flank attack, Getman's tank corps was decimated in the heavy and confused fighting. When they went into combat along the corps' flank, the 200th Tank Brigade and the 6th Motorized and 112th Tank Brigades went into battle in small packets but were then cut into even smaller units and almost destroyed before the survivors withdrew under cover of darkness. By

the evening of 10 July, the 3rd Panzer Division joined the fighting, sending its 70-tank armoured nucleus through Verkhopen'e and southward toward Berezovka into the midst of the VI Tank Corps' defences. As a result, the VI Tank Corps had become virtually combat-ineffective, with no more than 35 tanks and 10 antitank guns surviving.

A Soviet classified account graphically describes the fate of 6th Tank Corps on 10 July:

'Isolated and broken-up tank groups of the 200th and 112th Tank Brigades were encircled in the region north of Berezovka, where, during the course of the day, they fought with enemy tanks and infantry. Only at night were they able to link up with the main force of the VI Tank Corps. As a result of the combat on 10 July, the VI Tank Corps suffered heavy losses and counted in its ranks only 35 tanks and 10 antitank guns. Having withdrawn to the line Novoselovka–Noven'koe, the corps halved its defensive front

Below: In a secure area, Soviet infantry hitch a ride on a T-34. Many men marched into battle, though US supplied trucks would give Soviet forces increased mobility. Indeed, right up to 1945, ammunition and rations were also brought forward by horse- and camel-drawn carts.

KURSK: THE VITAL 24 HOURS

(from 20 to 10km [12.4 to 6.2 miles]) and again restored its smashed defences.'

General Getman, commanding the corps, summed up the action:

'Many of our soldiers and commanders fell heroically in the five days of ferocious battle. Hundreds of corps' soldiers were wounded and evacuated to the rear. We suffered especially heavy losses in equipment. By the end of 10 July, not more than 50 tanks, more than one half light, remained operational and three batteries of antitank guns, two in the 6th Motorized Rifle Brigade and one in the 22d Tank Brigade. Reinforcing units – the 60th Tank, and the 270th and 79th Guards Mortar Regiments – and two batteries of self-propelled guns, as well as the subunits of the 1st and 10th Mechanized Brigades, which were operating with us, were also considerably weakened. Nevertheless, the corps continued to resist the enemy. Having littered the field of battle with hundreds of his burned and destroyed tanks and guns and thousands of bodies, the enemy succeeded in pushing our lines back several kilometres. His attempt to seize fully the village of Noven'koe and advance further in a northern and western direction failed. Meeting organized fire resistance, he ceased his attacks at nightfall. But, certainly, only so that he could renew the attacks in the morning with new force. Understanding this, we prepared for the new battle.'

General Katukov was more laconic in his memoirs:

'Finally, the Hitlerites succeeded in penetrating to the northwest and reaching the population points of Noven'koe and Novoselovka. Clearly, they were attempting to encircle the VI Tank Corps and 90th Guards Division, which were defending southwest of Verkhopen'e. On Shalin's [the army chief of staff's] map, it was clear how the blue crayon line enveloped the positions of our forces from the northeast. He ordered the forces to withdraw to the west and, together with the X Tank Corps and the 184th Rifle Division, to create a dense defence. As a result of these measures, the enemy attack misfired on the army's right flank.'

Unlike his corps commander, however, Katukov failed to mention the heavy casualties.

In other command posts, the situation maps were being studied closely. The most significant aspect of Vatutin's extensive regrouping effort and his plans for a future decisive

Opposite: A machine gun crew work their way forward through the smoke rising from burning grass. The man in the foreground has the metal container for a spare barrel slung over his shoulder; the fast rate of fire made quick barrel changes vital to avoid overheating.

counterstroke was the movement of General P.A. Rotmistrov's powerful tank army into the Prokhorovka region. Rotmistrov's army received its alert order on 9 July, and during the next 24 hours moved 100km (62.1 miles) by road into designated assembly areas in the rear of Zhadov's Fifth Guards Army. Assigned to Sixty-Ninth Army control on 10 July, Rotmistrov met that day with Vatutin and STAVKA representative Vasilevsky at Front headquarters in Oboyan to review the situation.

The Front commander invited Rotmistrov closer to the map. Pointing with a pencil at the Prokhorovka region, Vatutin said:

'Having failed to penetrate to Kursk through Oboyan, clearly the Hitlerites have decided to shift the axis of their main blow farther east along the rail line to Prokhorovka. There, the forces of II SS-Panzerkorps have assembled, which must attack along the Prokhorovka axis in cooperation with XLVIII Panzer Corps and tank formations of Group Kempf.'

Vatutin glanced at Vasilevsky and then, turning to Rotmistrov, he continued: 'Thus, Pavel Alekseevich, we have decided to oppose the SS tank divisions with your tank guardsmen to deliver a counterstroke against the enemy with Fifth Guards Tank Army, reinforced by a further two tank corps.'

'Incidentally,' said Vasilevsky, 'the German tank divisions possess new heavy Tiger tanks and Ferdinand self-propelled guns. Katukov's tank army has suffered considerably from them. Do you know anything about this equipment and how do you feel about fighting with them?'

'We know, Comrade Marshal. We received tactical-technical information about them from the Steppe Front staff. We have also thought about means for combating them.'

'Interesting!' added Vatutin, and nodding to me, said, 'Continue.'

'The fact is that the Tigers and Ferdinands not only have strong frontal armour, but also a powerful 88mm [3.4in] gun with direct fire range. In that regard they are superior to our tanks, which are armed with 76mm [3in] guns. Successful struggle with them is possible only in circumstances of close in combat, with exploitation of the T-34's greater manoeuvrability and by flanking fire against the side armour of the heavy German machines.'

'In other words, engage in hand-to-hand fight and board them,' said the Front commander, and again he turned to conversation about the forthcoming counterstroke, in which First Tank Army, Sixth, Seventh and Fifth Guards Armies were to take part.

'Thus,' write historians David Glantz and Jonathan House, 'the most important and, subsequently, most apparent aim of Vatutin's counteroffensive was to halt the German advance on Prokhorovka and, hence, the German seizure of Oboyan and Kursk. However, the counterstroke Vatutin planned and carried out against the XLVIII Panzer Corps' left flank, although subsequently masked by the "noise" and furore of the Prokhorovka battle, was equally important, for it denied the Germans the opportunity of adding *Großdeutschland* Division to their main attack on Oboyan and Kursk. This, in no small measure, conditioned the German setback at Prokhorovka and the overall failure of Operation Citadel. No less critical to the success of the German offensive and the fate of Vatutin's counterattack plans was the situation east of the Northern Donets River, where General Breith's III Panzer Corps struggled to fulfil its offensive promise.'

Below: T-34 76/D tanks move up to the front. To the right, a truck driver lounges by his US-supplied vehicle. He has covered the windscreen with a tarpaulin to reduce the reflection, which could be seen from the air.

As they conferred, Hoth's Fourth *Panzerarmee* was in position to capture the town of Prokhorovka, secure a bridgehead over the Psel River and advance on Oboyan. The Psel was the last natural barrier between Manstein's Panzer divisions and Kursk. According to Soviet sources, the Fourth *Panzerarmee*'s attack on the town was led by SS General Paul Hausser's II *SS-Panzerkorps*, General Otto von Knobelsdorff's XLVIII Panzer Corps and General Ott's LII Army Corps. Even allowing for the losses these formations had suffered, it would be a formidable force – yet the reality of the fighting at Prokhorovka would prove to be the ultimate test.

THE SOVIET RESPONSE

The Fifth Guards Tank Army was the Soviet strategic armoured reserve in the south, the last significant uncommitted armoured formation in the sector, with more than 650 tanks. The Soviet operational armoured reserve, General Mikhail E. Katukov's First Tank Army, was already in action against Hoth's Fourth *Panzerarmee* south of the Psel. Katukov's army had been unable to prevent the Germans

Above: Flames lick around a knocked out T-34. Soviet tank forces suffered heavily at Prokhorovka but insisted they inflicted comparable casualties on the Germans. Whatever the figures, the outcome was a Soviet victory that was followed by a summer counteroffensive.

from reaching the river, however. His VI Tank Corps, which was originally equipped with more than 200 tanks, had only 50 left by 11 July, and the other two corps of Katukov's army had also sustained serious losses. On 10 July, *Totenkopf*, commanded by Hermann Priess, had established a bridgehead over the Psel, west of Prokhorovka. By 11 July, the division's panzer group had crossed the river on pontoon bridges and reached the bridgehead. What was left of Katukov's armour regrouped to oppose the XLVIII Panzer Corps below Oboyan or counterattack the Psel bridgehead. Reinforced with the XXXIII Rifle Corps and X Tank Corps, Katukov launched continuous attacks on the *Totenkopf* units on the north bank of the river.

Hausser's advance had caught Soviet defenders along the Prokhorovka axis at an awkward moment. During the hours of darkness before the German thrust began, Soviet forces frantically carried out Vatutin's regrouping orders, and their defences suffered accordingly. On the morning of 9 July, General Burkov's X Tank Corps withdrew from its sector north of the Prokhorovka road and began the long march to

join Katukov's First Tank Army defences along the Oboyan road. It left behind its 11th Motorized Rifle Brigade, which defended along the Psel River from Krasny Oktiabr to Mikhailovka, and the 52nd Guards Rifle Division and its 178th Tank Brigade, which defended on the II Tank Corps' left flank north of the Prokhorovka road. The 11th Motorized stoutly resisted *Totenkopf*'s drive to gain a bridgehead over the Psel and continued to defend Hill 241.6 after the Germans achieved their foothold north of the river.

When the X Tank Corps withdrew, General Popov's II Tank Corps assumed responsibility for defence of the Prokhorovka road. Popov deployed his brigades astride the road forward of Komsomolets State Farm and the railway line running south past Krasnaia Poliana. His 26th, 169th, and 99th Tank Brigades formed from left to right across the

Prokhorovka road, and the 178th Tank Brigade concentrated along his right flank to the Psel valley. At dawn on 10 July, protected by infantry from the 183rd Rifle Division, his brigades attacked down the road into the teeth of German antitank defences and were soon enmeshed in a running battle with the two advancing regiments of *Leibstandarte* and *Das Reich*.

Confused and costly fighting raged all day for possession of Komsomolets State Farm and Hill 241.6. Despite able support from the 1502nd and 48th Antitank Regiments, Popov's forces had been driven from both points by the end of the day. Yet despite heavy losses Popov remained optimistic, for lead elements of General Zhadov's Fifth Guards Army reached Prokhorovka shortly after nightfall, to back up the flagging armour defence.

On Vatutin's orders, Colonel A.M. Sazonov's crack 9th Guards Airborne Division had marched through the dusty streets of Prokhorovka and, by daybreak on 11 July, had dug into defensive positions anchored on the city's eastern suburbs to the rear of Popov's tired tankers. The sudden appearance of Sazonov's division marked the forward deployment of all of Zhadov's XXXIII Guards Rifle Corps into the II *SS-Panzerkorps*' path. The rifle corps' 95th and 97th Guards Rifle Divisions occupied defences along the Psel River to back up the depleted 51st and 52nd Guards Rifle Divisions. All four divisions prepared to meet the II *SS-Panzerkorps*' renewed advance north of the river. The 42nd Guards Rifle Division remained in reserve, prepared to reinforce the 97th Guards or 9th Guards Airborne should the need arise. Once these forces were in place, late on 10 July, the 183rd Rifle Division disengaged from combat and shifted its regiments southward by forced march to relieve V Guards Tank Corps forces, which, on Vatutin's orders, were also redeploying to join the First Tank Army.

GROßDEUTSCHLAND

Formed in 1939 from *Wacht* (Guard) Regiment Berlin and the infantry training battalion at Doeberitz, *Großdeutschland* (GD) was raised as a full four-battalion infantry regiment. The name 'Großdeutschland' (greater Germany) was chosen to reflect the fact that the regiment drew its members from all over Germany rather than specific regions as most army units did.

Großdeutschland developed as the army's premier armoured formation, comparable only to 1st *SS-Leibstandarte Adolf Hitler* and Hermann Göring Divisions. It progressively expanded from regiment to division and finally corps. Associated formations raised with the help of cadres from *Großdeutschland* were Brandenburg Division, *Führer Begleit* (escort) Panzer Division, *Führer Panzergrenadier* Division, *Panzergrenadier* Division *Kurmark* – all were entitled to wear *Großdeutschland* cuffbands.

The year 1942 saw the expansion of *GD* into a full motorized infantry division. The orders concerning this re-organization emphasized its status as an elite unit. Only fit men of a certain minimum height with perfect eyesight and no criminal record were admitted. Ideally, these men were volunteers who wanted the honour of serving with the forces of *GD*. These new orders also saw to it that *GD* was the first frontline unit to receive the latest and best equipment as it became available, notably the Panther tank.

In 1943, the Allies' growing strength was felt on all fronts. The Soviet army benefited enormously from two factors in its favour: firstly its ability to rebuild completely destroyed units from its vast pool of men and, secondly, the large amounts of lend-lease material coming in from the West. *GD*, however, received reinforcements in the form of additional artillery, a Tiger tank unit and more armoured personnel carriers.

For *GD*, 1944 was the year of the heaviest fighting yet. Many divisions were sent home or to France for rest and refitting, but *GD* was not to be so fortunate. This was one disadvantage of being an elite unit, expected to do the impossible against overwhelming odds. *GD*, as in the past, was continuously thrown into critical battles and weak points in the lines. The unit earned the nickname 'The Fire Brigade' for its efforts in saving critical military situations. A *GD* company commander at Kursk, Major Otto Remer, would become notorious as the officer who, following instructions from Goebbels, smashed the July Plot in 1944.

Early in 1945, *GD* was expanded into a full Panzer Corps, but this did not help in what was rapidly becoming a desperate situation. *Panzerkorps Großdeutschland* was shifted from battle to battle, but even the most dedicated troops could not hold against superior numbers and firepower indefinitely. In late March 1945, the last remnants of *GD* reached Pillau and some 4000 men were involved in heavy defensive fighting. Out of these, only 800 were able to reach Schleswig-Holstein. With this final move, *GD* ceased to exist as a fighting force.

Above: The commander of a Tiger tank unit of Waffen-SS Panzerdivision Das Reich *observes the terrain. The flat horizons made navigation difficult since there were few landmarks. A Swastika flag is just visible on the rear deck of the tank for air identification.*

The redeployment of the V Guards Tank Corps was also part of Vatutin's significant and tricky armoured regroupment aimed at bolstering First Tank Army's defences further west. Late on 10 July, after days of intense combat against the flank of II *SS-Panzerkorps* along the Lipovyi Donets south of Prokhorovka, Kravehenko's corps began its long march to join the battle of Katukov's First Tank Army against the XLVIII Panzer Corps. At the same time, General Burdeiny's II Guards Tank Corps, which during previous days had repeatedly attacked the right flank of II *SS-Panzerkorps* along the Lipovyi Donets south of Teterevino, itself regrouped. Replaced by the 93rd Guards Rifle Division and now under Sixty-Ninth Army control, the corps withdrew late on 10 July into assembly areas around Maloe Iablonovo to rest and refit. Once it was rested, Vatutin

planned to use the corps to support the future counterstroke of the Fifth Guards Tank Army, which was then also closing into the Prokhorovka region.

With only 18 hours remaining before his attack, Rotmistrov made final adjustments in his force deployments, confident that these could be completed before the appointed time. He chose for his jumping-off positions a swathe 15km (9.3 mile) wide, which went through the broad rolling fields west and southwest of Prokhorovka, from north of the Psel River and south across the road and rail line to Storozhevoe. This offered more than ample space for deploying Major-General B.S. Bakharov's XVIII and Major-General I.F. Kirichenko's XXIX Tank Corps in first echelon, adjacent to the II Tank and II Guards Tank Corps, which were to attack abreast along his left flank in the Vinogradovka and Belenikhino sectors. Rotmistrov held Major-General B.M. Skvortsov's V Guards Mechanized Corps in second echelon and a small task force commanded by his deputy army commander, Major-General K.G. Trufanov, in army reserve. During the final stages of the complex redeployment, late on

Right: A Waffen-SS MG42 machine gunner covers the edge of a track where Soviet trucks and tanks have been ambushed. He has stretched out the 50-round belt to ensure a smooth feed into the gun. The open hatches on the T-34/76D indicate that the crew escaped.

11 July, the II Tank Corps' 99th and 169th Tank Brigades, which were defending west of Prokhorovka along the road and railway line, were to withdraw and shift southward into their new attack sectors.

Hence, Rotmistrov planned to commit about 500 tanks and self-propelled guns in his initial assault. What he did not know was that the precipitous German advance the next day would severely disrupt his careful attack planning and the smooth regroupment of the II Tank Corps. His well-planned counteroffensive would quickly turn into a desperate and confused armoured meeting engagement.

11 JULY 1943

Early on 11 July, after the Soviet forces had completed their initial force regrouping but before Vatutin's counteroffensive preparations were complete, the II *SS-Panzerkorps* resumed its attack on Prokhorovka. Now it was supported by the bulk of *Luftflotte* IV, which, as before, was able to achieve tenuous air superiority along the Prokhorovka axis – at least on 11 July. While *Totenkopf* struggled to expand its narrow bridgehead north of the Psel, anchored on the southern slopes of Hill 226.6, the now fully assembled *Leibstandarte* drove forward from Hill 241.6 along both sides of the road to Prokhorovka, with *Das Reich*'s *Deutschland* Regiment protecting its right flank.

At 05:00, the 1st and 2nd Battalions of *Leibstandarte*'s 2nd *SS-Panzergrenadier* Regiment advanced eastward astride the road, destroying or bypassing dug-in tanks and antitank guns of the 169th Tank Brigade, II Tank Corps. Although under heavy flanking fire from Soviet forces on the northern bank of the Psel and from artillery firing from Prelestnoe and Petrovka, the panzer grenadiers covered over 2km (1.2 miles) in less than two hours and were halted only by heavy fire from Soviet troops dug in around Hill 252.4, just southeast of Oktyabrskiy State Farm.

All the while, the two battalions had fended off attacks by small groups of tanks against both of their flanks, launched by the Soviet 99th Tank Brigade from Andreevka in the Psel valley and the 169th Tank Brigade from Storozhevoe. These harassing attacks, the intense artillery and antitank fire, and the discovery of an immense antitank ditch, which covered the approaches to Oktyabrskiy State Farm, prompted the regiment to call for assistance.

Division headquarters responded promptly. At 06:30, it ordered its 1st *SS-Panzergrenadier* Regiment, supported by the four Tiger tanks of its 13th Company, to join the attack and clear Soviet forces out of Storozhevoe on the 2nd Regiment's right flank. Fifteen minutes later, it ordered the division's reconnaissance battalion into action to protect the division's left flank against Soviet attacks from Andreevka in the Psel valley. Meanwhile, the divisional artillery and

Nebelwerfer regiments opened intense fire on Soviet artillery positions north of the Psel, and Stuka dive-bombers began hourly strikes against Soviet defences to the front.

Up to now, *Leibstandarte* had been contending only with the already depleted II Tank Corps and small infantry elements from the 183rd Rifle Division. The initial German attack penetrated the 169th Tank Brigade's defence rather easily and forced the Soviet tanks to withdraw slowly up the Prokhorovka road and toward Storozhevoe. On the 169th's left, the 99th Tank Brigade wheeled back toward the Psel valley, from which it began launching periodic forays against *Leibstandarte*'s flank, supported by 52nd Guards Rifle Division infantry. When the Germans resumed their assault, however, they ran straight into the dug-in 9th Guards Airborne Division, which was now supported by the remaining tanks of the 169th Tank Brigade and the 57th Tank

Regiment and 301st Antitank Artillery Regiment, provided by the Fifth Guards Army. As the relative coolness of dawn gave way to the stifling heat and humidity of the full summer day, the fighting took on new ferocity.

Only the night before, the paratroops of Colonel A.M. Sazonov's division had occupied defences forward of Prokhorovka, both to back up the 183rd Rifle Division, which was supposed to be regrouping to the south, and to cover the forward deployment of Rotmistrov's tank army. Although they did not expect to go into action until the next day, they found themselves within hours at the focal point of the II SS-Panzerkorps' assault. Sazonov deployed his 26th and

Below: Sergeant Zhukov digs for mines near a knocked out 7.5cm (3in) Stug III Ausf 142/1 assault gun. Deep Soviet minefields slowed up the German attacks, and once AFVs were immobilized, they could be destroyed by antitank guns or even infantry tank hunting patrols with rudimentary weapons.

28th Guards Airborne Regiments in line abreast, covering to the south.

At 09:05, after a preliminary bombardment by artillery, Stukas and Nebelwerfers, Leibstandarte resumed its advance. Its 2nd Battalion, 2nd SS-Panzergrenadier Regiment, supported by Tiger tanks and assault guns, quickly pushed on toward Hill 252.2, where at 09:50 it ran into intense fire from the 26th Guards Airborne Regiment's 2nd Battalion and from Soviet positions covering Oktyabrskiy State Farm. Joined by the 1st Battalion, the two regiments fought an intense three-hour fight for the key hill but failed to dislodge the paratroops. At 10:15, the division's panzer group joined the attack, and finally, at 13:10, it captured the precious and now bloodsoaked crest of the hill.

Major D.I. Boriskin, the commander of the 3rd Battalion, Guards, reported on the situation to his regimental commander, Guards Lieutenant-Colonel G.M. Kashpersky, and ordered the commanders of his rifle companies and

batteries to open heavy fire as the tanks and infantry neared their positions.

'Oktyabrskiy State Farm, Hill 252.2, and Lutovo [village] shuddered from exploding bombs, shells, and mines. The soldiers attentively observed the approaching enemy from the foxholes they had dug the night before. When only several hundred meters remained to the edge of the state farm, infantry poured out of the armoured transporters. Sub-machine gunners opened fire on the run, and concealing themselves behind the tanks, they began the assault. The distorted faces of the Fascists bore witness to the fact that their warlike ardour was roused by a fairly large dose of schnapps.

'"Fire!" ordered the battery commander. A squall of 3rd Battalion fire met the Fascists. The long bursts of I.V. Khoroshikh's and P.N. Lyznikov's heavy machine guns struck the infantry in the flanks and were echoed by the guardsmen's light machine guns and submachine guns.

Divisional artillery and supporting artillery battalions of the RGK [Reserve of the High Command] 3rd Artillery Penetration Division laid down an immovable defensive fire in front of Oktyabrskiy State Farm. The battalion and regimental artillery of Guards Lieutenants I.G. Samykin and A.F. Shestakov delivered fire over open sights.

'The infantry were separated from the tanks, and facing a hurricane of fire from the state farm, they withdrew to the reverse slopes of Hill 215.4. The Fascists attacked the 3rd Battalion two more times before 14:00. However, these were only reconnaissance in force... At 14:00, up to 100 enemy tanks, and up to a regiment of infantry riding in armoured transporters, attacked Oktyabrskiy State Farm and Hill 252.2.

Below: Abandoned PzKpfw V Ausf D Panthers on the Kursk battlefield. These tanks do not appear to have any battle damage and may well have suffered engine failure due to overheating. This was resolved in later marks, which were equipped with a hull-mounted machine gun.

Above: Soft-skinned vehicles of the Leibstandarte SS Adolf Hitler *in the cover of a* balka *with half-tracks on the skyline. The unarmoured vehicles include a VW Typ 166* Schwimmwagen *and Mercedes-Benz Typ 1500, and may be part of an HQ group.*

Around forty tanks and up to a regiment of motorized infantry attacked the neighbouring 287th Guards Rifle Regiment of 95th Guards Rifle Division. Discovering the junction between the 95th Guards and 9th Airborne Divisions, the Fascists tried to drive a wedge between them. One hundred and forty tanks were attacking along a front of 3km [1.9 miles] in the sector from Iamki Farm to Andreevka. A powerful fire raid and bombing strikes by 50 dive-bombers preceded the assault. Once again, fierce battle raged, but the effort was unequal. The enemy possessed absolute numerical superiority and displayed special obstinacy at the junction of the 26th and 287th regiments....

'Having pressed back the 26th and 287th Regiments, up to forty enemy tanks concentrated against Prelestnoe and the southern edge of Petrovka and up to 60 tanks across Hill 252.2 and along the railway line toward Prokhorovka. The 26th Regiment withdrew to the positions of the 23rd Guards Airborne Regiment, on the southwestern slopes of Hill 252.4 [1km (0.6 miles) west of Prokhorovka].'

The day's bitter fighting ended in early evening. Although *Leibstandarte* had made considerable progress and taken Oktyabrskiy State Farm and Hill 252.2, its panzer group was unable to advance beyond the state farm and found itself in a precarious position with both of its flanks exposed and subject to heavy fire. The 2nd *SS-Panzergrenadier* Regiment's 1st Battalion was able to secure the rail embankment southeast of Hill 252.2, and, jointly with the division's 1st Regiment's 2nd Battalion, it cleared the small forest adjacent to the embankment. The remainder of the 1st *SS-Panzergrenadier* Regiment penetrated into the village of Storozhevoe, where by nightfall it was engaged in the nasty process of clearing the village house by house. However, the regiment was not able to seize Storozhevoe, and, since *Das Reich's* advance also lagged, this left the division's right flank still vulnerable.

Leibstandarte's day-long thrust had irreparably smashed the II Tank Corps' defences, isolated the corps' 99th Tank Brigade in the Psel valley, driven a wedge between the 95th Guards and 9th Guards Airborne Divisions, and carved a deep salient in the 9th Guards Airborne Division's defences forward of Prokhorovka. Most significantly, the German thrust had wholly pre-empted the Fifth Guards Army's careful counterattack plans.

THE 26TH GUARDS AIRBORNE REGIMENT

On the southern approaches to Prokhorovka and Rotmistrov's projected tank assembly area, Lt Colonel G.M. Kashpers's 26th Guards Airborne Regiment occupied the 'place of honour' astride the Prokhorovka road. His 3rd Battalion, commanded by Major D.I. Boriskin, was dug in around and south of Oktyabrskiy State Farm, protected, in part, by the deep antitank ditches; his 2nd Battalion defended from Hill 252.2 southward to Iamki; and his 1st Battalion was in second echelon, positioned north of Oktyabrskiy State Farm with a 76mm (3in) gun battalion of the regimental artillery regiment.

Sazonov's 28th Guards Airborne Regiment, under the command of Major V.A. Ponomarov, occupied a strong defensive position due south of Prokhorovka, having two battalions forward and one in reserve in the city's suburbs. His third regiment, the 23rd Guards, under the command of Lieutenant-Colonel V.S. Savinov, together with the 10th Guards Separate Antitank Artillery Battalion, provided backup for the forward regiments from positions just northwest of Prokhorovka. The airborne division also had at its disposal the 57th Army Heavy Tank Regiment's 21 KV heavy tanks and 24 antitank guns of the 301st Army Antitank Artillery Regiment.

Sazonov and his paratroopers heard and even felt the early-morning fighting to the south as it moved closer to their forward positions south of Oktyabrskiy and Hill 252.2. His artillery fired barrages in support of their comrades, but

Below: Smoke drifts across a tank graveyard as German infantry approach a T-34/76B. Many of the Soviet tanks deployed at Kursk were not new models and some were more vulnerable types, like the T-70; there were also British and US tanks, including the Lee Grant.

within a matter of hours the sounds of fighting had died out, to be replaced only by the near-constant rumble of artillery fire. Within hours, Sazonov expected to see and hear Rotmistrov's tank army. Instead, the more menacing spectre of massed German tanks soon emerged from the dust. At 13:30, the 26th Guards Airborne Regiment and 169th Tank Brigade tanks struck the 1st Battalion, 2nd *SS-Panzergrenadier* Regiment, on the southern slopes of Hill 252.4. At 14:40, the 99th Tank Brigade, then being forced out of the village of Vasil'evka by *Totenkopf*'s soldiers, again attacked the reconnaissance battalion protecting *LAH*'s left flank. This threat became more serious when the Soviet 95th Guards Rifle Division, which by evening of 10 July had occupied positions along and south of the Psel on the 9th Guards Airborne's right flank, lent its weight to the 99th Tank Brigade's counterattacks.

FRONT INSPECTION

On the Soviet side Marshal Vasilevsky had come forward to observe the battlefield with General Pavel Rotmistrov. Rotmistrov later provided his view of the day's surprising developments:

'At around 19:00 on 11 July, Marshal A.M. Vasilevsky arrived at my CP [command post]. I reported to him about the army's combat formation and the missions assigned to the corps and the attached artillery. He approved my decisions and reported that he had had a conversation with I.V. Stalin, who ordered him to locate himself permanently with Fifth Guards Tank and Fifth Guards Armies, to coordinate their operations during the course of battle, and to render necessary assistance. I.V. Stalin ordered the front commander, N.F. Vatutin, to remain at his CP in Oboyan. The front chief of staff, Lieutenant-General S.P. Ivanov, went to the Korocha axis.

'Sufficient daylight still remained, and the marshal proposed an inspection of the jumping-off positions which I had selected for XXIX and XVIII Tank Corps. Our route passed through Prokhorovka to Belenikhino, and the quick-moving Willies [jeeps], bobbing up and down over the potholes, skirted round vehicles with ammunition and fuel, which were heading to the front. Transports with wounded slowly went past us. Here and there, destroyed trucks and smashed transports stood by the roadside. The road passed

Right: A Soviet Pulemyot Degtyarova Pekhotnii obr 1928 g *light machine gun crew in a frontline position. The corpse of a* Waffen-SS *soldier has been pushed aside. The well equipped and tidy appearance of the soldiers suggests, however, that this is a posed photograph.*

through wide fields of yellowing wheat. Beyond them began a forest that adjoined the village of Storozhevoe.

'There, along the northern edge of the forest, were the jumping-off positions of the XXIX Tank Corps. The XVIII Tank Corps would attack to the right, I explained to A.M. Vasilevsky. He intently peered into the distance and listened to the ever-growing rumble of battle. One could divine the

front lines of our combined armies from the clouds of smoke and the explosions of aerial bombs and shells. The agricultural installations of Komsomolets State Farm could be seen 2km [1.2 miles] distant to the right.

'Suddenly, Vasilevsky ordered the driver to stop. The vehicle turned off the road and abruptly halted amid the dust-covered roadside brush. We opened the doors and went several steps to the side. The rumble of tank engines could be clearly heard. Then the very same tanks came into sight.

'Quickly turning to me, and with a touch of annoyance in his voice, Aleksandr Mikhailovich asked me, "General! What's going on? Were you not forewarned that the enemy must not know about the arrival of our tanks? And they stroll about in the light of day under the Germans' eyes. . . ."

Above: Waffen-SS Grenadiere *slog through the dust kicked up by a PzKpfw III. The lead man carries a Tellermine 42 antitank mine. Mines like this could be wedged under the rear overhang of the turret of the T-34/76B in a hazardous close combat technique.*

'Instantly, I raised my binoculars. Indeed, tens of tanks in combat formation, firing from the march from their short-barrelled guns, were crossing the field and stirring up the ripened grain.

'"However, Comrade General, they are not our tanks. They are German. . . ."

'"So, the enemy has penetrated somewhere. He wants to pre-empt us and seize Prokhorovka."

'"We cannot permit that," I said to A.M. Vasilevsky, and by radio I gave the command to General Kirichenko to move without delay two tank brigades to meet the German tanks and halt their advance.

'Returning to my CP, we knew that the Germans had launched active operations against almost all of our armies.

Thus the situation suddenly became complicated. The jumping-off positions that we had earlier selected for the counterstroke were in the hands of the Hitlerites.'

What Rotmistrov did not know was that the advancing German tanks were from *Leibstandarte*'s 1st *SS-Panzergrenadier* Regiment. He did, however, understand the grim and harrowing consequences: 'In this regard, we had to prepare for the offensive anew; in particular, select artillery firing positions and deployment and attack lines. In the compressed time, we had to refine missions, organize cooperation between corps and units, revise the schedule for artillery support, and do all to facilitate the precise command and control of forces in combat.' In short, within a matter of hours, the violent German assault had turned Rotmistrov's well-planned offensive into a hasty engagement.

During the evening of 11 July, Hausser readied his divisions for an assault on Prokhorovka. *Totenkopf* anchored the left flank of the corps, while *Leibstandarte*, commanded by *Brigadeführer* Theodore Wisch, was in the centre, assembled west of the town between a rail line and the Psel.

Das Reich, commanded by *Gruppenführer* Walter Krüger, moved into its attack zone on the corps' right flank, which was several kilometres south of Tetrevino and southwest of Prokhorovka.

While Hausser's SS divisions prepared for battle, there was feverish activity in the Soviet camp as well. On 11 July, the Fifth Guards Tank Army arrived in the Prokhorovka area, having begun its march on 7 July from assembly areas nearly 332km (200 miles) to the east. The army consisted of the XVIII and XXIX Tank Corps and the V Guards Mechanized Corps. Rotmistrov's 650 tanks were reinforced by the II Tank Corps and II Guards Tank Corps, which had increased its strength to about 850 tanks, 500 of which were T-34s. The Fifth Guards' primary mission was to lead the main post-Kursk counteroffensive, known as Operation Rumyantsev, and its secondary mission was as defensive insurance in the south. The commitment of Rotmistrov's army at such an early date is stark evidence of Soviet concern about the situation on the Psel. The Fifth Guards' arrival at the Psel set the stage for the Battle of Prokhorovka.

On 11 July, XLVIII Panzer Corps issued orders for *Großdeutschland* to be relieved by Lieutenant-General Wetshoven's 3rd Panzer Division during the night. *Großdeutschland* was to assemble astride the road south of Hill 260.8 and be ready to advance north.

At the close of 11 July, *Fremde Heere Ost* – Foreign Armies East – gave the following assessment of the fighting.

'The overall impression of the combat operations by the enemy is still unchanged…After the enemy committed frontally the groupings which had been formed at the flanks against the German spearheads any attack by large forces against German flanks is unlikely. The likelihood of such an operation will appear only after the enemy has shifted the direction of his main effort to another place, and after a corresponding movement of his forces from the depth has been detected.'

THE 'CLASH OF ARMOUR' BEGINS

At around 02:30 on 12 July, Soviet and German tank crews began to discern the outline of vehicles and men. The day dawned clear but would be punctuated by heavy rain squalls.

Below: The commander of a StuG III Ausf G assault gun keeps watch while Waffen-SS Panzergrenadiere, *dug in at the edge of a sunflower field, enjoy a moment's respite. The StuG has lost some of its* Schürzen *side armour, a common event during fast-moving armoured actions.*

OBERSTURMFÜHRER MICHAEL WITTMANN – TANK ACE

Born on 22 April 1914, Michael Wittmann was a farmer's boy, so he grew up familiar with machinery and the skills of the hunter. He joined the army in 1934 and transferred to the *Leibstandarte-SS Adolf Hitler* in 1937. In Poland and France, he was in an armoured car reconnaissance unit. In the Balkan campaign, he commanded a StuG III Ausf A assault gun. On his first day in Russia, he destroyed six T34/76 tanks and was awarded the Iron Cross First Class. The young NCO went to the officers' school at Bad Tolz in June 1942. He returned to train on the Tiger I and now in the 13th (Heavy) Company of the 1st SS Panzer Regiment built up a formidable crew – Berger, Kirschner and Pollman and his gunner Balthasar 'Bobby' Woll. The Tiger's slow rate of turret traverse was compensated for by Wittmann's experience with the turretless StuG: he swung the complete tank into the direction of the enemy, saving time and placing the heavy armoured front towards the enemy.

With 138 destroyed enemy tanks and 132 antitank guns and field artillery pieces, *Hauptsturmführer* Michael Wittmann would be by far the most successful tank commander of World War II. With a combination of acute observation and strategical intuition, he was able to create surprise assaults and cause havoc, throwing his enemy totally off balance. He regarded his crew members as individuals of an elite combat team, not as parts of his vehicle, allowing his gunner to exploit a tactical situation in the event that Wittmann, as vehicle commander, was involved with other tasks.

The crew fought at Kharkov in January 1943, and at Kursk they were in action with the *LAH*. Wittmann's Tiger destroyed 30 AFVs, mainly T34/76s as well as 28 antitank guns. He particularly hated antitank guns, which were often well-camouflaged and hard to see. When he left the Eastern Front, Wittmann had destroyed 119 enemy tanks and won the Knight's Cross with Oak Leaves. In fighting in Normandy, he proved a formidable opponent to the British and Canadian forces, holding up and practically destroying the 22nd Brigade of the British 7th Armoured Division. He was killed in action south of Caen on 8 August 1944.

Left: Wittmann in Normandy in 1944 seated on his Tiger. Besides the Knight's Cross, he has the Iron Cross First Class, Verwundeten-Abzeichen *(Wound Badge) and the* Panzerkampfabzeichen *(Tank Battle Badge). Though a Panzer ace, he always insisted that his victories were a crew triumph.*

Mark Healy sets the scene for Prokhorovka.

'As the morning light broke across the landscape, visibility was obscured by local showers falling from a sky of leaden clouds, driven by a cold eastern wind. Periodically the sun would break through, allowing the observer a clearer perspective, to scan the lie of the land in what was clearly a very constricted arena of combat. For the commanders of the *SS-Panzerkorps*, standing in the turrets of their tanks, a panoramic sweep of the battlefield would have shown its northern boundary firmly anchored by the winding ribbon of the River Psel. Swinging southeast, the view would have taken in a traditional, slightly rolling steppe landscape characteristic of the Upper Donets valley, with fields of rye and wheat broken here and there by the small, cultivated plots of collective farmers, by hedges and the odd wooded copse. Farther to the east and barely three miles away lay the agricultural town of Prokhorovka, its tall grain silo standing proud against the skyline. The southernmost boundary of the battlefield, only [6.4km] 4 miles from the Psel, was fixed by the cutting of the Kursk-Belgorod railway, for to its immediate south the land became hilly and broken up by mounds and ravines, rendering it unsuitable for large-scale tank warfare.'

At 06:50, *LAH* began to push northwards towards the railway halt of Prokhorovka. It was here that it encountered the tanks and assault guns of the Fifth Guards Tank Army. *Leibstandarte* units reported hearing loud vehicle engine noise, which indicated massing Soviet armour. Soon afterwards, hundreds of Soviet tanks, carrying infantry, rolled out of Prokhorovka and its environs in groups of 40 to 50. Waves of T-34 and T-70 tanks advanced at high speed, charging straight at the startled Germans. When machine-gun fire, armour-piercing shells and artillery fire struck the T-34s, the Soviet infantry jumped off and sought cover. Leaving their infantry behind, the T-34s rolled on. Those Soviet tanks that survived the initial clash with SS armour continued a linear advance, only to be destroyed by the Germans.

When the initial Soviet attack paused, *Leibstandarte* pushed its armour toward the town and collided with elements of Rotmistrov's reserve armour. A Soviet attack by the 181st Tank Regiment was defeated by several SS Tigers. One of these, the 13th (Heavy) Company of the 1st SS Panzer Regiment, was commanded by *Obersturmführer* Michael Wittmann, the most successful tank commander of the war. Wittmann's group was advancing in flank support of the German main attack when it was engaged by the Soviet tank regiment at long range. The Soviet charge, straight at the

Above: A Waffen-SS MG42 crew, with the gun unusually fitted with a 50-round drum magazine, provide cover while a Grenadier digs in. The MG42 weighed 11.6 kg (25.6lb) and was quick and cheap to build, between 1942 and 1945 over 750,000 were produced.

Tigers over open ground, was suicidal. The frontal armour of the Tiger was impervious to the 76mm (3in) guns of the T-34s at any great distance. The field was soon littered with burning T-34s and T-70s. None of the Tigers were lost, but the 181st Tank Regiment was annihilated. Late in the day, Rotmistrov committed his last reserves, elements of the V Mechanized Corps, which finally halted *Leibstandarte*.

Das Reich began its attack from several kilometres southwest of Prokhorovka and was quickly engaged by aggressive battlegroups of the II Tank Corps and II Guards Tank Corps. Fierce, somewhat confused fighting broke out all along the German division's axis of advance. Battlegroups of 20–40 Soviet tanks, supported by infantry and ground-attack planes, collided with *Das Reich* regimental spearheads.

Rotmistrov continued to throw armour against the division, and combat raged throughout the day, with heavy losses of Soviet armour. *Das Reich* continued to push slowly eastward, advancing into the night while suffering relatively light tank losses. Meanwhile, on the left flank, Soviet First Tank Army elements unsuccessfully tried to crush *Totenkopf*'s bridgehead. The SS division fought off the XXXI and X Tank Corps, supported by elements of the XXXIII Rifle Corps. In spite of the Soviet attacks, *Totenkopf*'s panzer group drove toward a road that ran from the village of Kartaschevka, southeast across the river and into Prokhorovka.

Untersturmführer Guehrs, a platoon commander in the 2nd *SS-Panzergrenadier* Regiment *LAH,* later described the fighting.

'They attacked in the morning. They went around us, over us, and between us. We fought man against man, jumped out of our trenches, fetched the magnetic antitank hollow charges from our armoured personnel carriers, jumped out of our vehicles, and attached them to the enemy. It was like hell! At 09:00, we held firm on the battlefield. We helped our tanks out quite a bit. My company alone destroyed 15 Russian tanks.'

At 08:00, the Soviets attacked *LAH* with an artillery barrage that lasted 80 minutes, switching at 08:30 to the likely German assembly areas. At the same time, tanks and infantry of the Second Guards Tanks attacked the *Das Reich* positions. The German advanced in wedge formation, with the small number of Tigers at the point flanked by lighter PzKpfw IV and the almost obsolete PzKpfw III.

At 09:00 came the first of the series of clashes with *LAH* when AFVs from the XVIII and XXIX Tank Corps ran straight into the *Waffen-SS* Division, hitting infantry and tanks of the *LAH*, who drove them off. Fifteen minutes later, over 40 tanks from the 29th Tanks, advancing from the direction of Jamki, were driven off by *LAH*. Five minutes later, the main weight of the attack from Prokhorovka fell on *LAH*. Of its seven remaining tanks, four were destroyed. While this was happening over 40 tanks, from either XXXI or

XVIII Tank Corps, attacked towards Hill 252.2 from the direction of Petrovka.

COUNTERATTACK AT PROHKOROVKA AND OKTYABRSKIY

At 09:20 an attack was launched out of Prokhorovka by 35 Soviet tanks against the *LAH* group, with 40 tanks out of Petrovka, on the crossroads a kilometre (0.6 miles) southeast of Oktyabrskiy. Soviet tactics were to advance as fast as possible towards the German armour to reduce the engagement range. This nullified the effectiveness of the 8.8cm (3.4in) gun of the Tiger, which could be used to kill armour at long range, and also allowed Soviet guns to fire at close range at the flanks of the big German tanks.

Below: The crew of a PzKpfw III of SS Panzerdivision Das Reich pause for a photograph as the smoke of battle rises on the horizon. This tank lacks the Schürzen track and turret armour added to older tanks as protection against shaped-charge projectiles.

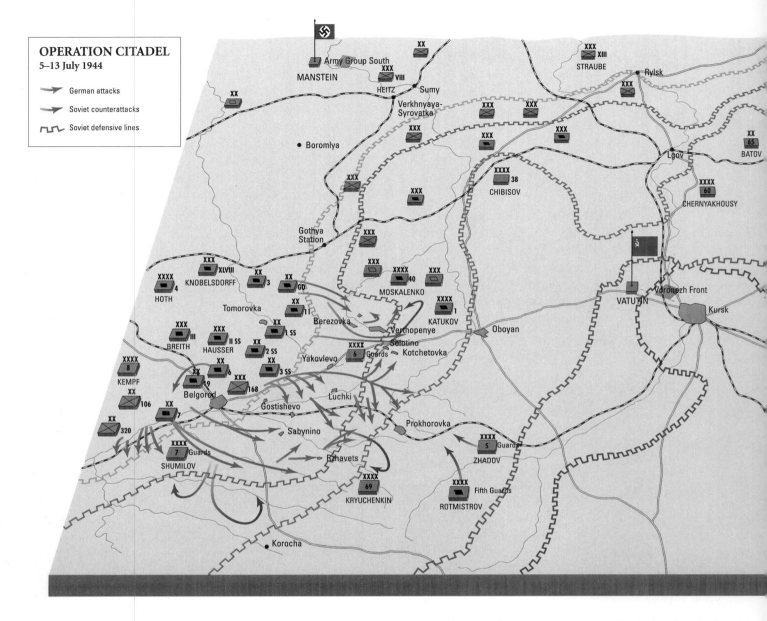

Above: The belts of Soviet defences that slowed down and eventually halted Operation Citadel can be seen as they appeared to Vatutin. The German attack from the north enjoyed little success, while the attack from the south pushed north until the tanks of LAH reached the town of Prokhorovka.

The attack near Oktyabrskiy knocked out four of the seven tanks of the 6th Panzer Regiment *LAH,* which was commanded by the 22-year-old *Obersturmführer* Manfred von Ribbentrop, the son of the German Foreign Minister Joachim von Ribbentrop. The surviving tanks linked up with the tanks commanded by *Sturmbannführer* Martin Gross, which were about 800m (874 yards) away.

Now at ranges of between 10 and 30m (10.9–32.8 yards), they fought a running battle with the Soviet tanks. Since they were moving on the same axis, it was hard for the Soviet tanks crews to distinguish between friend and foe. The 33 tanks attacked and destroyed over 60 T-34s and T-70s. Both Ribbentrop and Gross were subsequently awarded the Knight's Cross for this action.

Von Ribbentrop later wrote: 'A purple wall of smoke rose into the air, produced by smoke shells. It meant: "Tank warning". The same signals were to be seen all along the crest of the slope. The threatening violet danger signals also appeared farther to the right at the railway embankment. Everything immediately became clear: beyond the hill, still out of sight of those in the valley, a major Soviet armoured attack was under way.... On reaching the rest of the slope, we saw another low rise about 200m [219 yards] away on the other side of a small valley, on which our infantry positions

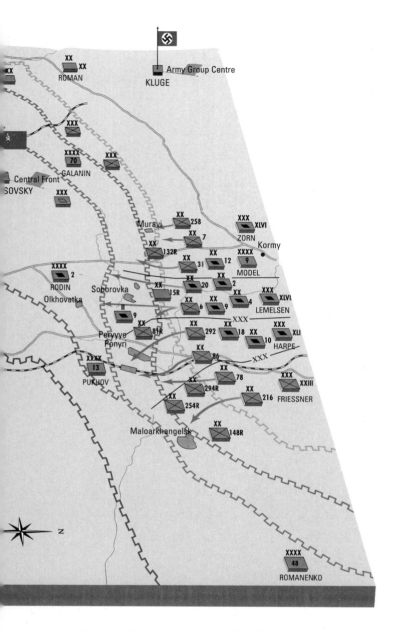

Hubert Neunzert from a platoon of the 3rd Company of the *LAH Panzerjäger* Battalion has left a powerful account of the day seen from a frontline position.

'It was approximately 04:00 as a new order was received by motorcycle courier: Secure the Stalinsk *Kolkhoz*. We were to secure generally to the right of the woods and in the direction of the railroad embankment. It was not much longer before we saw about 25 or 30 T-34s moving along to our right 6 or 7km [3.7–4.3 miles] away, heading straight for Division *Das Reich*'s battle line. They were too far away for us, but the artillery trained its sights on them and made sure that they did not pass our right flank unscathed.'

There followed a brief period of inaction as the *LAH* formation advanced.

'But at 08:00, the magic began with a bang. Salvo after salvo from "Stalin organs" rained down on our positions, with artillery and mortar shells in between. All in all, it looked like a preparation for a real attack, and it lasted almost one-and-a-half hours. A German reconnaissance plane fairly deep over Russian territory signalled to us with his wings, dropped a message canister, and released two violet smoke flares. That meant tanks. Left of the railroad embankment, there were also violet smoke signals going off, so there must be tanks there, too!

'At the same time, the fire slackened, and there – coming over the hill to the left of the railroad embankment – three, five, 10, too many to count. At full speed, T-34 after T-34 roared over the hill, and one after the other into the infantry defensive positions. As soon as the first tank appeared, we opened fire with our five guns, and perhaps a second later, the first T-34 was covered in a black cloud. At times we had to let a target go, as the infantrymen jumped onto the tanks loaded with Russian infantrymen and engaged them in hand to hand combat. However, another 40 to 50 were coming toward us on our side of the embankment. Now we had to swivel around and place these under fire.'

Not all the Soviet tank crews used such simple and vulnerable tactics. Neunzert described how three tanks used a depression to shield them and were soon on to the road and on their way to the *kolkhoz*. Now the action had become intense.

'I didn't have time to fire. The gun on the right jammed and apparently it could not be cleared. Also, the tanks moved between the buildings of the *kolkhoz*. I couldn't see, but I fired at the first T-34. I missed. It quickly moved between the buildings – and as I stood in front of one of the cabins, the jam was cleared. Again, the first one emerged and my loader shouted into my ear: "The last shell is in the breach".

were obviously located....The small valley extended to our left, and as we drove down the forward slope we spotted the first T-34s, which were apparently attempting to outflank us from the left.

We halted on the slope and opened fire, hitting several of the enemy. A number of Russian tanks were left burning. For a good gunner, 800m [874 yards] was the ideal range.

As we waited to see if further enemy tanks were going to appear, I looked around, as was my habit. What I saw left me speechless. From beyond the shallow rise, about 150–200m [164–219 yards] in front of me, appeared 15, then 30, then 40 tanks. Finally there were too many to count. The T-34s were rolling toward us at high speed, carrying mounted infantry.'

Von Ribbentrop's Tiger company had run directly into the Soviet XXIX Tank Corps' 31st and 32nd Tank Brigades.

I cranked the gun toward a T-34 about 150m [164 yards] range, and it was the next monster to pass by: The rear of the gun lurched and the barrel of the 7.5cm [2.9in] cannon raised in the air. I tried with all my might to depress the barrel. I succeeded in getting the turret of the T-34 into the cross-hairs and fired. It's a hit! The hatch opened and two men jumped out – one remained, and the other skipped between the buildings.

'After several firefights with the Russian infantrymen and dismounted tank crews, during which our infantrymen were magnificent, we were able to race through a gap between burning T-34s to the woods. Here, there was another Russian tank attack, supported by three to four waves of

Below: A German soldier supervises Soviet prisoners as they dig close to a knocked out T-34/76D. They may be constructing a field position or digging a grave for its crew. Using the protection afforded by the tank was a practice used by both sides.

infantry, that pushed our brave infantrymen back, breaking through.

'Burning tank carcasses were strewn about the sector at about 1500m [1640 yards] distance, destroyed in close combat and some perhaps by the 10 to 12 guns. One hundred and twenty attacked, perhaps more. Who could count them? Sammetreiter was awarded the Knight's Cross for the conduct of his platoon during this engagement.'

The high claims made by German tank and antitank crews fighting on the Eastern Front, particularly at Kursk, appear to some Western analysts to be wildly exaggerated, but they can be explained by the Soviet use of massed tanks and the relatively poor tactical training of their crews. German Tiger crews were carefully selected and highly trained – so even when outnumbered, Army and *Waffen-SS* tanks retained the edge on their opponents.

A company commander from the *LAH* wrote home from the front describing the fighting on 11 July: 'Then the hellish

Above: T-34/76Ds in a spectacular battle scene. The distinctive markings and lack of fuel drums suggests that this may be a still from a post-war Soviet film about Kursk. Kursk was justifiably celebrated even though it was bought at a very heavy price in Soviet casualties.

defensive battle began. It was a free-for-all battle on all sides, and some went all day without supplies. The Russians tried to cut off our panzer wedge with massed tank attacks. Tanks all day and all night. Four battles in one day. Then we withdrew. With half of my tanks, a portion in tow, I returned in a pouring rain to the attack departure area. Never have I experienced a ten-fold superiority in enemy tanks such as this. It was a raging turmoil. On this day, our regiment destroyed 62 enemy tanks. My company led the rest with 20 kills. Until today, my company had destroyed 43 enemy tanks and I had only one of the total. Now the company has become a blood brotherhood. It dominates the spirit and morale and can motivate us to uproot trees. One of my tanks was shot up, though I got there in time and only the radio operator was wounded.'

He ended his letter, 'I am writing this letter to you just before the start of another attack. We are at the halt behind a hill. In front of us, the infantry and artillery battle is simmering. All around us are the wide plains with the treacherous *balkas*. A wind blows between the rain showers,

exposing the sun for a few seconds. The battle is developing. Soon we must rattle across the infantry lines and attack into the enemy's depth.'

To the east, the men of *Großdeutschland* could see the battle unfolding from the heights of Hill 240. 'Seen dimly through the rain,' writes James Lucas, 'in and out of the smoke of battle, armour roared in desperate cavalry-type charges; while in an ambush position a squadron could be detected picking off enemy machines. For as far as they could see, and from their front away to their right and out of sight on their sectors held by II SS Corps and III Panzer Corps, the ground was covered with smashed and burning vehicles. From newly hit tanks the crews, dwarfed by the immensity of the machines, could be seen jinking furiously as they made their escape. Dimly seen through the fountains of earth flung up by the shell barrages the observers could see the thin lines of German infantry, moving slowly forward, or else the successive and unbroken infantry waves of a Soviet counterattack. Here and there, a ripple of flame would betray the presence of a *Pakfront* as the antitank guns opened fire upon some new panzer thrust.'

Though Rotmistrov had T-34s, his force had no SU-152s with their formidable gun. However, he recalled, 'The sun came to our aid. It picked out the contours of the enemy tanks and blinded the German tankmen. Our first echelon at full speed cut into the positions of the German troops. The appearance on the battlefield of a great number of our tanks threw the Germans into confusion. Control was soon disrupted. Our tanks were destroying the Tigers at close range, where the Germans could not use their armament to advantage in close combat. We knew their vulnerable spots, so our tank crews were firing at their sides. The shells, fired from very short distances, tore large holes in the armour of the Tigers. Ammunition exploded inside them, and turrets weighing many tons were flung yards away. At the same time over the battlefield furious aerial combats developed. Soviet as well as German airmen tried to help their ground forces to win the battle. The bombers, ground-support aircraft and fighters seemed to be permanently suspended in the sky over Prokhorovka. One aerial combat followed another. Soon the whole sky was shrouded by the thick smoke of burning wrecks. On the black, scorched earth, the gutted tanks burnt like torches. It was difficult to establish which side was attacking and which defending. The 2nd Battalion 181st Tank Brigade of the XVIII Tank Corps, attacking on the left bank of the Psel, encountered a group of Tigers which opened fire on the Soviet armoured fighting vehicles from a stationary position. The powerful long-range guns of the Tigers are exceedingly dangerous, and the Soviet tanks had to close with then to eliminate this advantage to the enemy.'

For Sigmund Landau, a member of the German-speaking minority in Transylvania, the memory of Kursk would be as blurred and confused as that of many frontline soldiers. Landau had volunteered for the *Waffen-SS* to avoid conscription into the Rumanian Army.

'I reached my unit in the midst of a terrible battle involving large numbers of tanks and found myself, once again, manning a machine gun. Before long, my *Schütze zwei* [Number 2] and myself became separated, my MG34 twisted into a scrap of iron under a Russian T34, and we ran for our lives. A self-propelled antitank gun, a Marder III, rattled past. I looked up as it went past me, noticed a sergeant who was covered in blood and on his own. Recognizing my tank

Opposite: Yakovlev Yak-9D *fighters on patrol. The aircraft performed well at low altitudes where it could out-turn any opposing fighters and consequently was popular with its pilots. Half of the 30,000 Yakovlev fighters were produced at the huge Factory No 153 in the Urals.*

destroyer's uniform, he beckoned me to jump up, which I did. The tank destroyer carried a 76.2mm [3in] gun and a crew of four. The sergeant and his driver were the only ones left and, like me, in a terrible state, but willing and ready to turn and fight at the first favourable position. That came sooner than expected. To our amazement and jubilation, a force of about one hundred German tanks were rolling towards us. I could make out Panzer III *Sturmgeschütz*, now sporting long gun barrels instead of the original short ones, some Panzer IVs and a number of various vehicles like our own. We immediately turned and joined this, for us, unusually massive cavalcade. The din was ear shattering, but our morale once again soared. No matter how many awesome reversals we suffered, we remained incorrigible optimists.

'The incredible sight of some 100 German tanks instantly rallied what remained of our valiant infantry and panzer-grenadiers.

'We pushed steadily forward and it was now the Russians who ran for their lives.

'I looked down to see a mass of mangled flesh and bone, bits of khaki and blue-coloured rags, among them the odd field grey one from days and weeks past and suddenly realized I was actually elated, glad to see these dead Ruskies, wanting to kill, kill, kill. "God," I thought, "I'm going round the bend."

'"Can you handle the gun? I am losing my sight but I'll load for you".

'"Sure, Sergeant, move over."

'We changed places, and it was only now that I noticed the blood running down his face from a wound. He noticed my concern.

'"Don't worry, it's not as bad as it looks."'

The fighting, characterized by massive losses of Soviet armour, continued throughout 12 July without a decisive success by either side – contrary to many accounts, which state that the fighting ended on 12 July with a decisive German defeat. These authors describe the battlefield as being littered with hundreds of destroyed German tanks and report that the Soviets overran the SS tank repair units. In fact, the fighting continued around Prokhorovka for several more days. *Das Reich* continued to push slowly eastward in the area south of the town until 16 July. This enabled the III

Above: A squad of Waffen-SS soldiers armed with MP40 submachine guns. The MP40 fired on automatic only with a cyclic rate of 500 rpm. It was an excellent weapon and between 1940 and 1944 factories in Germany and Austria produced over a million MP40s.

Panzer Corps to link up with the SS division on 14 July and encircle several Soviet rifle divisions south of Prokhorovka. *Totenkopf* eventually reached the Kartaschevka–Prokhorovka road, and the division also took several tactically important hills on the north edge of its perimeter.

On the night of 11/12 July *Großdeutschland* was relieved by 3rd Panzer Division, according to plan. However, von Mellenthin noted that 'the *panzergrenadiers* moved off with a sense of uneasiness. The last stages of the relief were carried out under heavy enemy shelling, and the men of *Großdeutschland* left their trenches to the accompaniment of the battle noises of a Russian counterattack. Their fears – alas – came true, for that very night 3rd Panzer Division was thrown out of its forward positions.'

Großdeutschland's history outlined von Knobelsdorff's intent: 'The divisional orders issued during the night of

11/12 July were in keeping with this notion. Elements of the *Panzergrenadier* Division *GD* were relieved by units of 3rd Panzer Division in their former positions and were transferred to the front of the attack lane in the area of Point 260.8 [along the Oboyan road] and to the north. The plan was for a continuation of the attack, primarily by the tanks and panzer-fusiliers, on 12 July in the direction of the Psel River, the last obstacle in front of Oboyan. It was learned from the division's neighbour on the right, II *SS-Panzerkorps*, that its spearheads had already crossed the river.'

Meanwhile, the 11th Panzer Division concentrated its efforts on consolidating its positions from the Oboyan road to Kochetovka and conducted reconnaissance forays forward to test Soviet defences. At the same time, the division extended its right flank and relieved elements of *LAH*, which was regrouping its forces eastward for the decisive drive on Prokhorovka. By nightfall on 11 July, the 11th Panzer was waiting expectantly for *Großdeutschland*'s panzer group to concentrate on its left flank along the Oboyan road and for the successful lunge at Oboyan, which it confidently assumed would follow.

A German account later poignantly recorded the opportunity at hand: 'The highest point on the approaches to Oboyan had thereby been reached and, at the same time, the deepest penetration made into the Russian front. From the high ground, one could see far into the valley of the Psel River, the last natural barrier this side of Kursk. With field-glasses the towers of Oboyan could be made out in the fine haze. Oboyan was the objective.'

VATUTIN'S PLANS

According to Hoth's carefully worked-out timetable the following should now have happened: XLVIII Panzer Corps to strike towards Oboyan and seize the crossings over the Psel. Its bulk to wheel eastward and-before thrusting on Kursk, to defeat, jointly with Hausser's *SS-Panzerkorps*, the enemy strategic armoured forces approaching across the strip of land of Prokhorovka. However, General Vatutin was also actively formulating new plans to thwart Hoth's and von Knobelsdorff's designs, within the context of an even greater counterstroke that was ultimately designed to 'encircle and destroy the main German grouping penetrating to Oboyan and Prokhorovka'.

The main concept of this operation consisted of delivering concentric blows against the enemy grouping. The forces of the V Guards and X Tank Corps, together with the Sixth Guards Army's XXII Guards Rifle Corps, were to move in the general direction of Jakovlevo and the Fifth Guards Tank Army and the Fifth Guards Army's XXXIII Guards Rifle Corps were to move in the general direction of Gresnoe, Jakovlevo and Bykovka. The left flank, XXIII Guards Rifle Corps of Sixth Guards Army, and the right flank, XXXII Guards Rifle Corps of Fifth Guards Army, were to deliver a secondary strike in the general direction of Prokhorovka. With part of its forces, Seventh Guards Army was to deliver a secondary blow on Razumnoe.

These offensive plans, which were scheduled to be implemented on the morning of 12 July, reflected Vatutin's unremittingly offensive mindset. Dspite the damage done in previous days to his once mighty VI Tank Corps and the remainder of his tank army, Vatutin issued these new orders to Katukov on 11 July, reflecting his unquenchable audacity.

Later on the evening of 11 July, as part of these larger plans, Rotmistrov finalized his attack planning and issued new orders to his corps. By this time, the German advance of the previous day, as well the increased likelihood that the Germans would attack even earlier than predicted on the morning of the 12th, prompted Rotmistrov to advance his H-hour to 08:30.

Rotmistrov also adjusted his plan to Vatutin's new order and to accommodate harsh and unpleasant combat realities. It was now clear that General Popov's II Tank Corps was in no condition to participate in the counterstroke. In fact, his few remaining tanks were still locked in desperate combat for Storozhevoe or trapped in the Psel valley, out of contact with their parent headquarters. In addition, Rotmistrov had to designate new jumping off positions, which, because of the German advance, were now in the very suburbs of Prokhorovka. His decision was as follows:

'To strike a blow with the forces of XVIII, XXIX and II Guards Tatsinskaia Tank Corps in the sector: to the right – Beregovoe, Andreevka, and Iasnaia Pohana; to the left – Pravorot', Belenikhino, Marker 232.0 and, by the end of the day, reach the line Krasnaia Dubrova–Iakovlevo. The V Guards Zimovnikovskii Mechanized Corps, located in army

Below: Waffen-SS *medics work on a wounded* Luftwaffe *pilot. Though the* Luftwaffe *achieved local air superiority over parts of the Kursk battlefield, the Soviet air defences on the ground and in the air were formidable. Kursk would see Soviet air aces achieve their first kills.*

Left: Vatutin emerges from a farm that has been taken over as a HQ. His death in 1944 meant that he never had to endure Stalin's suspicion and jealousy after 1945, something that plagued the careers of many of the popular and successful Soviet senior commanders.

second echelon, received the mission of being prepared to exploit the success of XXIX Tank Corps and II Guards Tatsinskaia Tank Corps in the general direction of Luchki and Pogorelovka. The tank corps had to occupy jumping-off positions from Prelestnoe through Storozhevoe to Mal Iablonovo by 24:00 on 11 July and be ready to attack by 03:00 on 12 July.'

To accomplish this daunting mission, Rotmistrov placed his two full-strength tank corps and the still-strong II Guards Tank Corps in first echelon to maximize the force of his initial blow. General Bakharov's XVIII Tank Corps formed up on the army's right flank in a 2km (1.2 mile) sector east of Petrovka in the Psel valley just to the rear of the 9th Guards Airborne Division's dug-in 23rd and 26th Regiments.

Bakharov placed his 181st and 170th Tank Brigades in first echelon, supported by the 1000th Antitank Regiment, with orders to attack southeast along the narrow plain between the Psel River and German defences at Oktyabrskiy State Farm, to reach Andreevka and Komsomolets State Farm. This force of over 100 tanks would be followed by the 32nd Motorized Rifle Brigade, 36th Guards Tank Regiment, and the 10th Tank Brigade in second and third echelon. Bakharov's full force of about 190 tanks would strike *Leibstandarte*'s 2nd *Panzergrenadier* Regiment and the right flank of *Totenkopf*'s Regiment Eicke and, he hoped, link up with the remnants of the 99th Tank Brigade en route. Overnight, Rotmistrov reinforced Bakharov's corps with a regiment of 57mm (2.2in) antitank guns from the 10th Antitank Artillery Brigade.

General Kirichenko's XXIX Tank Corps occupied a dubious place of honour in the centre of Rotmistrov's formation astride the Prokhorovka road. Deprived of its intended jumping-off positions in the open fields south of

Prokhorovka, his corps instead formed for the attack in the city's southern suburbs. Kirichenko's 31st, 32nd and 25th Tank Brigades and the 1446th Self-propelled Artillery Regiment, with 191 tanks and self-propelled guns, supported by 21 additional self-propelled guns of the 1529th Self-propelled Artillery Regiment, were to lead the assault against German forces dug in between Oktyabrskiy State Farm and Storozhevoe. They would be accompanied by the 9th Guards Airborne Division's 28th Regiment, and the corps' 53rd Motorized Rifle Brigade would follow in second echelon.

On the evening of 11 July, under the watchful eye of Vasilevsky, Vatutin and Rotmistrov did all in their power to deny the Germans their prize. Vatutin ordered Rotmistrov: 'On 10:00 12 July, deliver a counterstroke in the direction of Komsomolets State Farm and Pokrovka and, in cooperation with Fifth Guards Army and First Tank Army, destroy the enemy in the Kochetovka, Petrovka and Gresnoe regions and do not permit him to withdraw in a southern direction.'

During the night of 11/12 July, General A.S. Burdeiny's II Guards Tank Corps regrouped its 120 surviving tanks into new assembly areas east of Belenikhino. This corps would attack with its 4th, 25th, and 26th Tank Brigades in single echelon against German forces of *Das Reich* occupying positions from west of Vinogradovka along the railway line to Belenikhino. In the gap between the XXIX and II Guards Tank Corps, Popov's two weakened brigades of the II Tank

Corps would attempt to join the effort. By attaching the remaining regiments of 10th Antitank Artillery Brigade (forty-eight 57mm/2.2in guns), Rotmistrov hoped Popov could at least protect the flanks of his main shock groups between Storozhevoe and Ivanovskii Vyselok. For insurance, he deployed the army's reserve 53rd Guards Tank Regiment (with 21 KV heavy tanks) near Yamki in Popov's rear area and kept the 228 tanks and self-propelled guns of General Skvortsov's V Guards Mechanized Corps in reserve east of Prokhorovka, ready to respond to any eventuality. General Trufanov's small reserve group assembled near Pravorot' to await further orders.

In addition, Vatutin provided Rotmistrov with five artillery or mortar regiments, the 17th Artillery Brigade and the 26th Antiaircraft Artillery Division. All told, Rotmistrov was to commit about 430 tanks and self-propelled guns in his initial assault, followed by another 70 from the second echelon. Except for the 261 lightly-armoured T-70 tanks in his army, most of his tanks were reasonably effective weapons. However, the superior armour and armament of the newest German tanks and assault guns made it

Below: The encounter battle at Prokhorovka. The fact that tanks drawn from Steppe Front had to be committed to halt the advance of the II SS Panzerkorps is seen by some historians as an indication that the Germans were actually close to victory.

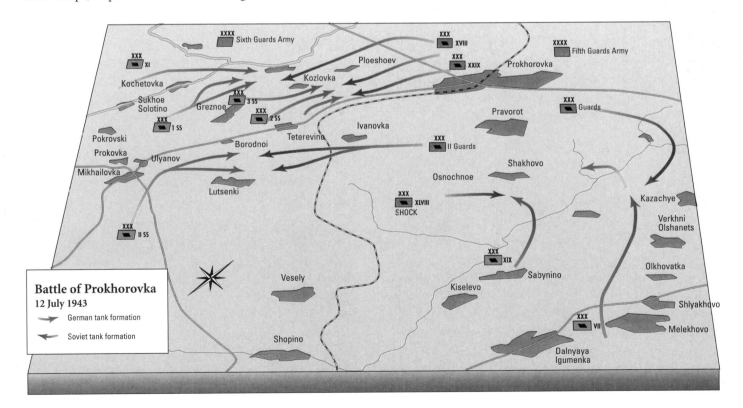

135

imperative that Rotmistrov's tank crews fight at ranges of 500m (546 yards) or less, where the German technical advantage would be almost neutralized. Engaging at such close ranges would also make it more difficult for the Germans to use artillery or air support against the Soviet tanks. Accordingly, Rotmistrov ordered all of his commanders to close with German armoured formations at high speed and 'gang up' on each German target – in particular, the heavy Tigers.

By 02:00 on 12 July, Rotmistrov's forces had completed most of their battle preparations, and the army commander was relatively satisfied with his day's labours. By pure dint of will and superb STAVKA support, his tank force had maintained its imposing strength despite the many long days of near constant movement. Rotmistrov also knew that his troops were already exhausted, and he hoped that the inevitable and obligatory last-minute political meetings in the combat battalions would inspire them. They would, of course, receive spiritual inspiration from their vodka ration.

Rotmistrov himself and his staff had little sleep that fateful night. No sooner had attack preparations been completed than at 04:00 Vatutin called and ordered him to dispatch his reserve southward. Disturbing word had arrived that Kempf's armoured spearhead had broken through in the south and was already on the outskirts of the Northern Donets River town of Rzhavets, less than 20km (12.4 miles) from Prokhorovka. Without reflection, Rotmistrov radioed his deputy General Trufanov and ordered him to march south with all haste and throw his group in the advancing Germans' path. This incident prompted Rotmistrov, and probably Vatutin and Vasilevsky as well, to reflect that, while the upcoming engagement around Prokhorovka was critical, it would not be the only critical battle the next day.

THE 'GREATEST TANK BATTLE IN HISTORY'?

By 12 July, the *LAH* had captured the area around Prokhorovka and the railway station, and could therefore recover their wounded and damaged tanks. Manstein, at this point, felt that he was very close to success as the Guards Tank Army did not resume any offensive actions after 12 July, but dug in and waited while Soviet reserves were committed.

On the flank, *Das Reich's Deutschland* Regiment had no sooner begun its advance from the eastern end of Ivanovskii

Right: A squad of Soviet infantry await the German attack at Kursk, armed with an array of Soviet side arms, including the PPsh-41 submachine gun (foreground) – one of the most popular and reliable weapons produced in the war – and the DP light machine gun.

Vyselok than it was struck in its front by the Soviet 26th Tank Brigade, with heavy antitank support. While *Deutschland's* 3rd *Panzergrenadier* Battalion recoiled from the shock, its 1st Battalion confronted a strong armoured thrust against its right flank. This force, spearheaded by Colonel A.K.

Brazhnikov's 4th Guards Tank Brigade, swept past the SS battalion, through the forward defences of neighbouring *Der Führer* Regiment's 1st Battalion, across the rail line north of Belenikhino, and into the eastern edge of the village of Krasnaia Pohana. Simultaneously, 1st and 4th Battalions of

Der Führer, under attack by Lieutenant-Colonel S.M. Bulygin's 25th Guards and Colonel S.K. Nesterov's 26th Guards Tank Brigades at and south of Belenikhino, were themselves forced back to the outskirts of Krasnaia Poliana and Kahnin. A history of *Das Reich* described the action:

KURSK: THE VITAL 24 HOURS

'*Deutschland* Regiment continued to protect the flank of the advancing *Leibstandarte*, while the rest of *Das Reich*, still on the defensive, flung back a succession of infantry and tank attacks. One interesting incident was the employment against the Russians of T-34s, which *Das Reich* had seized from a factory in Khar'kov. During the day, a column of 50 Russian vehicles was seen driving along one of the *balkas* or valleys.... The direction of the column's advance showed that it was moving to attack *Der Führer*. On the high ground above the Russian column stood the division's group of T-34s, which opened a destructive fire upon the Russian tanks. The panzermen's tactic was one which they had learned early in the war with Russia; kill the enemy's command tank first. It was the only machine fitted with both a radio receiver and transmitter. The other vehicles had only receivers and could not communicate by wireless with one another. This was yet another weakness in Red Army tactics. Russian tanks carried

Below: A Soviet reconnaissance team or forward observation post use a knocked out PzKpfw III or StuG III as cover as they spot suitable targets. The rear deck of the wrecked vehicle offers excellent overhead protection, and hopefully the AFV will not attract enemy fire.

on their rear decks a metal drum containing reserve fuel supplies. A hit on the drum ignited the fuel and caused the tank to "brew up".'

Another account captured the frustration in German ranks and, at the same time, underscored the source of that frustration: 'Heavy fighting developed on the right flank of *Das Reich* Division. There the Soviet II Guards Tank Corps attacked repeatedly from the gap between Hausser's corps and Breith's divisions, which had not yet arrived. That accursed gap! "The Russian attacks on our flanks are tying down half of our effectives and taking the steam out of our operation against the enemy at Prokhorovka," growled the regimental commander, Sylvester Stadler.'

For the popular readership in the Soviet Union, General Rotmistrov would describe the action of 12 July with almost apocalyptic images:

'Till late in the evening the unending roar of engines and the clatter of treads hung over the battlefield. Shells were bursting all around; hundreds of tanks and self-propelled guns were in flames. Clouds of dust and smoke rose to the sky. The enemy had not expected to meet with an armoured encounterattack in the Prokhorovka sector....

Above: Soviet 152mm Pushka obr. 1910/34 g howitzers under camouflage. German gunners did not rate their Soviet counterparts, though all combatants respected the volume of fire they could deliver. The howitzer fired a 43.5kg (95.9lb) shell to 17,600m (19,247yds).

Soviet soldiers performed an unparalleled feat. In a ferocious tank battle, they bled the Nazi force white and forced it onto the defensive.'

However, in 1974 Rotmistrov, now Chief Marshal of Armoured Forces and an avuncular bespectacled figure with a moustache, contributed to a Soviet Army study of Kursk in more measured tones.

'A big role was assigned to the Fifth Guards Tank Army, which had been transferred to the Voronezh Front from the GHQ reserve…

'On the morning of 12 July, it was to mount a counterattack in the direction of Yakovlevo and Tomarovka and, together with the First Tank and Fifth Guards and Sixth Guards armies, destroy the Nazi panzer grouping…

'It was in this complex situation and in the absence of detailed information about the strength of the enemy grouping and its intentions that the Voronezh Front launched a counterattack in the morning of 12 July…

'No sooner had the Fifth Guards Tank Army gone into the offensive than the German panzer force resumed its advance on Prokhorovka. The two mighty waves of armour precipitated towards each other. In the ensuing meeting engagement, both sides sought to gain the upper hand.

'The battle formations of the opposing tank units got intermingled in the very first hours of the encounter. The battle went on the whole day. At some points, the units of the Fifth Guards Tank Army gained ground, at others the enemy made some progress. Both sides suffered heavy losses on that day, losing about 300 tanks each.'

Writes Professor John Erickson, describing 12 July, 'With the coming of the deep night, when thunderclouds piled over the battlefield, the gunfire slackened and the tanks slewed to a halt. Silence fell on the tanks, the guns and the dead, over which the lightning flickered and the rain began to rustle. The *Prokhorovskoe poboishche*, the "slaughter at Prokhorovka" was momentarily done.'

The number of SS tanks involved in the battle has been reported as high as 700 by some authorities, while others have estimated it at between 300 to 600. Even before the Battle of Kursk began, however, the II *SS-Panzerkorps* never had 500 tanks, much less 700. On 4 July, the day before Operation *Zitadelle* was launched, Hausser's three divisions possessed a total of 327 tanks between them, plus a number of command tanks. By 11 July, the II *SS-Panzerkorps* had a total of 211 operational tanks –*Totenkopf* had 94 tanks, *Leibstandarte* had only 56 and *Das Reich* possessed just 61. Tanks damaged tanks or undergoing repairs are not listed. Only 15 Tiger tanks were still in action at Prokhorovka, and no SS Panthers were available. The battalions equipped with Panthers were still training in Germany in July 1943.

ZHUKOV ARRIVES

The clash at Prokhorovka overshadows the action on the western flank of the salient. For *Großdeutschland*, it was the first day without fighting. The division was assembled and

Below: A Soviet 76.2mm (0.3in) Pushka obr. 1939 g (76-39) dual-purpose field gun employed in the antitank role. The gun fired a 6.4kg (14.1lb) shell to a maximum range of 13,290 metres (14,534 yards). Captured guns were used by the Germans as the 76.2cm Pak 39(r).

concentrated astride the road south of Novosselovka, where it replenished fuel and ammunition and repaired damaged equipment. There was a degree of optimism: 'Reconnaissance to the north reported that Novosselovka only seemed occupied by insignificant forces,' noted von Mellenthin. But he added that 'Heavy fighting could be heard to the west and the news from 3 Panzer Division was not encouraging'.

In Moscow, Stalin was following the action closely and ordered Zhukov to fly to Prokhorovka to coordinate operations of the Voronezh and Steppe Fronts. In his memoirs, Zhukov writes:

'On 13 July I arrived at the command post of the Voronezh Front, 'where I also found General I.S. Konev, who was then commanding the Steppe Front. In the evening, I met Vasilevsky at the command post of the Sixty-Ninth Army. After examining the situation and the actions of our own and the enemy troops, I fully agreed with Vasilevsky's measures and decisions. Stalin had instructed him to go to the South-Western Front and organize offensive operations in that quarter to dovetail with the counteroffensive that was to be mounted by the Voronezh and Steppe Fronts.'

The visit as described by Zhukov sounds like a measured meeting between military professionals. However, General Popel in his book *The Tanks Turned to the West*, published in 1960, gives a different picture of a visit by Zhukov to General A.L. Getman's HQ, whose tank formation was experiencing difficulties in the fighting near Kursk.

PAVEL ROTMISTROV

Pavel Alekseevich Rotmistrov was born in 1901 in a village in the Tver province. In 1919, he joined the Red Army. Rotmistrov participated in the suppression of the Kronstadt revolt, and returned to his village after being hospitalized by a wound.

After graduating from the Smolensk infantry school, Rotmistrov, a Communist Party member, was sent to Ryazan as the political officer of the 149th Rifle Regiment, then to Vladimir as the political officer of a divisional horse patrol.

In 1922, Rotmistrov was admitted to military school. In 1924 he became the commander of an infantry platoon. In 1931 he graduated from the Frunze Academy, and by 1937 he was in command of a rifle regiment. In October 1937 he arrived in Moscow to take up a post as tactical instructor at the Military academy of mechanization and motorization. In December 1940, Rotmistrov was appointed the Assistant to the Commander of 5th Tank Division of III Mechanized Corps of the Baltic Special Command. In 1941, he was promoted to the Chief of Staff of III Mechanized Corps. Within two months, III Mechanized Corps, withdrawing with forces of Eleventh Army, were trapped in Shaulyay. After breaking out of encirclement, Colonel Rotmistrov was promoted to commander of 8th Tank Brigade of Northwest Front. In 1942,

Rotmistrov was appointed the Commander of VII Tank Corps. At the end of June 1942, the Corps transferred to Fifth Tank Army. Near Yelets, the tank corps attacked the 11th German Panzer Division and crushed it. In 1942, the corps was transferred to First Guards Army. During the Stalingrad counterattack, VII Tank Corps distinguished itself near Rachkovsky. Then as part of Second Guards Army, the corps participated in the crushing defeat of the Kotelnikovsky unit of Don Army Group. In 1943, Rotmistrov was promoted to Commander of Fifth Tank Army, and participated in the tank battle at Prokhorovka and later in the crossing of the Dneipr as a part of armies of the Steppe Front. From October 1943, Rotmistrov's army fought at Pyatikhatki, Krivoy Rog and Kirovograd. In January 1944, Rotmistrov participated in the Korsun-Shevchenko operations. In 1944, Rotmistrov was given the rank of the Marshal of Armoured forces, and in August 1944 was appointed the Assistant of the Commander of Armoured and Mechanized forces of Red Army.

Following the war, Rotmistrov commanded Soviet armoured forces in the Far East, and then taught at the Armoured and Mechanized Forces Academy in Moscow. In 1962, he was appointed Chief Marshal of Armoured Forces. He died in 1982.

'Slamming the door, Marshal Zhukov got out of his vehicle. While he walked to Getman's tent, quickly glancing all around, the news spread like a breeze through the headquarters. The commanders looked on Zhukov with apprehension and hope. With apprehension, for they knew that the rare visit by Zhukov would not be without just and unjust dressings down, dismissals, demotions. With hope, because the representative of the STAVKA, vested with authority, was able to get units moving and at any time – since he knew the situation well – could prompt a decision.

'This time, the reasons for Zhukov's indignation were understandable. The situation was actually turning tragically; Leonov's brigade had got itself cut off. But why must he, without grasping the meaning, accuse someone and give vent to his impetuous irritation? They say a commander's rebukes are supposed to get the subordinates working better, moving faster and thinking. I don't believe this. Not five minutes ago, Getman was decisive and firm; now he had lost his nerve…'

Popel adds:

'The rudeness [*grubost*], which many commanders of my generation connect with name of Marshal Zhukov, was not his only self-indulgence. His belief in his right to insult, to humiliate his subordinate was transmitted like an infection. Martinet-like arrogance, which is alien to the truly democratic nature of our army, was adopted by some of the commanders, and at times even became their style.'

However, like so much of the Soviet historians of Kursk, Popel had his own agenda. An army political commissar, he was a future propagandist for the role played by Khrushchev in the battle. He shows his hand when he adds: 'Zhukov's hostility toward the political workers – at times completely open – could be explained, we thought, by the fact that they opposed to the extent of their power, petty tyranny of such "Napoleons". Like many successful commanders, Zhukov did not try to cultivate popularity and knew that he was required to deliver victory to Stalin – whatever the cost.

At 06:00 on 13 July, Rotmistrov knew that he too must deliver victory. With a small operational group of staff officers, he joined his XXIX Tank Corps commander, General Kirichenko, at the corps' forward command post. He used the CP, which was located on a small hillock southwest of Prokhorovka and afforded an excellent view of the battlefield, as his army observation post during the assault. German Messerschmitt aircraft appeared at 06:30 to sweep the skies clear of Soviet aircraft, and waves of German bombers followed a half hour later. As Rotmistrov gazed up, squadrons of Soviet fighters and then bombers began an air battle that swirled overhead.

At 08:15, Soviet artillery roared and for 15 minutes pounded German positions until giving way to fiery sheets of *Katyusha* multiple rocket fire, which announced the end of the artillery preparation. Soviet gunners then shifted their thousands of tubes from fire on preplanned concentrations to creeping barrage fire, which inched forward toward

Below: Accompanied by infantry support, Tiger tanks of the Waffen-SS *take up a defensive position following a lull in the fighting at Prokhorovka. The Tigers and Panthers of the II SS Panzer Corps were the chief cause of the Soviet army's heavy tank losses.*

German advanced positions. From his OP, Rotmistrov could already see German forces advancing. 'Indeed,' he wrote later 'It turned out that both we and the Germans went over to the offensive simultaneously.' At precisely 08:30, Rotmistrov's radio operator transmitted the code words, '*Stal', Stal', Stal'*' (Steel, Steel, Steel) and Rotmistrov's command to attack was passed to his assembled corps, brigades, regiments and battalions. Shortly thereafter, his 500 tanks and self-propelled guns carrying mounted riflemen from the 9th Guards Airborne Division lurched forward into action. It would prove to be a costly battle.

THE TRUE SCALE OF PROKHOROVKA

On 13 July, Fourth *Panzerarmee* measured the cost of the fighting around Prokhorovka. Its reports declared that the II *SS-Panzerkorps* had 163 operational tanks, a net loss of only 48 tanks. Actual losses were somewhat heavier, the discrepancy being due to the gain of repaired tanks returned to action. A closer study of the losses of each type of tank reveals that the corps lost about 70 tanks on 12 July. In contrast, Soviet tank losses, which were long assumed to be

moderate, were actually catastrophic. In 1984, a history of the Fifth Guards Tank Army, which written by Rotmistrov himself, revealed that on 13 July the army lost 400 tanks to *repairable* damage. He gave no figure for tanks that were destroyed or not available for salvage. Evidence suggests that hundreds of additional Soviet tanks were lost. Several German accounts mention that Hausser had to use chalk to mark and count the huge jumble of 93 knocked-out Soviet tanks in the *Leibstandarte* sector alone. Other Soviet sources maintain that the tank strength of the army on 13 July was 150 to 200, a loss of about 650 tanks. Those losses brought a caustic rebuke from Stalin. Subsequently, the depleted Fifth Guards Tank Army did not resume offensive action, and Rotmistrov ordered his remaining tanks to dig in among the infantry positions west of the town.

Historians have tended to inflate the numbers of tanks in action. One reason for this is that they have assumed that all three SS divisions participated at Prokhorovka. In fact, only one, the *LAH*, fought the battle. The other two were on the flanks of the *LAH* (*Totenkopf* on the left, and largely across

Above: An exhausted Panzergrenadier *rests his head on a Tellermine 35 (Stahl). Weighing 9.75kg (21.5lb), the mine operated under a pressure of 225–295kg (496–650lb). This mine will probably be fitted with a pull igniter for use as an improvised infantry antitank weapon.*

the Psel River, and *Das Reich* on the right) and were fighting their own separate battles. At the time of the battle, LAH had already been in combat for about a week and was substantially depleted. By 11 and 12 July, the two main days of the battle, *LAH* was down to about 103 tanks, assault guns and tank destroyers (not including observation tanks). The Soviet units that participated in the battle at Prokhorovka were the XVIII and XXIX Tank Corps, along with a separate detachment under General Trufanov. Combined, these units were able to field about 421 tanks, assault guns, and tank destroyers. So, contrary to the popular claims of 'thousands' of tanks fighting it out in front of Prokhorovka, we have about 517, of which 455 were actually 'tanks'.

In all, the Soviet Fifth Guards Tank Army and the Fifth Guards Army probably fielded over 1000 tanks and assault

Right: Two PzKpfw VI Tiger Ausf H have been hitched together with steel cables to tow out a Tiger that has become stuck in a swampy stream. Even with their wide tracks, Tigers were as vulnerable as other tanks to the danger of boggy ground.

guns, a significant percentage of which were obsolete T-70 light tanks and the SU-76 assault gun. Although the fighting was fierce and a large number of AFVs were involved, it certainly was not the vast battle favoured by popular myth. Furthermore, most of the 'battle' was a series of *distinct* attacks, counterattacks and withdrawals involving separate and distinct units, often very far apart. It is a misconception that there was just one large, swirling, running, three-day tank battle.

On the Soviet side, the entire Fifth Guards Tank Army was able to field about 800 tanks. However, not all of these were positioned to engage the *LAH* at Prokhorovka. Only the XXIX Tank Corps and the XVIII Tank Corps did battle with the *LAH* on 11 and 12 July. The II Guards Tank Corps was significantly further south, in action against *Das Reich*. II Tank Corps was positioned defensively just behind XXIX Tank Corps and stayed in a defensive posture for the course of the battle. 9th Guards Airborne Division participated in the battle, but had no tanks. V Guards Motorized Corps had a significant number of tanks, but was in reserve and remained there until after the Soviets went on the counteroffensive. So, the Fifth Guards Tank Army brought about 600 tanks and self-propelled guns to the battle with *LAH*, including the II Tank Corps, which did not enter the action between 11 and 12 July. The myth that the Germans fielded huge numbers of tanks, including numerous Tigers, probably arose because Soviet commanders had to justify their heavy losses. In fact, the *LAH* went into the battle on 11 July with more PzKpfw Is and PzKpfw IIs than Tigers and had Marder IIIs in the order of battle. On 11 July, there were only four Tigers available for combat, while there were two PzKpfw Is and four PzKpfw IIs available. These obsolete tanks were probably signals or observation vehicles.

Another misconception about the battle is the notion that all three SS divisions attacked shoulder-to-shoulder through the narrow lane between the Psel and the railway line west of Prokhorovka. Only *Leibstandarte* was aligned directly west of the town, and it was the only division to attack the town itself. Contrary to the impression given in many accounts, the II *SS-Panzerkorps* zone of battle, was approximately 14.4km (9 miles) wide, with *Totenkopf* on the left flank, *Leibstandarte* in the centre and *Das Reich* on the right flank. *Totenkopf*'s armour was committed primarily to the Psel

bridgehead and in defensive action against Soviet attacks on the Psel bridges. In fact, only *Leibstandarte* actually advanced into the corridor west of Prokhorovka, and then only after it had thrown back initial Soviet attacks.

Another myth is that Soviet tanks rammed German ones during the battle. This assumes that the Soviet tank crews, knowing their guns to be ineffective against the tough

German armour, chose instead to close to point-blank range and ram the tanks, thereby knocking them out. Many of the stories typically focus on big KV tanks ramming Tigers. Such stories are probably a product of embellished and propagandized Soviet versions, which were designed to 'play up' the fierceness of the battle and justify the extent of their losses. In reality, hardly any of the German AFVs present had armour that was consistently able to withstand Soviet firepower.

One version of the ramming story appeared in 'The speed of attack of a Tank Army', an article in *Voyenno-istoricheskiy Zhurnal*, written in 1964 by General Rotmistrov.

'On the black, scorched earth, the gutted tanks burnt like torches. It was difficult to establish which side was attacking and which defending. The 2nd Battalion 181st Tank Brigade of XVIII Tank Corps, attacking on the left bank of the Psel, encountered a group of Tigers, which opened fire on the Soviet armoured fighting vehicles from a stationary position. The powerful long-range guns of the Tigers were exceedingly dangerous, and the Soviet tanks had to try to close with them

as quickly as possible to eliminate the advantage of the enemy. Captain P.A. Skripkin, the battalion commander ordered: "Forward, follow me!" The first shell of the commander's tank pierced the side of a Tiger. Instantly another Tiger opened fire on Skripkin's T-34. A shell crashed through its side and a second wounded the battalion

JOSEPH STALIN

Stalin was born on 21 December 1879 in Gori, the son of Georgian peasants. Christened Joseph Vissarionovich Dzhugashvili, he was known by his friends as 'Soso'. Between 1888 and 1894, he was obliged to learn Russian at the Gori church school. A good student, he won a scholarship to T'bilisi Theological Seminary.

Studying for the priesthood, he read widely, including Karl Marx's *Das Kapital*, and became a Marxist. Leaving the seminary before graduating, he joined the Social-Democratic party in 1899 and worked as a propagandist among T'bilisi rail workers. Arrested in Batum in 1902, he spent over a year in prison before being exiled to Siberia, from which he escaped in 1904. On his return, Stalin married Yekaterina Svanidze, who died in 1910, the year he adopted the name 'Stalin' – Steel Man. A second wife, Nadezhda Alliluyeva, whom he married in 1919, committed suicide in 1932.

Between 1902 and 1913, Stalin was arrested eight times and exiled seven times, and he escaped six times. The longest exile lasted from 1913 until 1917. In the last years of Tsarist Russia (1905–17), Stalin was a follower rather than a leader, supporting the Bolshevik faction of the party. Lenin promoted him in the party by co-opting him into the Bolsheviks' Central Committee in 1912. The next year, Stalin briefly edited the new party newspaper, *Pravda* (Truth), and at Lenin's urging wrote his first major work, 'Marxism and the Nationality Question'. Stalin was sent to Siberia in 1913 before the article appeared in 1914.

After the March 1917 Revolution, Stalin returned to Petrograd (St Petersburg), again editing *Pravda*. Before Lenin's return in April, he and Lev Kamenev dominated the party, advocating a policy of moderation and co-operation with the provisional government. As the Bolsheviks' expert on nationalities, he became head of the Commissariat for Nationality Affairs. Together with Yakov Sverdlov and Leon Trotsky, he helped Lenin with emergency decisions in the first period of the Civil War. Stalin participated in that war as a commander on several fronts. He was commissar for state

control in 1919–23 and in 1922 became secretary-general of the party, which enabled him to build a power base.

In 1929, following Lenin's death, Stalin secured his position as Lenin's successor and sole leader of the Soviet Union. He reacted to lagging agricultural production in the late 1920s by expropriating grain from the Ukraine. When other crises threatened in late 1929, he expanded a moderate collectivization programme into a nationwide offensive against the *kulaks* – landowning peasantry. This caused mass starvation and the death of about 60 million *kulaks*. The industrialization and electrification programmes in the 1930s were much more successful; these raised the backward Union of Soviet Socialist Republics to the rank of the industrial powers. Liberal and intellectual Western visitors were impressed and described the Soviet Union as 'the future'. This industrial base would prove critical in World War II, when women workers and the young and old built the weapons that helped defeat Nazi Germany. In the 1930s, the purges of any opposition, real or imagined, made Stalin the most murderous tyrant of the twentieth century. More people were executed or imprisoned in the *Gulags* – slave labour camps operated by the NKVD (*Narodnyi Kommissariat Vnutrennikh*, or People's Commissariat for Internal Affairs) – than suffered under Hitler.

Stalin participated in the Allied Conferences at Tehran (1943), Yalta (1945), and Potsdam (1945). He obtained recognition of a Soviet sphere of influence in Eastern Europe, and after the war extended Communist control over the countries liberated by the Soviet armies. His single-minded determination to prevent another attack on the USSR produced the arms race and Cold War, leading to the Berlin Airlift of 1948–9 and the Korean War of 1950–3.

In his last years, he became increasingly paranoid and frail, in January 1953 he ordered the arrest of many Moscow doctors, mostly Jews, charging them with medical assassinations. The trials in the so-called 'Doctors' Plot' were halted by his sudden death on 5 March 1953.

commander. The driver and wireless operator pulled their commander from the tank and took him to the cover of a shell crater. As a Tiger was making straight for them, Aleksandr Nikolayev, the driver leapt back into his damaged and already smouldering tank, started the engine and raced up to meet the enemy tank. Like a flaming ball of fire, the T-34 raced over the ground. The Tiger halted. But it was too late. The blazing tank rammed the German Panzer at full speed. The detonation made the ground shake.'

The last great myth is that Prokhorovka was the 'death ride of the Panzers', in which the Germans lost many tanks. Western sources, citing Soviet accounts, place tank losses for both sides at about 1200. If it was anything, the battle was the 'death ride' of the Soviet XXIX Tank Corps, which suffered 75 per cent AFV losses in one day. Some commentators now state that the Germans barely noticed the effects of the battle at Prokhorovka. The *LAH* permanently lost a total of seven AFVs. A further 25 were damaged and sent to repair shops, only one of which was a Tiger. The Soviets, on the other hand, permanently lost at least 134 AFVs, more than 19 times the losses of the Germans. A further 125 were temporarily lost due to damage. Therefore total AFV losses due to combat at Prokhorovka come out at 32 German against 259 Soviet.

'Immediately after Prokhorovka' says Professor Erickson, writing in 1983, 'Soviet tank strength was certainly down to half what it had been eight days before; the losses in antitank guns were heavy indeed, and battle casualties high. The *Ostfront* had more than once seen some appalling fighting, but German infantrymen insisted that there had never been anything like this. Ponyr in the north had been the site of one of these savage, blood-soaked grapples; in the south at the Belgorod blood-bath, *"die Blutmühl von Belgorod"*, the arrogant, merciless ideological shock-troops of Nazi Germany, whose very emblem was so often their automatic death-warrant once they were prisoners in Soviet hands, had

Below: In the aftermath of a Soviet attack, German soldiers in a shallow trench scan the horizon while others examine the T-34/76D that got closest to their positions. Other knocked-out tanks engaged at longer ranges can be seen in the distance.

been impaled on the stakes of Oboyank and Prokhorovka. When the Russians came to excavate the Prokhorovka battlefield, they reported coming upon 400 shattered tank-hulls. In the small outlying woods they found the tank workshops, and though in previous battles the time won by covering troops had always been used to tow off damaged machines, this time the Tigers stood mostly where they had been knocked out, some straddling Soviet trenches, others inert in firing positions, the crews splayed out beside them or interred within these steel tombs, mainly fragments of men in a horrifying litter of limbs, frying-pans, shell-cases, playing cards and stale bread.'

Charles Sydnor writes of *Totenkopf*:

'Though outnumbered four-to-one in both tanks and infantry the *Totenkopf* division managed successfully throughout the 12th, the 13th, and into late afternoon of the 14th to contain the two Soviet corps [XXXI Guards and XXXIIIrd Guards Rifle] and prevent any penetration into

Hausser's flank. In the process, however, SSTK absorbed terrific punishment, and by the time the Russians broke off their attacks at dusk on 14 July *Totenkopf* had lost over half its tanks and vehicles and had taken heavy casualties among all its combat units.'

On 4 July, *Das Reich* had 48 PzKpfw IIIs, 30 PzKpfw IVs (of which 15 were short-barrel versions), 12 Tigers, 8 PzKpfw III command tanks, 18 captured T-34s, 33 StuGs and 10 Marders combat-ready. On the first day of *Zitadelle*, its Tigers knocked out 23 tanks in some six hours of heavy fighting near Beresoff and Hill 233.3 to the north. On 6 July, south of Lutschki, 1st Battalion's Tigers destroyed ten tanks of the II Guards Tank Corps, but antitank fire killed the 6th Panzer Company commander, *Untersturmführer* Worthmann. It was *Hauptsturmführer* Dieter Kesten who took over the company. By 13 July, *Untersturmführer* Hans Mennel in PzKpfw IV number 621 had knocked out 24 tanks during the campaign. From 5 to 16 July, *Das Reich* accounted for 448 Soviet tanks and assault guns, losing a total of 46 panzers and assault guns destroyed.

ARMY DETACHMENT KEMPF

The first six days of the German offensive had been expensive and frustrating for General Werner Kempf and his Army Detachment. Try as it might, Kempf's force seemed unable to penetrate deeply and rapidly through the dense fortifications of the Soviet Seventh Guards Army. Its failure to do so deprived the II *SS-Panzerkorps* of its flank support, disrupted its full concentration along the Prokhorovka axis, and threatened the viability of Hoth's offensive plans.

Kempf's problem was similar to but more severe than that of von Knobelsdorff. While the XLVIII Panzer Corps' attention was constantly distracted by the endless battles along its left flank, Kempf's force had to contend with near constant threats to both its flanks. On its left flank, Soviet forces held the front anchored on the Northern Donets and Lipovyi Donets Rivers north and east of Belgorod, and the 19th Panzer Division had to divert significant forces to support the 168th Infantry Division, which was inching its way northward from the city along the banks of both rivers. Simultaneously, Kempf had to defend his increasingly long right flank southward to Maslovo Pristan' against ever more active Soviet forces.

Left: A Soviet Army women's battalion near Kursk in 1943. Many of the women who fought in the Red Army realized how many men had been killed and ruefully said that they were destined to be 'soldiers forever' since they would never find a husband.

Above: A PzKpfw III grinds past the SdKfz 251 half-tracks of a Panzergrenadier formation prior to a renewed attack on Soviet positions. Here the weather appears good, but the reality was bursts of heavy rain that made the air humid and thunderous.

These twin flank threats denied Kempf the opportunity to concentrate Breith's critical armour for a decisive thrust to the north and Prokhorovka. Moreover, Kempf's slow northward progress required the II *SS-Panzerkorps* to use its 167th Infantry and *Das Reich* Divisions to protect its long and unprotected light flank along the Lipovyi Donets River, where Soviet armoured forces were still most active.

Vatutin capitalized on this situation. He ordered Shumilov's Seventh Guards Army to maintain pressure against Kempf's flank east of the Northern Donets and to prepare even stronger counterattacks for 12 July. General Kriuchenkin's Sixty-Ninth Army, now reinforced with the entire XXXV Guards Rifle Corps, took over responsibility for

defence between Prokhorovka and Miasoedovo, east of Belgorod. Kriuchenkin employed successive defence lines to block the III Panzer Corps' forward progress, while he orchestrated the tricky phased withdrawal of his forces from the Northern Donets salient north of Belgorod.

Accordingly, the Sixty-Ninth Army's 92d Guards, 94th Guards and 305th Rifle Divisions, with modest armour and antitank support, contained the III Panzer Corps' spearhead 6th Panzer Division around Melikhovo. By the end of 10 July, Soviet defenders had used a mixture of antitank ditches, antitank guns, mines and artillery to reduce the 6th Panzer's armoured strength to only 47 running tanks, out of an original total of over 100. Try as it might, the 6th Panzer could not break out northward until it received support from either the 7th or 19th Panzer Divisions or both, yet these divisions were tied down in fighting along Kempf's flanks.

To the south, the 7th Panzer Division covered Kempf's long western flank to Miasoedovo and lent support to Corps

Rauss's infantry divisions, which were under renewed pressure. This pressure was already heavy in the Rzhavets region, where the 72nd Guards and 213th Rifle Divisions were launching nearly constant attacks, but it also materialized near Batratskaia Dacha, where Shumilov's 15th Guards Rifle Division went into action. Rauss's 320th and 106th Infantry Divisions had already suffered losses totalling over 40 per cent of their original strength, and the newly arrived 198th Infantry Division had its hands full dealing with the threat posed by the Soviet 15th Guards Division's attacks. In combination, these actions kept the 7th Panzer tied down for days, helplessly out of supporting range of the 6th Panzer.

While the 6th and 7th Panzer Divisions were stalled at and south of Melikhovo, the 19th Panzer Division and the 168th Infantry cleared Soviet troops from the eastern bank of the Northern Donets River. They were assisted in this effort by Kriuchenkin's 10 July order to his 375th and 81st Guards Rifle Divisions. Kriuchenkin had instructed these two divisions to disengage, withdraw from the region south of the Lipovyi and Northern Donets Rivers, and turn over their defensive sector south of Gostishehevo to the 89th Guards Rifle Division. This shortening of lines permitted Kriuchenkin to create reserves to contend with a German advance northward from Mefikhovo, which Kriuchenkin knew was inevitable.

Late on 10 July, at von Manstein's urging, Kempf had moved to break the stalemate east of the Northern Donets. Slipping elements of the 7th Panzer Division northward to occupy 6th Panzer positions around Mefikhovo, he concentrated the latter for a northward drive in concert with an advance along the eastern banks of the Northern Donets by 19th Panzer Division. At dawn on 11 July, the 6th Panzer struck, with the Tigers of the 503rd Panzer Detachment in the vanguard. While the 19th Panzer lunged northward along the left bank of the Northern Donets through Khokhlovo and Kiselevo to Sabynino, 6th Panzer advanced 12km (7.4 miles) northward and seized Kazach'e. This headlong advance by massed Tiger tanks tore through the Soviet 305th Rifle Division's defences and wedged into the prepared defence line of the 107th Rifle Division, 10km (6.2 miles) to the rear.

MOVE AND COUNTER-MOVE
In addition to unhinging Kriuchenkin's defences, Kempf's audacious thrust rendered the 89th Guards Rifle Division's defences south of Gostishchevo untenable. In desperation equal to that which propelled the Germans forward,

Kriuchenkin threw his already battle-scarred 81st Guards Rifle Division into combat to block the German northward advance and ordered the 89th Guards Division to withdraw to new defences just south of Gostishehevo. Kriuchenkin understood that his situation was precarious. While he had held Kempf's force at bay for several days, and Kempf's armoured spearheads were still 25–30km (15.5–18.6 miles) from Prokhorovka, he doubted that his remaining reserves (the threadbare 375th Rifle Division) could halt further German advances. Soviet records describe Kriuchenkin's subsequent decision:

'To liquidate the existing penetration, the Sixty-Ninth Army commander made the decision to regroup his forces on the night of 12 July and to withdraw some formations to new defensive positions. After regrouping in accordance with this plan, by dawn on 12 July, the army formations occupied the following positions: the 93d Guards Rifle Division continued to defend its positions along the Rozhdestvenka–Druzhnyi line [southwest of Gostishchevol]; the 89th Guards Rifle Division, having left no more than two battalions with antitank guns on the front from Kalinin to Petropavlovka, occupied defences along the front Kiselevo-Krivtsevo; the 81st Guards Rifle Division occupied defences along the western bank of the Northern Donets from Krivtsevo to Rudinka; the 92d Guards Rifle Division with the 96th Tank Brigade occupied a prepared defence line along the front Vypolzovka–NovoAlekseevskü Vyselok; the 107th and 305th Rifle Divisions occupied defences along the line Razumnoe balka-Gremiach'e; the 94th Guards Division with the 31st Antitank Brigade occupied defences along the fine Shhakhovtsevo Mazildno-Sheina-Ushakovo, with one rifle regiment and a regiment of the 31st Antitank Brigade in second echelon along the line Ploskoe-Novoselovka, along the eastern bank of the Koren' River. To the left, Seventh Guards Army's 15th Guards Rifle Division continued to defend along the line Sheina (excl.) SoloVev State Farm.'

Despite these elaborate defensive preparations, Kriuchenkin knew he could not successfully contain a renewed German assault. Therefore, late on 11 July, he appealed to Vatutin for help. The call for help came none too soon, for early on 12 July, the III Panzer Corps continued its desperate drive northward toward Prokhorovka.

German commanders were still optimistic and still prepared to use the imagination and initiative that had characterized their early *blitzkrieg* victories. *Oberst* von Oppeln-Bronikowski summoned his commanders and gave his orders for a surprise attack to cross the Donets and swing north behind the Soviet Sixty-Ninth Army.

'Gentlemen, we will carry out our mission in a big night attack. The terrain suits such an attack. Our night advance road is also a Russian route of retreat. We will not attack the Russian columns at first in order to conceal our movements for as long as possible. And now everyone get ready. Departure after last light. Bäke, you and your battalion will drive point, I will join you in my command vehicle.'

Major Dr Franz Bäke commanded the 2nd Battalion 11th Panzer Regiment with the 2nd Battalion 11th *Panzergrenadier* Regiment under Lieutenant Roembke in support. He put a captured T-34 at the head of the column

Below: In the aftermath of Citadel, wrecked Porsche Ferdinands straddle Soviet trenches. The Ferdinand had a powerful antitank gun but no machine gun for localized defence against infantry attack. Without infantry support, it was doomed since Soviet tank hunters could attack at short range.

Opposite: A Waffen-SS tank crew examines the damage to their Tiger tank following the battle of Kursk. The heavily-armoured Tiger tanks could afford to take a number of hits without necessarily being put out of action, and the Soviet T-34 76As would normally need to outnumber the Tigers by four or five to one to ensure victory.

in the hopes that the familiar silhouette would deceive the Soviet forces. The approach march went according to plan with Soviet infantry unaware that the tanks rumbling past were enemy vehicles. However, after about 12km (7.4 miles) Dr Bäke recalled:

'Our T-34 went on strike. Moved no doubt by national sentiments, it stopped and blocked the road. So our men had to climb out of their tanks and in spite of the Russians standing all round them, watching curiously, they had to haul the T-34 off the road and push it into the ditch in order to clear the way for the rest of the formation. In spite of the

order that not a word of German was to be spoken, a few German curses were heard. Never before had I winced so much under a curse as at Rzhavets. But the Russians still did not notice anything. The crew of our T-34 was picked up. And on we moved.'

Soon after this encounter, seven T-34s from a column that had initially driven past them swung back and surrounded the command tank of Dr Bäke – this tank had a dummy gun

and extra radio communications. In the darkness, Bäke led a daring attack on foot armed with magnetic antitank charges. The Germans knocked out the T-34s, three of which were personally destroyed by Bäke and now, with surprise gone, the column drove hard for the Donets bridge. Even though the bridge had been blown, combat engineers managed to reach the far bank via a footbridge. A lodgement on the north bank was established and the demolished bridge

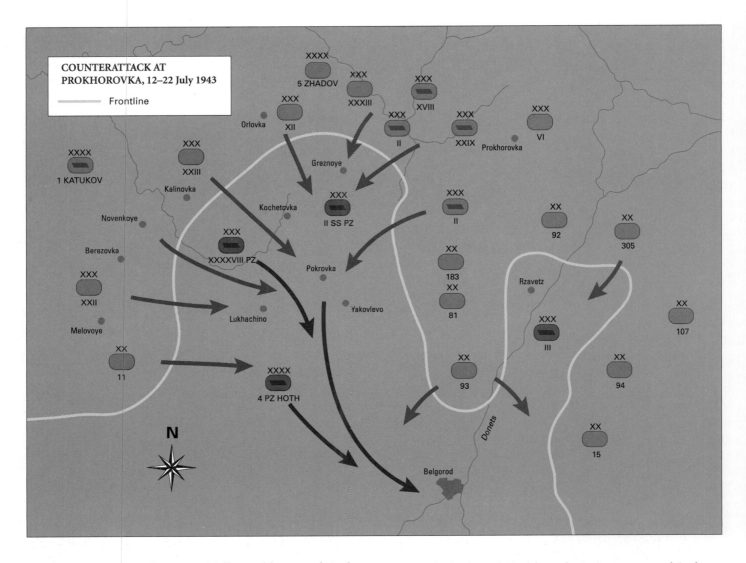

COUNTERATTACK AT
PROKHOROVKA, 12–22 July 1943

—— Frontline

repaired. However, Bäke was initially unable to exploit the coup. The bulk of the 6th Panzer Division had been attacking the important high ground of Alexsandrovka 12km (7.4 miles) further east. It was vigorously defended.

However, General von Hünersdorff, commanding the division, committed six Panthers to an outflanking manoeuvre, and bypassed the village. By 13 July, the 6th Panzer Division was free to thrust northwards and the tanks of the 7th and 19th Panzer Divisions were pouring through the bridgehead at Rzhavets towards Prokhorovka.

On 1 August, Bäke became the 262nd recipient of the Knight's Cross with Oak Leaves, and six days later von Oppeln was awarded the German Cross in Gold. However, von Oppeln was wounded when his command vehicle was hit by fire from an antitank gun and he was evacuated to Germany. He was not the only casualty: the charismatic 45-year-old commander of the 6th Panzer Division, Walter von Hünersdorff, who had already been wounded in an

Above: The final act of Citadel saw the Soviet counterattack in the south, following the Germans' failed offensive at Prokhorovka. Surprisingly the German forces were able to disengage, even launching localized counterattacks. The German withdrawal remained coherent because Soviet forces had suffered heavy losses in the earlier fighting.

accidental attack on his HQ by a *Staffel* of He-111s, was hit by a sniper. Despite expert medical attention from Oberst Dr Tönjes, it proved a fatal head wound and he died in hospital in Kharkov on 17 August. His wife, a senior Red Cross nurse serving in Russia, was by his side for the last three days. His sacrifice and those of his men would be in vain. The violence and confusion of the fighting in the southern Kursk salient was described by General Kirill Moskalenko.

'It was hard to tell who was attacking and who was defending…there was no place for manoeuvre. The tankmen were forced to fire point-blank. Villages and heights changed hands repeatedly. The enemy lost heavily…[and] the Germans were compelled to go over to the defensive…the Nazis had dreamed of reaching Kursk in four days but, in the first eleven days of fighting failed to penetrate deep even half our defensive lines…'

Hundreds of miles to the west at Zossen, the HQ complex of camouflaged bunkers to the east of Berlin, Gehlen wrote ruefully to his staff.

Below: German graves in Maloarkhangel'sk, with markers improvized from local birch trees and the wood from ammunition boxes. Numerous deaths went unrecorded and memorials have only vague information about the place and time of death of soldiers on the Ostfront.

'*Der Chef*
Fremde Heere Ost HQ, 13 July 1943

The course of the fighting on the eastern front these last few days has once again confirmed precisely every detail of the enemy-Intelligence picture we produced…The chief of staff expressed particular commendation for this a few days ago. I know this excellent result is the result of the hard work and magnificent co-operation of all this branch's staff and experts and of the support it enjoyed from the other agencies like Air Intelligence, the controller of signals reconnaissance . . . .

I wish to express my thanks to all the staff and my hope that they will continue to do their utmost for the job assigned to us with the same effort and enthusiasm.

Gehlen'

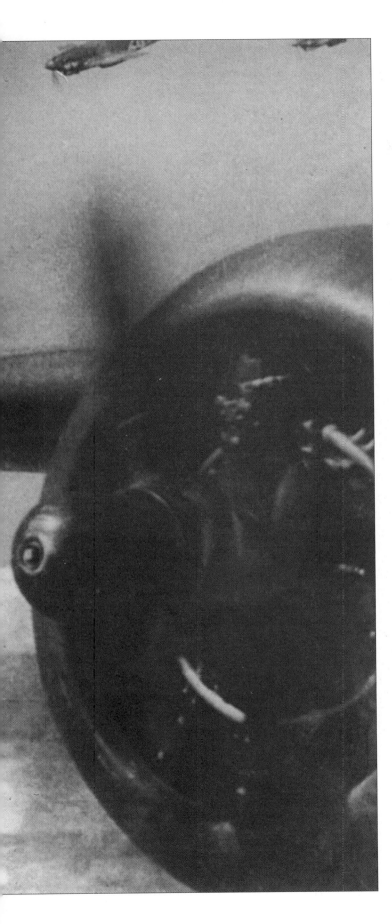

CHAPTER FIVE

AIR POWER

**The air war over the Kursk salient
was a critical factor in the fighting on the ground.
Both German and Soviet armoured tactics relied
on the freedom to move rapidly without having
to look for cover or camouflage against
attacks from the air.**

IF FIGHTERS COULD dominate the skies, then bombers and
particularly ground-attack aircraft could destroy enemy
armour and artillery before it had a chance to play a part in
the battle. *Luftflotte* IV had allocated 1st Air Division in
support of the Ninth Army, while the whole of *Luftflotte* VI
was available to support the attack on the right flank. The
German aircraft were grouped on airfields around Orel,
Belgorod and Kharkov and included the He 111s and Ju 88s
of KGs 3, 27 and 55; fighter units flying Focke-Wulf Fw
190A-5s and Messerschmidt Bf 109G-6s were drawn from
JGs 3, 51, 52 and 54.

GERMAN AIRCRAFT

Among the German aircraft that would see action was the
unique Henschel Hs 129B twin-engined ground-attack
fighter. Heavily armoured, it was armed with two 7.92mm
(0.312in) MG 17 (or two 13mm/1.1in MG 13) machine guns
in the wings, two fixed forward-firing 20mm (0.8in) MG 151
cannon in the fuselage, one (optional) 30mm (1.1in) MK 101
or 37mm (1.4in) BK 3.7 cannon in a ventral pack, and a
maximum bomb load of 350kg (771lb). The Hs 129 would be
plagued by powerplant failures throughout its operational
life. The two 700hp Gnome-Rhône 14M 4/5 engines

*Left: Yakovlev Yak-9-D fighters seen from the cockpit of a bomber they
are escorting. The Yak-9 equipped the French Normandy-Niemen
Squadron and Polish 1st Fighter Regiment Warszawa. It was armed
with a 37mm (1.45in) cannon and a 12.7mm (0.5in) machine gun.*

produced a maximum speed of 407km/h (253mph) at a height of 3830m (12,570ft), and a range of 690km (429 miles). It saw action in North Africa at the close of the campaign and besides Kursk was employed in Normandy in 1944. Besides their cannon armament, ground-attack aircraft would also be carrying SD-1 and SD-2 bombs – these were the world's first 'cluster bombs', containing respectively 180 2kg (4.4lb) or 360 1kg (2.2kg) bombs. When the SD-1 and SD-2 were dropped, they opened at a pre-determined height

and the smaller 'bomblets' were then scattered across the target area.

On 8 July, a section of Hs 129B-2s, which were based at Mikoyanovka and led by *Gruppenkommandeur* Bruno Meyer, located a Soviet tank brigade west of Byelgorod and moving towards the positions of the Fourth *Panzerarmee*. Meyer alerted the IV (Antitank) *Gruppe* of *Schlachtgeschwader* 9. The force consisted of four squadrons, each with 16 Hs 129 aircraft. Meyer ordered it to attack by squadrons, and within

Opposite: Hans-Ulrich Rudel (right), Stuka pilot and tank-buster, with his rear gunner. By the end of the war, Rudel would be the most highly decorated man in Germany with the Knight's Cross with Golden Oak Leaves, Swords and Diamonds. He died in 1982.

a few minutes six tanks were burning. Fw 190s with fragmentation bombs joined the attack, hitting the escorting infantry. The Soviet forces realized that they were in a one-sided battle and withdrew to the cover of woods.

The powerful and versatile single-seat Focke-Wulf Fw 190 fighter would also be deployed in the ground-attack role. The Fw 190G had been developed from the Fw 190A and had bomb racks fitted as standard equipment and the machine guns deleted, leaving it with two 20mm (0.8in) MG 151 cannon in the wings and a maximum bomb load of 1250kg (2755lb). The 8.95m (29ft 4in) long Fw 190G was powered by one 1700hp BMW 801D-2 radial engine, which produced a maximum speed at sea level of 573km/h (356mph) and a range of 635km (395 miles). It first saw action in Tunisia but played a significant role at Kursk. It would serve until the end of the war, including attacks at night on the Ludendorf Bridge on 7 March 1945, with aircraft each carrying a single 1800kg (3968lb) bomb.

HANS-ULRICH RUDEL

German ground-attack pilots in action at Kursk included Hans-lrich Rudel, the only recipient of the *Ritterkreuz mit goldenen Eichenlaub, Schwerten und Brillianten* – Knights Cross with Golden Oak Leaves, Swords and Diamonds – awarded on 1 January 1945. A dashing *Luftwaffe* officer, he was hailed by the Nazi propaganda machine.

Rudel was born at Konradswaldau (Silesia) on 2 July 1916. In 1937, he entered the *Luftwaffe*. In 1941, during the invasion of the USSR, he flew a Ju 87 and sank the battleship *Marat* in Leningrad harbour and damaged her sister-ship the *October Revolution*. Flying the Ju 87G at Kursk, he was a formidable tank killer: his total confirmed kills were over 518 tanks, 700 trucks, over 150 anti-aircraft and artillery positions, nine fighter or ground-attack aircraft and hundreds of bridges, bunkers and railway lines. Rudel was shot down 32 times and in March 1944 escaped capture by Soviet troops, swimming across the River Dnyestr, which is 300m (984ft) wide. In the spring of 1945, he was badly wounded, the result being that his right leg was partially amputated. Despite this injury, he flew into Berlin in the last days of the war.

After World War II, he moved to Argentina, where he worked for the State Airplane Works. He also wrote two books on politics. In *We Frontline Soldiers and Our Opinion on Rearmament of Germany*, he advocated a new war with the Soviet Union. He followed this with *Daggerthrust or Legend*, a book that attacked those members of the German Army that had not given their full support to Adolf Hitler. In both these books, Rudel was seen to be promoting Nazi ideals and attempts were made to stop the publication of his war diary, *Nevertheless*, being published in West Germany.

Rudel returned to West Germany in 1953 and joined the neo-Nazi German Reich Party. His memoirs, *Stuka Pilot*, was published in 1958. A successful businessman in post-war Germany, Hans Ulrich Rudel died in Rosenheim on 18 December 1982. At his burial, West German fighter pilots

Below: The Focke-Wulf Fw 190G, developed as a ground attack aircraft from the Fw 190A fighter, had a maximum bomb load of 1250kg (2755lb). Hitler was obsessed with the idea of fitting bomb racks to aircraft that had originally been designed as fighters.

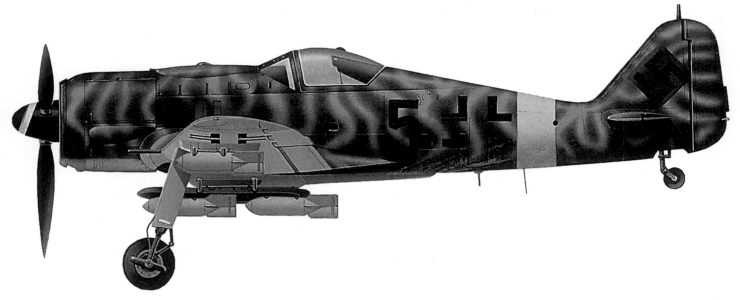

JUNKERS JU 87G-1

The Ju 87G-1 was one of the marks of the slow but battle-proven, 11.5m (37ft 8in) long, 6600kg (14,550lb), two-seater, single-engined Ju 87 Stuka. This antitank version saw action almost exclusively in the East until the end of hostilities. It was supplied to the Romanians and used by their air force against Soviet ground troops and later against the Germans when Romania switched sides. The armament was formidable: two fixed forward-firing 37mm (1.5in) BK 3.7 (Flak 18) cannon underwing and one flexible MG 15 in the rear cockpit. The cannon could easily punch through the thin deck armour of Soviet tanks. Powered by one 1400hp Junkers Jumo 211J-1 engine, it had a maximum speed at 4100m (13,500ft) of 410km/h (255mph) and a maximum range of 1535km (954 miles).

caused a scandal that led to the resignation of two senior officers: while officially on a routine training mission, they contrived to fly in salute over the cemetery in the 'missing man' formation.

Rudel would recall the ground-attack tactics that were the most effective in his Ju 87: 'We have always to try to hit a tank in one of its most vulnerable places. The front is always the strongest part of every tank; therefore every tank invariably tries as far as possible to offer its front to the enemy. Its sides are less strongly protected. But the best target for us is the stern. It is there that the engine is housed, and the necessity for cooling this power centre permits of only a thin armour plating. In order to further assist the cooling, this plating is

Below: The Junkers Ju 87G-1, a D-5 conversion fitted with 37mm (1.5in) BK3.7 (Flak 18) cannon. Stuka *pilots like Rudel used the powerful armament to attack Soviet tanks, aiming at the thin armour of rear deck. Hits normally destroyed the tank or immobilized it.*

perforated with large holes. This is a good spot to aim at because where the engine is there is always petrol. When its engine is running, a tank is easily recognizable from the air by the blue fumes of the exhaust. On its sides, the tank carries petrol and ammunition. But there the armour is stronger than at the back.'

Rudel describes his first attack in his cannon-armed *Stuka*: 'In the first attack, four tanks explode under the hammer blows of my cannons; by the evening, the total rises to twelve. We are all seized with a kind of passion for the chase from the glorious feeling of having saved much German bloodshed with every tank destroyed.'

Rudel would remember August 1943 as hot in every sense of the word. 'To the south, there is bitter fighting for the possession of Kromy. In one of our first attacks in this area, directed against the bridge in this town, a very odd thing happens to me. As I am diving, a Russian tank just starts to cross the bridge; a moment before, the bridge was clear in my sights. A 500kg [1102lb] bomb aimed at the bridge hits him when he is half-way across it; both tank and bridge are blown to smithereens.'

SOVIET AIRCRAFT

As Soviet forces moved on to the offensive, the Soviet Air Force began harrying the retreating German forces, and among the aircraft spearheading the attack was the three- or four-man Petlyakov Pe-2 dive bomber. Its armament was formidable: two fixed 7.62mm (0.3in) ShKAS or one 12.7mm (0.5in) Beresin and one 7.62mm (0.3in) ShKAS in the nose; one flexible 7.62mm (0.3in) ShKAS or one 12.7mm (0.5in) Beresin UBT machine gun in each dorsal and ventral position, and a maximum bomb load of 1200kg (2645lb). Powered by two 1100hp Klimov M-105R engines, it had a maximum speed at 5000m (16,400ft) of 540km/h (336mph) and a range of 1500km (932 miles).

It was a demanding aircraft to fly, but equipped several élite Guards Regiments. The most remarkable was the 125th M.M. Raskova Borisov Guards Bomber Regiment, whose air and ground crew were all women. Between 1943 and 1945, the Regiment flew 1134 sorties, with some crews flying three sorties a day, and it dropped 980 tons (1080 tonnes) of bombs. By the close of the war, Soviet aircraft factories had built 11,427 Pe-2 bombers.

The United States supplied aircraft to the USSR during the war, and almost half of the production run of the Douglas A-20G Havoc or Boston bomber went to the Soviet Union. With a crew of three, this light bomber could carry a bomb load of 1814kg (4000lbs). It was employed at Kursk and was also used in anti-shipping missions from the North Cape to the Black Sea.

The heavily armoured Ilyushin Il-2 *Shturmovik* was a formidable antitank and ground attack aircraft. Originally designed as a fighter, the two-seater version was armed with two fixed, forward-firing 23mm (0.9in) VYa cannon in the wings, two 7.62mm (0.3in) ShKAS machine guns in the fuselage and a flexible 12.7in (0.5in) UBT machine gun in the rear cockpit. It could carry up to 600kg (1323lbs) of external ordnance. Powered by a 1770hp Mikulin AM-38F engine, it had a top speed at 1500m (4920ft) of 404km/h (251mph) and a normal range of 765km (475 miles). By 1943, *Shturmovik* pilots had refined their tactics. Flying in attack groups of 8 to 12, in open country, they would attack 'soft' targets, such as infantry or trucks, simply skimming in at an altitude of 5–10m (16–32ft). Against stationary 'hard' targets such as bunkers, they would use near-vertical dive-bombing attacks, while against armour moving in a column, they would proceed straight down the column or weave over it in a shallow S-curve, dropping their PTAB antitank bombs from an altitude of 100–150m (320–480ft). Against armour in offensive formation, however, they preferred the 'Circle of Death' attack, in which a *Shturmovik* group would flank around the enemy and then peel off successively, each Il-2 making a shallow diving attack, then pulling up and around for another pass. The beauty of the 'Circle of Death' was that it kept the enemy under continuous fire for as long as the aircraft had fuel and ammunition.

One *Shturmovik* pilot, Senior Lieutenant Alexander Yefinov, used tactics very similar to those adopted by Hans-Ulrich Rudel. He wrote: 'We usually tried to attack from the rear, where the armour was thinner and where the most vulnerable components of the vehicles were located: the engines and the gas tanks.' He proudly added that 'the effect was staggering as Hitler's celebrated Tigers burned under the strikes.' Il-2M3s armed with 37mm (1.5in) guns were able to destroy Panthers and Tigers with their guns alone, blasting through their thinner top armour.

The *Shturmovik*'s armour made it generally invulnerable to anything less than 20mm (0.8in) fire. Even that had to be accurate and precise to do the aircraft damage, and an Il-2 moving fast and jinking wildly at low altitude was very hard to hit. Rudel recalled an attack by Il-2s against his airfield: 'One morning on dispersal we are surprised by a strong formation of Il-2 bombers which has approached our aerodrome unobserved at a low level. We take off in all directions in order to get away from the airfield; but many of our aircraft are caught on the ground. Miraculously, nothing

Above: The Henschel Hs 129B ground attack aircraft had a variety of powerful guns in the ventral pack, including a 30mm (1.18in) MK 101 or a 37mm (1.5in) BK 3.7 cannon. The A models of the aircraft were seriously under powered while the B were prone to overheating.

happens; our A.A. guns on the airfield open up for all they are worth and this evidently impresses the Ivans. We can see normal 2cm [0.8in] flak ricocheting off the armour of the Russian bombers.'

Despite their survivability, *Shturmovik* losses were high, for they fought in the teeth of the worst combat and had no place to hide. Soviet factories continued to churn out the simple, reliable aircraft, and those that fell were quickly replaced with new aircraft whose weaknesses had been eliminated. Soviet pilots refined their tactics to help reduce the losses. The *Shturmovik* was a significant contributor to the victory at Kursk. According to Soviet historians, Il-2s

destroyed 70 tanks of the 9th Panzer Division in a mere 20 minutes. In two hours, they inflicted losses of 2000 men and 270 tanks on the 3rd Panzer Division, and effectively destroyed the 17th Panzer Division in four hours of strikes, smashing 240 vehicles out of their total of almost 300.

One *Shturmovik* pilot, Georgii Timofeevich Beregovoi, was unlucky enough to be hit by effective ground fire at Kursk, which set fire to his aircraft. He attempted to keep the aircraft flying, but when his gunner's clothing began to burn, Beregovoi and the gunner jumped, at less than 300m (1000ft). They survived. After the war, Beregovoi was promoted to Colonel, became Deputy Chief of the Test Department, and was named 'Honoured Test Pilot of the USSR.' In 1962, after sitting in the *Vostok* spaceship, he successfully requested assignment to the Centre for Cosmonaut Training. After the death of Vladimir Komarov in *Soyuz* 1, Beregovoi was selected to test *Soyuz* 3. He

GROUPE DE CHASSE 3 (GC 3), NORMANDIE-NIÉMEN

In a remarkable example of Allied collaboration, a Free French Fighter Group, *Groupe de Chasse 3* (GC 3), was established in September 1942 and sent to assist the Red Air Force. It travelled to the USSR via Persia. Flying Soviet *Yakovlev* Yak-9 fighters, it went into action in 1943 and scored its first victory when two pilots downed an Fw 190 on 5 April.

The armament of the Yak-9 was not as heavy as that on some *Luftwaffe* fighters, consisting of one 20mm (0.8in) ShVAK cannon firing through the propeller hub and one 12.7mm (0.5in) Beresin MG in the upper cowling. One version of the Yak-9, the Yak 9-DK that had a dedicated antitank role, mounted a single 45mm (1.7in) NS-P-45 cannon in the nose. Its 1360hp, Klimov VK-105PF-3 engine gave a maximum speed at 2000m (6560ft) of 602 km/h (374mph) and a range

of 1410km (876 miles). Total production of the Yak-9 was a staggering 16,769 aircraft.

The French pilots of GC 3 were in action over Kursk and operated in Russia until December 1944. In that time, its 96 pilots flew 5240 missions and scored 273 conformed victories with 36 probables. On 31 July 1944, for its part in the air battle over the River Niemen, Stalin honoured GC3 with the title 'Normandy-Niémen'. Among the 46 men from GC3 who were killed in action was Marcel Lefèvre, commander of the Cherbourg Squadron and the GC3's ace with 14 victories. Badly burned when shot down on 28 May 1944, he died in hospital in Moscow on 5 June 1944. At a ceremony in Berlin on 18 February 1953, his body was returned to the French along with those of other comrades from the group.

rocketed into space on 26 October 1968; four days later, he returned to Earth. He was named 'Pilot-Cosmonaut of the USSR' and received his second Gold Star as a 'Hero of the Soviet Union'. In 1972, as a Major General, he became Director of the Centre of Cosmonaut Preparation.

'IVAN THE TERRIBLE'

Kursk would be the combat debut of Ivan Kozhedub, the top-scoring fighter pilot with the Soviet Air Force (VVS). His reputation would earn him the nickname 'Ivan the Terrible'. Born in Ukraine in 1920, Kozhedub began his career in the VVS in 1941, when he graduated as a pilot at Chuguyey military flying school. He was initially prevented from joining a fighter squadron because his skill as a pilot made him more useful as an instructor and only flew his first combat mission on 26 March 1943. He was posted as a Sergeant in the 240th Air Regiment with Voronezh Front flying La-5s. He did not make his mark against the *Luftwaffe*

until several months later, when the regiment began operations over Kursk.

On 6 July, while three fellow pilots provided cover for ground forces in the Pokrovka area, Kozhedub stormed into a formation of 22 Ju 87s, succeeding in destroying one of them. He claimed another of these the following day. Then, on July 9, Kozhedub and his flight were assigned to a frontline patrol and became involved in a melee with nine Ju 87s, four Bf 109s and two Fw 190s. During this combat, he downed a Bf 109 on his first pass and with his fourth kill met the conditions for the award of his first Order of the Red Banner.

Below: Luftwaffe *objectives at the beginning of* Zitadelle *included communications choke points, headquarters and frontline positions like gun batteries and tank concentrations. What the* Luftwaffe *could not hit were the tank factories mass producing the T-34, for these were now completely out of range.*

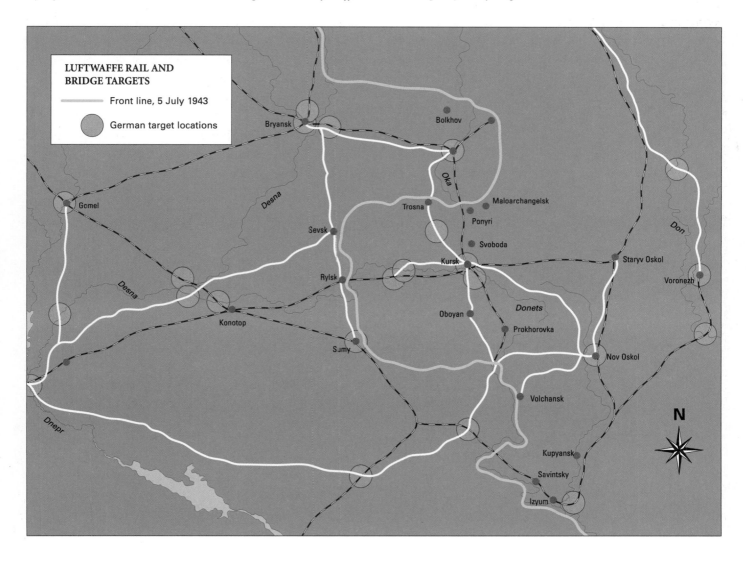

Above: A Soviet Air Force major pulls on his parachute prior to flying a mission in a North American B-25 Mitchell in spring 1943. The United States supplied 862 B-25B, D and G Mitchells to the USSR. The B-25 had a bomb load of 1361kg (3000lb).

A short time later, he took command of a fighter squadron which was to be credited with downing 12 Bf 109s, 11 Ju 87s and a Fw 190 during 165 combat sorties between August and October 1943. Kozhedub favored the surprise attack, closing right in before firing, and he piled up the victories. By the end of October, he had 20 personal kills and was well qualified for his first award of the title Hero of the Soviet Union, having gained a reputation for aggressiveness, skill and tenacity. It is particularly noteworthy that he required only 27 encounters to secure his kills, made during the course of 146 sorties, 90 of which were as escorts, 39 as ground force cover, and 9 as armed reconnaissance, with just 8 scrambles.

In 1944, he participated in intense activity that flared up along the Yuzhnyj Bug River and subsequently took part in the brutal battles over Romania. At the same time, he was in a highly competitive scoring race with another great fighter

ace, Kirill Yevstigneyey. In an outstanding effort, Kozhedub's squadron was credited with 65 enemy planes downed since August 1943: 23 Bf 109s, 30 Ju 87s, 5 He 111s, 2 Hs 129s, one Fw 190, three Fw 189s and one PZL-24 during 710 sorties (318 ground force cover, 357 escorts, 35 armed reconnaissance). Kozhedub's score had now risen to 34 and he was recommended for his second Gold Star award.

Victory number 50 came on 10 February 1945, and in that same month Kozhedub is believed to have shot down one of the first Messerschmidt Me 262 jets to be encountered on the Eastern Front. The date given by Kozhedub himself is the 19th while others suggest the 15th or 24th. It seems most likely that this claim has never been officially accepted, as it cannot be traced in his 'nagradnoj lisf' – the recommendation submitted by Chupikov, the commander of the 176th Air Regiment, for the award of his third title of Hero of the Soviet Union on 31 March 1945. By then, Kozhedub had reached 60 confirmed kills, becoming the top Allied fighter pilot of the war.

During the Korean conflict, he again displayed exceptional leadership, his unit claiming 207 U.N. aircraft destroyed for

HEAD TO HEAD

Luftwaffe	Soviet Air Force
Fighters	
Messerschmidt Bf 109	Lavochkin La-5
Focke-Wulf Fw 190	Yakovlev Yak-1
Messerschmidt Bf 110	Yakovlev Yak-7
	Yakovlev Yak-9
Ground-Attack	
Henschel Hs 129	Ilyushin IL-2 'Shturmovik'
Junkers Ju 87 'Stuka'	Petlyakov Pe-2
Bombers	
Heinkel He 111	Boston A-20
Junkers Ju 88	
Reconnaissance/Evacuation	
Henschel Hs 123	Polykarpov U-2/Po-2
Junkers Ju 52	Polykarpov R-5
Fieseler Fi 156 'Storch'	

the loss of 27 MiG-15 jet fighters in combat and nine pilots. Between 1956 and 1963, he was assigned as an inspector of VVS flight training, and in January 1964 became deputy commander of the Moscow PVO (air defence) forces. In 1967, he was appointed president of the Aviation Sports Federation and vice president of the International Federation of Aviation (FAI). He later rose to Air Marshal and was assigned as an inspector of the Soviet Ministry of Defence. Air Marshal Ivan Nikitovich Kozhedub died in August 1991.

Perhaps the last words should be left to Kozhedub:

'I destroyed my first enemy aircraft in the air during the Battle of Kursk. Historians have been setting forth my total score as 62 victories. As a matter of fact, this figure requires revision. There were many victories that either remained unconfirmed or were credited to fellow pilots. I reckon that my personal score actually is in excess of 100 victories while I never counted enemy aircraft destroyed jointly with my comrades.'

Below: The Ilyushin Il-2m3 Shturmovik ground attack fighter. Its two 23-mm (0.9in) wing-mounted cannon and two 7.62mm (0.3in) fuselage-mounted machine guns, as well as a 600kg (1321 lb) bomb load, wrought havoc against German transport and armour.

CHAPTER SIX

HUSKY INTERVENES

The Allied landings on Sicily
on 10 July prompted Hitler to order a halt to
Zitadelle. He insisted that the II *SS-Panzerkorps*,
which he rated as the equivalent of 20 Italian
divisions, should be withdrawn and sent south
to Italy to halt the landings.

A WAR ON TWO FRONTS – which had plagued the Imperial German Army in World War I until Russia pulled out of the conflict following its Revolution – had become a grim reality for Nazi Germany. Now that the Western Allies had a toehold in Europe, the pressure would increase from East and West. Soviet historians would assert that Hitler's decision to halt *Zitadelle* was not because of the Allied invasion but because the Germans had been beaten at Kursk. The impact of Operation Husky would be dismissed as 'Bourgeois Historiography'. It is therefore worth examining what was happening in the Mediterranean.

On the night of 9/10 July 1943, British and American airborne forces landed on Sicily as the advanced guard for the US Seventh Army and British Eighth Army. Of the 137 gliders released, some 69 landed in the sea, and though the amphibious invasion force managed to rescue some of the soldiers, about 200 were drowned. The British 1st Airlanding Brigade was tasked with the capture of the Simeto Bridge, north of the town of Primasole. The gliders carrying the

Left: German soldiers fill in an antitank ditch near a village. The depth and steep sides would trap a tank while antitank guns covered any viable access points. Soviet defences at Kursk had been dug by impressed civilians, soldiers and even prisoners-of-war.

force were widely scattered, but 12 landed near the bridge and the troops on board managed to hold the bridge until they were forced to withdraw. The troops who forced them out were men of *Fallschirmjäger Regiment 3 (FJR 3)*, the Machine Gun and Engineer Battalions and elements of FJR 4. They had flown from bases in southern France, via Italy, to Sicily and jumped at Catania airport on July 12 as part of a rapid reinforcement for the island. The US airborne forces were also badly scattered and 2781 men were spread over a 80km (50 mile) radius.

The Anglo-American amphibious landings by the 15th Army Group, commanded by General Alexander, were in the southeast tip of Sicily. The US Seventh Army, commanded by

Below: A German MG34 crew with the machine gun on its buffered MG-Lafayette 34 sustained fire mount. By 1943, the MG34, the world's first general purpose machine gun, was being replaced by the faster firing, less highly engineered (and less costly) MG42.

Patton, landed at Licata and the US II Corps under General Omar Bradley between Gela and Scoglitte. Here they were faced respectively by the Italian 207th Coastal Division and the 18th Coastal Brigade. On 11–12 July, tanks of the *Panzerdivision Herman Göring* launched a counterattack against the American 1st Infantry Div at Gela and had actually reached the coastal dunes before it was broken up by naval gunfire. It is estimated that over 5000 naval shells rained down on the 60 tanks of *Panzerregiment Herman Göring*, knocking out 40 PzKpfw III and IV and 17 tanks of the Army *Tiger-Kompanie* 2/504.

The British Eighth Army under Montgomery, composed of the XXX Corps under General Oliver Leese and the XIII Corps under General Miles Dempsey, landed at Pachino and between Avola and Cassible respectively. They were faced by the Italian 204th Coastal Division. Kesselring moved the XIV Panzer Corps onto the island to bolster the Italian garrison. As the Allies piled on the pressure following their landings,

Above: Under cover of a rudimentary smoke screen, Soviet engineers construct a pontoon bridge. Tough and courageous engineers not only breached obstacles like minefields and rivers, but re-used explosives they had extracted from mines and unexploded shells and bombs to construct mines and demolition charges.

Kesselring did not wait for clearance from Hitler before he began to withdraw his forces across the Straits of Messina to mainland Italy. On 29 July, the German press saluted Mussolini on his 60th birthday. It was a demonstration of Hitler's loyalty to his Fascist ally.

The German forces put up strong resistance, and their demolitions and rearguard actions meant that Messina did not fall until 17 August 1943. Its capture became a race between the British under Montgomery and the US Army under Patton, both very competent men and both men with huge egos. The Germans realized that Messina was critical and fought hard against the British Eighth Army. At 10:15, the US 3rd Division entered Messina – Patton and the Americans had won by 50 minutes. Prior to the capture of Messina, Operation *Lehrgang* saw the German and Italian navies evacuate 40,000 German, 60,000 Italian troops, nearly 10,000 German vehicles and 47 tanks across the straits to the Italian mainland in six days. The cost of the Sicilian campaign was high. The British and Canadians lost 2721 killed, 2183 missing and 7939 wounded. The Americans suffered 2811 killed, 686 missing and 6471 wounded. Axis losses were estimated at 164,000 killed or captured.

MANSTEIN'S 'LOST VICTORY'

In Russia, as the battle for Kursk raged, Manstein believed that the Soviet reserves were running out and that Model, by keeping the pressure on the northern flank, would achieve a breakthrough. What was undoubtedly true was that instead of being held back for a strong counterattack, Soviet reserves were being drawn into the fighting.

A violent battle is underway along the coast of eastern Italy, where Italian and German troops are vigorously combating enemy forces who have landed there and are bravely withstanding their pressure. Enemy aerial forces are active. Axis fighter planes have shot down 22 enemy aircraft, anti-aircraft guns 9.

Italian Forces High Command.
Sunday 11 July 1943

Opposite: The Soviet counteroffensive. Having halted Zitadelle and inflicted heavy losses, the Bryansk and West Fronts attacked in the north on July 15 while the Voronezh and South-West Fronts attacked in the south on July 17. Incredibly, the Germans were able to fight a cohesive withdrawal.

One of the great 'what ifs' of Kursk is whether it would have been a German victory if Manstein had been allowed to keep up his attacks. The Voronezh Front had been obliged to call on the Steppe Front to contain the attacks, and despite heavy rain Manstein's forces had trapped the Soviet Sixty-Ninth Army and two tank corps between Rzhavets, Belenikhino and Gostishchevo. Since the beginning of the operation, Manstein had taken 24,000 prisoners and destroyed or captured 1000 tanks and over 100 antitank guns. However, the goal was to encircle Soviet forces inside the salient, and destroy those who were in the way. Fourth *Panzerarmee*'s spearhead, II *SS-Panzerkorps*, would indeed

have broken through the fighting around Prokhorovka and into open ground, but Model had been forced to redeploy to meet attacks that were trying to cut off the Orel salient from which he was operating. He could not, therefore, continue the thrust and there was also an unknown number of Soviet reserves that could still be committed in the fight against the spearheads of Fourth *Panzerarmee*. There were still 130km (81 miles) to go to link up with Model's Ninth Army, all heavily fortified and backed by Soviet armour.

The decision to disengage from the action would not be easy. Writing in 1955, von Mellenthin commented:

Below: Villagers greet a T-34 that has camouflage doubling as victor's garlands. People living in areas that had been under German control were regarded with suspicion by the NKVD, who suspected that they might have collaborated or seen an alternative to Communism.

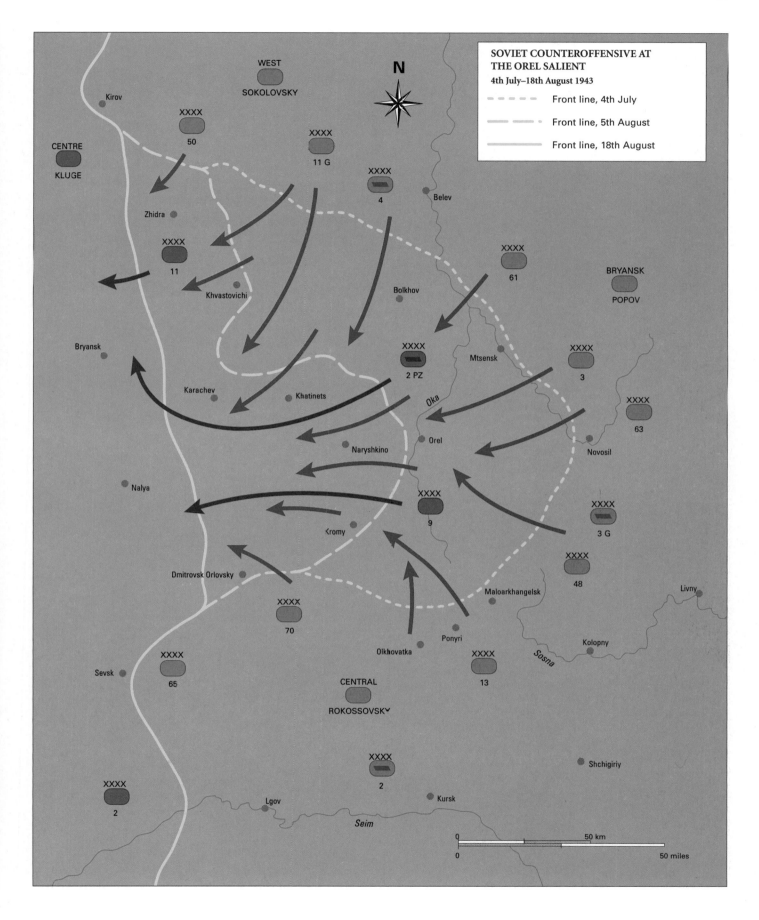

SOVIET COUNTEROFFENSIVE AT THE OREL SALIENT
4th July–18th August 1943

- - - - Front line, 4th July
–·–·– Front line, 5th August
——— Front line, 18th August

N

WEST
SOKOLOVSKY

Kirov

XXXX
50

CENTRE
KLUGE

XXXX
11 G

XXXX
4

Belev

Zhidra

XXXX
11

Khvastovichi

Bolkhov

XXXX
61

BRYANSK
POPOV

Bryansk

Karachev

Khatinets

XXXX
2 PZ

Mtsensk

Oka

XXXX
3

XXXX
63

Naryshkino

Orel

Novosil

Nalya

XXXX
9

XXXX
3 G

Kromy

XXXX
48

Dmitrovsk Orlovsky

Maloarkhangelsk

Livny

XXXX
70

Ponyri

Kolopny

Olkhovatka

Sosna

XXXX
65

Sevsk

XXXX
13

CENTRAL
ROKOSSOVSKY

Shchigiriy

XXXX
2

XXXX
2

Lgov

Kursk

Seim

0   50 km

0   50 miles

171

Opposite: Arguably the most able German general of the war, Erich von Manstein could plan set-piece attacks like the attack on France in 1940 and siege of Sevastopol in 1942 and also handle fast-moving tank battles like Kharkov 1943, where quick decisions were critical.

'Manstein had not committed all his forces and was in favour of continuing the offensive as a battle of attrition; by smashing up Soviet armoured reserves in the Kursk salient, we might forestall major offensives in other sectors. This situation should have been foreseen before *Citadel* was launched; we were now in the position of a man who has seized a wolf by the ears and dare not let him go. However, Hitler declared that the attack must stop forthwith.'

Unrelenting fighting continued on 13 July, and *Leibstandarte* pulled back to rest and re-arm while *Totenkopf* took over, together with *Das Reich*. The latter was ordered to attack via Pravorot to Prokhorovka, exploiting a gap in the enemy lines. Hausser was aware that his troops were in need of rest, to ensure that if *Das Reich* lacked the necessary strength to push on, *Leibstandarte* could be thrown in the line again. However, the fighting was taking a heavy toll and by the end of the day the II *SS-Panzerkorps* was down to 180 operational tanks and 64 assault guns. Moreover, the attacks by the XLVIII Panzer Corps were suspended as its flanking formations came under heavy attack. The Germans now had only one option: to relinquish control of Beresovka and Hill 247.0.

ZITADELLE HALTED

On the same day, Manstein and Kluge were summoned to the *Wolfsschanze* – Hitler's 'Wolf's Lair' HQ at Rastenburg in East Prussia. Hitler ordered them to break off *Zitadelle* and direct troops to Western Europe, in order to contain the Allies. Pressed by Manstein, Hitler agreed that Hoth and Kempf could continue their attacks in the south, despite the fact that Manstein was deprived of the *SS-Panzerkorps*, which was now broken up. *Leibstandarte* was rushed to Italy, while *Das Reich* and *Totenkopf* now made up II *SS-Panzerkorps*. Before being entrained for Italy, *Leibstandarte* handed over all its tanks to *Das Reich* and *Totenkopf*.

ERICH VON MANSTEIN

Manstein was born in Berlin on 24 November 1887, and following the death of his parents, the von Lewinskis, he took the name of his adopted father, Georg von Manstein. An Imperial court page, he then spent six years in the cadet corps. He joined the German Army and in 1906 was commissioned in the 3rd Foot Guards.

Following the outbreak of World War I, Manstein served in Belgium before being wounded in Poland on November 1914. After recovering, he returned to the Eastern Front before being sent to France in 1917. Manstein remained in the army after the war and in 1936 was appointed Chief of Operations. Promoted to the rank of major-general, he served under General Ludwig Beck as *Oberquartermeister*. Considered to be uncooperative by Adolf Hitler, he was sent to Silesia as commander of the 18th Division.

In the invasion of Poland, Manstein served as chief of staff to the Group South under General Gerd von Rundstedt. In 1940, Manstein worked with Guenther Blumentritt and Henning von Tresckow to develop the plan to invade France. Manstein and his colleagues suggested that the German Army attack through the wooded hills of the Ardennes. Hitler originally rejected the proposal but eventually approved a modified version of what became known as the Manstein

Plan. Manstein was sent back to Silesia and did not take part in the successful operation until the final stages, when he served under General Gunther von Kluge.

Promoted to Field Marshal, he conducted the successful siege of Sevastopol during 1941–2. He commanded the forces that attempted to relieve Stalingrad in 1943 and subsequently the counterattack at Kharkov in 1943. After the failure of the attack at Kursk, he argued with Hitler about overall strategy, and in March 1944 he was dismissed.

Subsequently, he was associated with the July Plotters but never closely involved. Captured by the British at the close of the war, he was charged with war crimes. In court, Manstein argued that he was unaware that genocide was taking place in the territory under his control. However, evidence was produced that Manstein had ordered that 'the Jewish Bolshevik system be wiped out once and for all' although he requested that officers should not be present during the killing of Jews.

Found guilty, Manstein was sentenced on 24 February 1950 to 18 years' imprisonment. However, he was freed for medical reasons on 6 May 1953. His war memoirs, *Lost Victories*, was published in Germany in 1955. He died at Irschenhausen near Munich on 11 June 1973.

KURSK: THE VITAL 24 HOURS

PARTY JOKES

The SD (*Sicherheitsdienst* – SS security police) monitoring domestic morale in Germany reported on 16 August 1943 that 'the people at present feel their powers of emotional resistance are being strained to the breaking point...Those wearing [Nazi] Party insignia have frequently been addressed by other Germans who say: "What, are you still wearing that thing?" There have also been numerous reports of the following joke: Anyone who recruits five new members into the Party gets to leave himself. Anyone who recruits ten new members gets a certificate testifying that he was never in the Party.'

On 14 July, *Das Reich* opened up with a barrage, followed at 04:00 by an infantry attack that had reached the outskirts of Pravorot by 12:00. Here, troops from I. and III. Abt from '*Der Führer*' destroyed 12 T-34s, using *Haft-Hohlladung* 3kg. These were portable 3.49kg (7.6lb) magnetic mines with a 0.89kg (1.9lb) shaped-charge TNT warhead. To operate it, the soldier used the three powerful magnets on the outer edge of the cone to fix it to the hull of a tank, and then pulled the friction igniter, which gave him between four and seven seconds to escape. (The Germans developed a special textured cement coating for their tanks to protect them from magnetic weapons.)

The XLVIII Panzer Corps counterattacked in an effort to regain Heights 247.0 and 243.0. As the Germans advanced, they came under intense artillery fire. Soviet attacks from the north and west were beaten off but disrupted the German operations. Despite this, they recaptured Height 243.0.

The fighting continued until the night of July 15, when heavy rainfall washed away the terrain and roads. *SS-Panzerkorps* managed to link up with III Army Corps, which destroyed several pockets of Soviet troops. But by now the German forces in the southern sector were beginning to pull back to their original start lines. *Zitadelle* was over.

Among the many historians who have re-examined the battle of Kursk, and particularly the action at Prokhorovka, the American historian George M. Nipe, Jr provides a telling analysis:

'*Waffen SS* formations' records of their Eastern Front operations were not declassified until 1978–81. By that time, many of the major works about the Eastern Front had already been published. Later authors accepted the accounts of the battle as given in the earlier books and failed to conduct additional research. As a result, one of the best known of all Eastern Front battles has never been understood properly. Prokhorovka was believed to have been a significant German defeat but was actually a stunning reversal for the Soviets because they suffered enormous tank losses. . . . As Manstein suggested, Prokhorovka may truly have been a lost German victory, thanks to decisions made by Hitler. It was fortunate for the Allied cause that the German dictator, a foremost proponent of the value of will, lost his own will to fight in southern Ukraine in July 1943. Had he allowed Manstein to continue the attack on the two Soviet tank armies in the Prokhorovka area, Manstein might have achieved a victory even more damaging to the Soviets than the counterattack that had recaptured Kharkov in March 1943'.

The British historian Brian Taylor agrees that the figures for tanks destroyed and prisoners captured by both sides are exaggerated, but offers a different analysis of the battle:

'The failure of Citadel broke the panzers, just as Guderian had feared. His fears were realized as the Soviets demonstrated that their own armoured losses, although severe, were relatively easily replaced....Defeat at Kursk had cost Germany the initiative in the east for good. Hitler's gamble with his reconstituted panzer force had squandered the German army's last sizeable force. Never again would the *Ostheer* field such a generously equipped force, and from here on it would fight a battle of attrition against a massively superior foe. Despite this, though, the German Army remained fundamentally intact as it waited for the expected Soviet counteroffensive.'

SOVIET COUNTEROFFENSIVES

Kursk might have had the makings of a victory, but the strategic balance was changing, both in the Mediterranean and with the opening of the Soviet counteroffensives. By 23 July, as Soviet pressure increased, Fourth *Panzerarmee* had been forced back to its start line of 4 July. Operation *Rumyantsev*, the attack by the Voronezh Front and Steppe Front, was launched on 3 August. It began with a five-minute barrage that ripped apart Ott's LII Army Corps.

This was part of a well-constructed fire plan: 30 minutes later, Soviet artillery resumed their fire while ground attack aircraft added their weight. This attack lasted for over two

Opposite: A Waffen-SS *officer watches as a T-34/76D crew dismount from their bogged-down tank. Though Soviet and later German tanks both had wide tracks to give mobility on snow and mud, waterlogged terrain could be deceptive and halt even these vehicles.*

Left: *For the common infantryman, close
combat actions with tanks on the Eastern
Front called for strong nerves and quick
judgement. Here, in an action during the
months following Kursk, a German soldier
armed with a* Panzerfaust *watches a T-34
burn after a classic infantry tank ambush
at a farm.*

The Soviet writer Vasili Grossman
wrote lyrically about the liberation of
Orel:

'The sun rose over the city. Amid
the smoke of still-burning fires, amid
yet-unsettled dust raised high into the
sky by explosions, along pavements
covered with the debris of brick and
glass moved our troops. They were
men in dust-covered boots and sun-
bleached shirts, with faces dark from
the sweltering August sun; men who
for many weeks, in parching heat and
in pouring rain, defying fire and death,
step by step breaking through wire
entanglements and demolishing
trenches, resolutely and persistently
moved towards Orel from the north
and east, from the south and southeast....That first parade looked so
austere amid the smoke caused by fires
and dust raised by explosions, amid
the high haze shading the sky above
the city in ruins. And hundreds of
people came out of doorways and
crawled out of basements, and ran to
meet the soldiers and officers
marching under a Red banner.'

hours. The Fortieth and Twenty-Seventh Armies to the
north, and Fifty-Seventh Army from the South West Front to
the east, launched attacks on the shoulder of the German
salient. The massed artillery of the Soviet Sixth Guards Army
laid down a barrage of several hours' duration on the
German 167th Infantry Division. When the artillery lifted its
fire, 200 tanks roared into the German line, followed by
waves of close-packed infantry. Before nightfall, the German
division was reduced to a few dazed survivors. Pouring
through the gap, the Soviets reached and took Belgorod and
Orel on 5 August.

The Fourth *Panzerarmee* and Army Detachment Kempf
fought a hard action as they withdrew, counterattacking on
11–17 August against the Voronezh Front south of
Bogudukhov, delaying the Soviet advance but not halting it.
By the end of the fighting, each side had lost about 1500
tanks, but many of the Soviet ones could be recovered and
repaired. On the northern shoulder of the Kursk salient,
General Nikolai Pukhov, in command of the Soviet
Thirteenth Army, surveyed the battlefield. 'Everywhere were
signs of recent fighting. The entire expanse had been
ploughed up by artillery and mortar shells and bombs.

Everywhere were deep craters, tangles of barbed wire, cut down or broken trees. The grass and crops had been crushed by thousands of booted feet. . . . Chimneys were all that was left of the villages burnt down by the retreating Nazis. Everything was broken, crushed. Only a distant hillock somehow left untouched by artillery shells would sometimes bristle with crosses over countless German graves. The enemy paid with thousands of such graves for his attempt to topple us on the Kursk bulge…'

On the northern flank, Model had fought a rear-guard action in which the weather as well as the ability of his exhausted troops had played a significant part. As his troops pulled back, they instituted a 'scorched earth' policy. The crops that were ready for harvesting were torched, as were farms, and 250,000 civilians, taking whatever they could carry, were forced to trek westward.

THE EASTERN WALL

Manstein informed Hitler that he lacked enough divisions to close the northern flank or to hold the long line on the Donets below Kharkov. He would either have to yield the Donets Basin or receive 20 divisions from somewhere else. As he had done on other occasions when confronted with unpleasant choices, Hitler avoided the decision by moving in an altogether different direction. He suddenly revived the idea of an East Wall, which he had rejected earlier. On 12 August, he ordered construction to start on a fortified line that was to begin in the south at Melitopol, run due north to the Dnieper River near Zaporozhe, follow the Dnieper to Kiev and the Desna to Chernigov, thence take a line almost due north to the southern tip of Lake Pskov, and, running along the west shores of Lakes Peipus and Pskov, anchor on

the Gulf of Finland at Narva. While it appeared that this order indicated that Hitler had accepted a general retreat on the Eastern Front as inevitable, subsequent decisions revealed that he actually intended to establish a barrier behind which the armies could not retreat and, since no work of any kind had as yet been done on the so-called East Wall, give himself an excuse for holding out farther east.

On 13 August, Soviet forces reached the outskirts of Kharkov and Germans were forced to withdraw to avoid encirclement. The city was liberated on 23 August. It was a shell, gutted, burned and blasted. In the days that followed, Soviet engineers working patiently in the dirt and rubble removed 61,000 mines and 320 aircraft bombs rigged as mines. In the last two weeks of August, the Soviet High Command expanded the offensive to the south and north. To the southeast, the Soviets broke through on the Donets south of Izyum and on the Mius River line east of Snigirevka. In the last week of the month, they penetrated Army Group Centre's front in three places.

On 31 August, Hitler gave the Sixth Army permission to retire from the Mius to the Kalmius River 'if necessary'. Three days later, he took a second positive step, ordering Army Group A to begin evacuating the useless beachhead which it still held on the Taman Peninsula. The Sixth Army could not halt on the Kalmius. During the morning of 6 September, a Soviet mechanized corps and nine rifle divisions broke

Below: A column of T-34/76D tanks on the move. The tanks incorporated lessons learned from combat: the hexagonal turret did not have the overhang at the rear, where German soldiers had learned to position Teller mines fitted with pull switches in hazardous close-combat actions.

Above: The SU-76 tank hunter was widely built during the war. The concept had been adopted from the Germans, since in 1941 the Red Army had tanks but no SP guns. The open topped SU-76 was not popular with its crews, hence the nickname 'Sucha', or 'Bitch'.

through on the boundary between the Sixth Army and First *Panzerarmee*. The next day, a tank corps slipped through the gap, and, leaving the infantry behind, the two armoured corps moved westward. By 8 September, they were approaching Pavlograd, 48km (30 miles) east of the Dnieper and 161km (100 miles) behind Sixth Army's front. On that day, Hitler allowed the Sixth Army and First *Panzerarmee* to start withdrawing to the line on which he had intended to build the East Wall, from Melitopol to the Dnieper north of Zaporozhe.

By 14 September, the northern flank of Army Group South was disintegrating. Fourth Panzerarmee was split into three parts, and the Soviets had a clear road open to Kiev. To the north, Army Group Centre fared no better. The Second Army's front on the Desna, which was to have been part of

the East Wall, was riddled with Soviet bridgeheads, and on 14 September the Soviets began an offensive directed at Smolensk. The next day, Hitler gave the two army groups permission to retreat to the line of the Dnieper, Sozh and Pronya rivers. In most places, the retreat was already under way, and in the last week of the month it developed into a race with the Soviets for possession of the river lines. At the end of the month, as the last German troops crossed the rivers, the Soviets had five bridgeheads on the Dnieper between the confluence of the Pripyat River and Dnepropetrovsk.

In two-and-a-half months, Army Groups South and Centre had been forced back for an average of 241km (150 miles) on a front 1046km (650 miles) long. The Germans had lost the most valuable territory they had taken in the Soviet Union. In an effort to deny the Soviets the fruits of those economically rich areas, Hitler instituted a scorched-earth policy, but in the end even that satisfaction was denied him. Nearly all of the factories, power plants, mines and railroads could be destroyed, but the Germans lacked the personnel to transport or destroy more than a fraction of the agricultural and economic produce.

PUSH TO THE DNEIPER

The River Dnieper affords the strongest natural defence line in western Russia, especially when the battle is moving from

Tonight at twenty-four hundred hours, on 5th August, the capital of our country, Moscow, will salute the valiant troops that liberated Orel and Belgorod with twelve artillery salvoes from 120 guns. I express my thanks to all the troops that took part in the offensive....Eternal glory to the heroes who fell in the struggle for the freedom of our country. Death to the German invaders.

Josef Stalin, Order of the Day
Moscow, 5 August 1943

Opposite: The Soviet autumn and winter offensive of 1943 cut off the Crimea and pushed deep into Belorussia. US-supplied trucks gave the Soviet Army greater mobility, which let it sustain offensive operations through the muddy season, giving the German forces no rest.

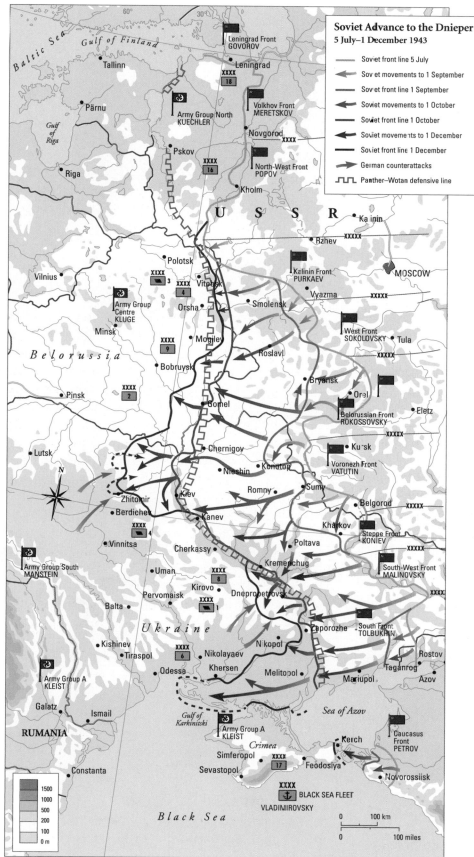

Soviet Advance to the Dnieper
5 July–1 December 1943

- Soviet front line 5 July
- Soviet movements to 1 September
- Soviet front line 1 September
- Soviet movements to 1 October
- Soviet front line 1 October
- Soviet movements to 1 December
- Soviet front line 1 December
- German counterattacks
- Panther–Wotan defensive line

east to west. Fortified and adequately manned, the Dnieper line could have constituted an ideal defensive position, but Army Group South was so badly battered that the river provided at most a degree of natural protection and a tenuous handhold. Of the East Wall nothing was in existence; much of the proposed line had not even been surveyed.

On reaching the Dnieper, the Soviet Army had attained the original objectives of its summer offensive. Ordinarily, the shortening of the German front, the defensive advantages of the river, the lengthening Soviet lines of communications, and the attrition of the Soviet forces could have been expected to bring the two sides into temporary balance. But Hitler had sacrificed too much of his strength east of the river. In contrast, the Soviets' numerical superiority had enabled them to rest and refit their units in shifts, and they reached the Dnieper with their offensive capability largely intact. Before the last German troops crossed the river, the battle for the Dnieper line had begun.

In the first week of October, the whole Eastern Front was quiet as the Soviets regrouped and brought up new forces. To underscore the victories achieved so far, they began renaming the front commands. Opposite Army Group South and the Sixth Army, which had passed to Army Group A, the Voronezh, Steppe, South West and South Fronts became the 1st, 2nd, 3rd, and 4th Ukrainian fronts.

On 9 October, the 4th Ukrainian Front launched 45 rifle divisions, five tank and mechanized corps, and two cavalry corps against the Sixth Army's 13 divisions in the line between Melitopol and the Dnieper. Within three weeks, it drove the Sixth Army back across the flat, dusty Nogai Steppe to the lower Dnieper.

Opposite: Fatigue lines the face of a Grenadier as he waits with his Kar 98k rifle in his shoulder. Aware of the excesses committed in Russia in 1941–42, German soldiers now fought not for victory but to keep a vengeful Red Army from the borders of the Reich.

Hitler refused last-minute requests to evacuate the Seventeenth Army from the Crimea, claiming that the Soviets would thereby gain airfields from which to bomb the vital Rumanian oilfields.

When the Sixth Army retreated beyond the Perekop Isthmus, the Seventeenth Army was cut off, and in the first week of November, Soviet troops gained beachheads on the Sivash Sea near the base of the isthmus and on the Kerch Peninsula. The defence of Sevastopol would turn out to be a forgotten epic of the Eastern Front.

The German Seventeenth Army under *Generalleutnant* Erwin Jaenecke held out until the spring of 1944, besieged by the 4th Ukrainian Front under General Fyodor Tolbukhin and the Independent Coastal Army of General Yeremenko. Hitler had demanded that the port be held as a fortress – *festung*. Though some defences had been prepared, the old Soviet emplacements were largely unusable. The shattered

galleries of the Maxim Gorky battery were used as a field hospital. The Soviet commanders were aware of the natural defensive advantages and prepared their attack thoroughly. Cn 5 May 1944, they opened fire with twice the weight of artillery deployed by the Germans in 1942. It took only a week for the Soviet forces to drive the German and Rumanian forces back to Cape Kherson. Here Junkers Ju 52s operating from an improvized airstrip were able to evacuate some of the wounded.

During these last days, vessels from the German and Rumanian fleets, which were commanded by Rear-Admiral Schulz, attempted to supply and then evacuate the garrison and lost 27 ships or landing barges with 8000 men drowned. Notable among the losses were the transports *Totila* and *Teja*, the sinking of which accounted for the bulk of the Axis casualties. On shore, 78,000 men were killed or taken

Below: The Tiger tank remained a formidable adversary fighting defensive actions. Waiting in ambush, the veteran crews could destroy T-34s at long range before moving to new hide positions. These skills would later be demonstrated against British and American tanks in Normandy in June 1944.

> There are two things I need for the war above everything else – Rumanian oil and Turkish chrome ore. Both will be lost if I abandon the Crimea.
>
> Adolf Hitler,
> October 1943

prisoner, but despite attack from bombers, torpedo boats and submarines of the Black Sea Fleet, the German and Rumanians saved about 130,000 men. The last ferry convoy left at 03:00 on 11 May. The last region to be defended was the Kherson peninsula, and though the defences around Sevastopol were inadequate, the trenches and obstacles blocking access to the area (some 200 square kilometres/ 77 square miles) held long enough for men to escape across the Black Sea to the Rumanian port of Constanta. At this late stage in the war, some, however, considered escaping to internment in neutral Turkey to the south. On 12 May 1944, STAVKA declared the Crimea free of Axis troops.

THROUGH THE UKRAINE

However, back in the autumn of 1943, while the 4th Ukrainian Front was engaged below the Dnieper bend, the 2nd and 3rd Ukrainian fronts operated against the First *Panzerarmee* and 8th Army, carving a bridgehead 322km (200 miles) wide and 96.5km (60 miles) deep on the river between Cherkassy and Zaporozhe. In the south, the 3rd Ukrainian Front threatened important iron and manganese mining areas near Krivoi Rog and Nikopol, which Hitler was determined to hold at any cost. The Soviets had taken a large bridgehead at the confluence of the Pripyat and the Dnieper in September.

To the south, the 1st Ukrainian Front broke out of two smaller bridgeheads on 3 November, and three days later it took Kiev. During the rest of the month, it drove the Fourth Panzerarmee back west and south of the city, threatening to demolish the entire left flank of Army Group South. To the north, the Belorussian Front forced the right half of Army Group Centre back from the Sozh River. Around Nevel, on the boundary between Army Groups Centre and North, the 1st and 2nd Baltic Fronts made a deep salient in the German front.

December 1943 brought some relief to the German armies, which for a few weeks regained their balance and even managed to counterattack west of Kiev. By this time, the best solution for the German predicament would have been to withdraw Army Group South and the Sixth Army to the next major river, the Bug (Southern Bug), but Hitler would not consider it. He talked vaguely of retaking Kiev and of reopening the Crimean Front. Actually, German prospects were worse than they had been in the two preceding winters. Opposing three million German troops, the Soviet Army had 5.7 million men and an overwhelming superiority in tanks and artillery. In the summer and autumn offensives, the Soviets had repeatedly laid down artillery barrages heavier than any since the great battles of World War I. Moreover, the German Army faced two new dangers: its manpower reserves were rapidly being exhausted, and an Anglo-American invasion on the coast of northwest Europe within the next six months was almost certain.

In November, Hitler had notified commanders on the Eastern Front that they would have to manage with their own resources until the invasion had been defeated. The danger in the West, he said, was greater than that in Russia, and he could no longer take the responsibility for allowing the Western Front to be weakened for the benefit of other theatres of war. He suggested that possibly the Eastern Front might trade space for time, but events soon were to prove that he was constitutionally incapable of adopting this course. Moreover, the Soviet Army was now a more mobile and flexible force and the OKW knew that after the frosts of winter had hardened the autumn mud, the depleted German forces in the East would be faced by a new offensive. They knew that the men and women of the USSR would be seeking revenge for the brutal occupation of the western states of the Soviet Union. The tough new confidence that now permeated Soviet forces, and which would take them to Berlin in a little over 18 months, was summed up by Ivan Boloto, a veteran interviewed 30 years after the battle of Kursk.

'When a tank came at me the first time, I was sure that that was the end of the world, honest to God. Then as that tank came nearer and started burning and I thought to myself – it's the end for him, not me. You know, by the way, I rolled and smoked about five cigarettes during that battle. Well, perhaps not right to the end, I don't want to lie to you, but I did roll five cigarettes. . . . When you're in combat it's this way: you put your gun aside and light a cigarette, when time allows. You can smoke when a battle's on, what you can't do is miss your aim. If you miss, you won't need that cigarette. That's the way it is.'

Opposite: A German Obergefreiter *advances along a trench, carrying Tellermine 35 antitank mines. The Teller 35 weighed 8.7kg (19.1lb). Operating pressure was 80–180kg (176–396lb) and the mine had threaded wells in the side and base to take anti-handling pull igniters.*

KURSK: THE VITAL 24 HOURS

APPENDIX 1

ZITADELLE ORDERS

Hitler issued two 'Orders of the Day' to be read on the eve of *Zitadelle*. One was addressed to the soldiers and read:

'Soldiers of the Reich!

This day you are about to take part in an offensive of such importance that the whole future of the war may depend on its outcome. More than anything else, your victory will show the whole world that resistance to the power of the German Army is hopeless.

The powerful strike, which you will direct at the Soviet armies this morning, must shake them to their roots…

The German homeland…has placed its deepest trust in you!'

The other was addressed to officers and read:

'My Commanders!

I have given the order for the first offensive of this year.

You and your subordinate soldiers are designated to successfully execute this mission no matter the circumstances. The importance of this first offensive of the year is extraordinary.

The initiation of this new German operation will not only strengthen our own people in the eyes of the rest of the world, but, most importantly, will also instil new self-confidence in the German soldier himself. Our allies will be reaffirmed in their belief in our final victory, while neutral countries will become more cautious and reserved. We must wrest the initiative from the Soviet leadership and create the conditions for Russian defeat during this offensive. It can have far-reaching effects on the morale and composure of the Soviet soldier.

The armies scheduled to participate in the attack have been provided with all the weapons that German ingenuity and technology can produce. Personnel strengths have been raised to the highest levels possible. The supply of ammunition and fuel have been secured in sufficient quantities for this and future operations. The *Luftwaffe* has concentrated all of its strength to destroy the enemy's air capability, to bomb his field fortifications and support the infantrymen with continuous sorties

I, therefore, turn over this battle to you, my commanders. More than ever, the decisive battles of this fourth year of the war depend on the commanders, on their leadership, on their enthusiasm and drive, on their ruthlessness, their unbending

desire for victory and, when necessary, their personal heroic commitment.

I know that you have given much in the preparation for this battle, I thank you for this. You must also realize that much depends on the successful execution of this first great battle of 1943, such as final victory.

I don't doubt that, under these circumstances, I can count on you, my commanders.'

Adolf Hitler

APPENDIX 2

APPRECIATION OF THE ENEMY'S MOVES IF OPERATION 'CITADEL' IS CARRIED OUT, BY *FREMDE HEERE OST*, 3 JULY 1943

'Once Operation "Citadel" begins, the enemy can either restrict his counter-measures to the "Citadel" operational area, so as to block our attack – if necessary by bringing up reserves from neighbouring areas – remaining generally on the defensive apart from minor counterattacks; or he will launch the offensives he has already prepared against Army Group South and Army Group Centre…In view of their own degree of readiness to attack, and with regard to the situation in the Mediterranean, the latter course appears the more probable. We therefore have to expect that, probably soon after our offensive begins, the Russians will mount strong diversionary counterattacks…

This suggests that the German offensive will bring about the following probable development in the enemy situation, which broadly conforms to our appreciation of the Russian intentions so far:

A] In the area of the German offensive:

The powerful enemy forces assembling at Kursk, Yaluyki, Voronezh and Yelets will probably be split up by the German offensive so that the bulk of them end up east of our attacking spearheads, and the rest, west of Kursk. Our attacking forces will therefore probably be exposed to particularly strong flank attacks from the east – from northeast of Bolgrad and west of Livny.

B] In the area of Army Group South:

We must expect the Russians to launch the offensives they have prepared against the southern wing and centre of this Army Group's front, soon after the German offensive begins. We expect both an encirclement action against the Sixth Army and the First Panzer Army, in the direction of the Donets basin, and a thrust by strong enemy forces from Kupyansk towards Kharkov, striking at the deep flank of the German attacking armies.

C] In the area of Army Group centre:

The enemy will probably seek to relieve the pressure on his own forces, by attacking our Second Army with strategic reserves believed to be held in the region bounded by Tula, Kaluga, Sukhinichi and Plavsk. We must be prepared for early and powerful attacks on the eastern and north-eastern front of the Second Panzer Army, heading for Orel with the object of breaking through in the rear of the German attacking armies.'

Gehlen
Fremde Heere Ost
3 July 1943

APPENDIX 3

SOVIET SITUATION REPORT ON THE CENTRAL FRONT, 21 MAY 1943

The excellent Soviet intelligence and the analysis of the impending battle for the Kursk salient can be seen in the report on the Central Front sent by Marshal Zhukov to Stalin. He conducted a similar study of the Voronezh Front. To ensure greater security, Zhukov used the code name 'Yuriev', while Rokossovsky was 'Kostin' and Stalin 'Ivanov'. It is clear that Zhukov is working on the concept of fighting a defensive action to be followed by a counterattack.

'To: Comrade Ivanov

The situation on the Central Front on 21 May 1943 was as follows:

By 21 May reconnaissance of all kinds has established that before the Central Front the enemy has 15 infantry divisions in the first line and 13 divisions, including panzer divisions, in the second line.

There is moreover, information about the concentration of the 2nd Panzer Division and 36th Motorized Infantry Division south of Orel. The information about these two divisions requires verification.

The enemy's 4th Panzer Division, formerly deployed west of Sevsk, has been moved somewhere. Besides, there are three divisions, two of them panzer, in the Bryansk and Karachev area.

Consequently as of 21 May the enemy can operate with 33 divisions, six of them panzer divisions, against the Central Front.

The Front's instrumental and visual reconnaissance has detected 800 artillery pieces, mainly 105mm [4.1in] and 150mm [5.9in] guns.

The enemy keeps the bulk of his artillery opposite the Thirteenth Army, the left flank of the Forty-Eighth Army and the right flank of the Seventieth Army, i.e. in the Prosno-Pervoye-Pozdeyevo sector. Behind this main artillery grouping, there are 600–700 tanks on the Zmeyeyka–Krasnaya Roshcha line. The bulk is concentrated east of the River Oka.

In the area of Orel, Bryansk and Smolensk, the enemy has concentrated 600–650 warplanes. The main enemy air grouping is in the Orel area.

Both on the ground and in the air the enemy has been passive in the last few days, confining himself to small-scale air reconnaissance and occasional minor artillery attacks.

In his forward line and his tactical depth, the enemy is digging trenches and intensively fortifying his positions in front of the Thirteenth Army in the Krasnaya Slobodka–Senkovo sector, where he already has a second defence line beyond the River Neruch. Observation reveals that the enemy is building a third defence line in this sector, 3–4km [1.8–2.4 miles] north of the Neruch.

Prisoners say the German Command knows about our grouping south of Orel and our planned offensive and that the German units have been warned. Captured airmen claim that the German Command is itself preparing for an offensive and concentrating aviation for this purpose.

I personally visited the forward lines of the Thirteenth Army, observed the enemy defences from various points, watched his activity and talked with divisional commanders of the Seventieth and Thirteenth Armies, with commanders Galanin [Lt Gen I.V. Galinin, Seventieth Army], Pukhov [Lt Gen N.P. Pukhov, Thirteenth Army] and Romanenko [Lt Gen P.L. Romanenko, Forty-Eighth Army], and came to the conclusion that in the forward line the enemy was not making direct preparations for an offensive.

I may be mistaken. It may be that the enemy is camouflaging his preparations for an offensive very skilfully. But an analysis of the deployment of his armour, the inadequate density of infantry formations, absence of heavy artillery groupings, as well as the dispersion of reserves, lead me to believe that the enemy will not be ready to launch an offensive before the end of May.

2. The defences of the Thirteenth and Seventieth Armies are correctly organized and echeloned in depth. The defences of the Forty-Eighth Army are thin, with insufficient or low artillery density, and if the enemy strikes at Romanenko's army with the idea of bypassing Maloarkhangelsk from the east in order to envelop Kostin's main grouping, Romanenko will be unable to withstand the enemy's blow. The reserves of

will not be able to come to Romanenko's assistance in time.

I consider that Romanenko should be reinforced from the STAVKA reserve with two infantry divisions, three T-34 tank regiments, two antitank regiments and two mortar or artillery regiments of the STAVKA reserve. If this is provided, Romanenko will be able to organise a stable defence and, when necessary, go over to the offensive as a fairly concentrated force.

The main flaw in the defences of Pukhov, Galinin and other armies of the Front is the absence of antitank artillery regiments. The Front has at present four antitank artillery regiments only; two of them are in the Front's rear, without any traction facilities.

Because of a big shortage of 45mm [1.7in] guns in the battalions and regiments, the antitank defences of the first echelons and forward lines are weak.

I consider it necessary to give Kostin four antitank artillery regiments six with Romanenko's and three regiments of self-propelled 152mm [6in] guns as quickly as possible.

3. Kostin's preparations for the offensive have not been completed. Having discussed this question on the spot, Kostin, Pukhov and I came to the conclusion that it was necessary to move the penetration area 2–3km [1.2–2.4 miles] west of the area chosen by Kostin, i.e., to Arkhangelskoye inclusive, and to put in the first echelon a reinforced corps with a tank corps west of the railway.

Kostin will not be able to effect the planned breach with the artillery grouping because the enemy has considerably strengthened and deepened his defences in this sector.

To make a breach a certainty, Kostin must be given another artillery assault corps.

The Front has on average one-and-a-half fire units of ammunition.

Please bind Yakovlev [Col Genl N.D. Yakovlev, Chief of the Main Artillery Administration] to supply the Front with three fire units of basic calibre within two weeks.

4. Pukhov now has 12 divisions, six of them united in two corps. Pukhov himself six divisions. For the good of the cause I ask you to order the immediate formation and dispatch to Pukhov of two corps HQ staffs, and to form and dispatch one corps HQ staff to Galanin, who now has five separate divisions in addition to an infantry corps.

Awaiting your decision.'

Yuriev

ORDER OF BATTLE, 5TH JULY 1943

SOVIET FORCES

STALIN

STAVKA representatives for Kursk:
Marshal Zhukov and Marshal Vasilevsky

CENTRAL FRONT (Gen of the Army K.R. Rokossovsky)

THIRTEENTH ARMY (Lt Gen N.P. Pukhov)
17th, 18th Guards (Gds) Rifle Corps, 15th, 29th Rifle Corps
Army Troops
field artillery
4th Breakthrough Artillery Corps, 5th, 12th Breakthrough Art. Div., 5th Gds Rocket Art.Div., 19th Gds Cannon Regt., 476th, 477th Mtr.Regt., 6th, 37th, 65th, 86th, 324th Gds Rocket Art.Regt.
others
275th Eng.Bn., 1st, 25th AA Div., 1287th AA Regt., 874th Anti-Tank (AT) Regt., 129th Tank Bde, 27th, 30th Gds Tank Regt., 43rd, 58th, 237th Tank Regt., 1442nd SU Regt., 49th Armoured (Armd) Train Bn.

FORTY-EIGHTH ARMY (Lt Gen P.L. Romanenko)
42nd Rifle Corps, 73rd, 137th, 143rd, 170th Rifle Div.
Army Troops
field artillery
1168th Cannon Regt., 479th Mtr.Regt.
others
313th Eng.Bn., 16th AA Div., 461st AA Regt., 615th AA Bn., 2nd AT Bde., 220th Gds AT Regt., 45th, 193rd, 229th Tank Regt., 1454th, 1455th, 1540th SU Regt., 37th Armd Train Bn.

SIXTIETH ARMY (Lt Gen V.D. Kryuchenkin)
24th, 30th Rifle Corps, 55th Rifle Div., 248th Rifle Bde
Army Troops
field artillery

1156th Cannon Regt., 128th, 138th, 497th Mtr.Regt., 98th Gds Rocket Art.Regt., 286th Gds Rocket Art.Bn.
others
59th Eng.Sapper Bde, 317th Eng.Bn., 221st Gds AA Regt., 217th AA Regt., 1178th AT Regt., 150th Tank Bde., 58th Armd Train Bn.

SIXTY-FIFTH ARMY (Lt Gen P.I. Batov)
18th, 27th Rifle Corps, 37th Gds Rifle Div., 181st, 194th, 354th Rifle Div.
Army Troops
field artillery
143rd Gds Mtr.Regt., 218th, 478th Mtr.Regt., 94th Gds Rocket Art. Regt.
others
14th Eng.-Mine Bde., 321st Eng.Bn., 29th Gds Tank Regt., 40th, 84th, 255th Tank Regt., 120th, 543rd AT Regt., 235th AA Regt.

SEVENTIETH ARMY (Lt Gen I.V. Galanin)
28th Rifle Corps, 102nd, 106th, 140th, 162nd, 175th (NKVD) Rifle Div.
Army Troops
field artillery
1st Gds Art.Div., 136th Mtr.Regt.
others
169th, 371st, 386th Eng. Bn., 3rd Destroyer Bde., 240th, 251st, 259th Tank Regt., 378th AT Regt., 12th AA Div., 581st AA. Reg.

SECOND TANK ARMY (Lt Gen A.G. Rodin)
3rd, 16th Tank Corps
Army Troops
357th Eng.Bn., 11th Gds Tank Bde., 87th MC Bn.

FRONT RESERVES
9th, 19th Tank Corps, 115th, 119th, 161st Fortified Sectors

Support Troops
field artillery
68th Cannon Art.Bde., 21st Mtr. Bde., 84th, 92nd, 323rd Gds Rocket Art. Regt.
others
1st Gds Special Purposes Eng. Bde., 6th Mine Eng.Bde., 12th Gds Mine Bn., 120th, 257th Eng.Bn., 9th, 49th, 50th, 104th Pont. Bn., 1541st SU Regt., 4th Destroyer Bde., 14th Destroyer Bde., 40th Armd Train Bn., 1st AT Bde., 13th AT Bde., 130th, 563rd AT Regt., 10th AA Div., 997th, 1259th, 1263rd AA Regt., 13th Gds, 27th, 31st AA Bn.

VORONEZH FRONT (Gen of the Army N.F. Vatutin)

SIXTH GUARDS ARMY (Lt Gen I.M. Chistyakov)
22nd, 23rd Gds Rifle Corps, 89th Gds Rifle Div.
Army Troops
field artillery
27th, 33rd Cannon Art.Bde., 628th Cannon Art.Regt., 263rd, 295th Mtr.Regt., 5th, 16th, 79th, 314th Gds Rocket Art.Regt.
others
205th, 540th Eng.Bn., 96th Tank Bde., 230th, 245th Tank Regt., 1440th SU Regt., 60th Armd Train Bn., 27th, 28th AT Bde., 493rd, 496th, 611th, 694th, 868th, 1008th, 1240th, 1666th, 1667th AT Regt., 26th AA Div., 1487th AA Regt.

SEVENTH GUARDS ARMY (Lt Gen M.S. Shumilov)
24th, 25th Gds Rifle Corps, 213th Rifle Div.
Army Troops
field artillery
109th, 161st, 265th Gds Cannon Art.Regt., 290th Mtr.Regt.
others
60th Eng.Sapper Bde., 175th, 329th Eng.Bn., 27th Gds Tank Bde., 201st Tank Bde., 262nd, 148th, 167th Tank Regt., 1529th, 1438th SU Regt., 34th, 38th Armd Train Bn., 30th AT Bde., 114th, 115th Gds AT Regt., 1669th, 1670th AT Regt., 5th AA Div., 162nd, 258th Gds AA Regt.

THIRTY-EIGHTH ARMY (Lt Gen N.Y. Chibisov)
167th, 180th, 204th, 232nd, 240th, 340th Rifle Div.
Army Troops
field artillery
111th Gds How. Art. Regt., 112th Gds Cannon Art.Regt., 491st, 492nd Mtr.Regt., 66th Gds Rocket Art.Regt., 441st Gds Rocket Art.Bn
others
235th, 268th Eng.Bn., 1505th Mine Eng.Bn., 108th Pontoon Bn., 180th, 192nd Tank Bde., 29th AT Bde., 222nd, 483rd, 1658th, 1660th, 981st, 1288th AA Regt.

FORTIETH ARMY (Lt Gen K.S. Moskalenko)
100th, 161st, 184th, 206th, 219th, 237th, 309th Rifle Div.

Army Troops
field artillery
36th Cannon Art.Bde., 29th How. Art. Bde. (–), 76th Gds Cannon Art. Regt., 493rd, 494th Mtr. Regt., 9th, 10th Mtn. Mtr. Regt.
others
14th Eng.Bn., 86th Tank Bde., 59th, 60th Tank Regt., 32nd AT Bde., 4th Gds AT Regt., 12th, 869th, 1244th, 1663rd, 1664th AT Regt., 9th AA Div., 1488th AA Regt.

SIXTY-NINTH ARMY (Lt Gen Kryuchenkin)
107th, 111th, 183rd, 270th, 305th Rifle Div.
Army Troops
field artillery
496th Mtr.Regt.
others
328th Eng.Bn., 1661st AT Regt., 225th Gds AA Regt., 322nd AA Bn.

1st TANK ARMY (Lt Gen M.Y. Katukov)
3rd Mech. Corps, 6th, 31st Tank Corps
Army Troops
field artillery
316th Gds Rocket Art.Regt.
others
71st, 267th Eng.Bn., 8th AA Div.

FRONT RESERVES
2nd, 5th Gds Tank Corps, 35th Gds Rifle Corps
Support Troops
field artillery
1528th How.Art.Regt., 522nd, 1148th Super Hvy.How.Art.Regt., 12th Mtr. Bde., 469th Mtr.Regt., 36th, 80th, 97th, 309th, 315th Gds Rocket Art. Regt.
others
4th, 5th Mine Eng.Bde., 42nd Special Purposes Eng.Bde., 6th Pontoon Bde., 13th Gds Mine Bn., 6th, 20th Pont. Bn., Separate Tank Regt. (unnumbered), 14th, 31st AT Bde., 1076th, 1689th AT Regt., 22nd Gds AA Bn.

STEPPE (RESERVE) FRONT (Col General I.S. Konev)

FOURTH GUARDS ARMY (Lt Gen Kulik)
20th, 21st Gds Rifle Corps, 3rd Gds Tank Corps
Army Troops
field artillery
466th Mtr.Regt., 96th Gds Rocket Art.Regt.
others
48th Eng.Bn., 452nd, 1317th AT Regt., 27th AA Div.

FIFTH GUARDS ARMY (Lt Gen A.M. Zhadov)
32nd, 33rd Gds Rifle Corps, 10th Tank Corps, 42nd Gds Rifle Div.
Army Troops
field artillery
308th Gds Rocket Art.Regt.
others
256th, 431st Eng.Bn., 301st, 1322nd AT Regt., 29th AA Div

TWENTY-SEVENTH ARMY (Lt Gen S.G. Trofimenko)
71st, 147th, 155th, 163rd, 166th, 241st Rifle Div.
Army Troops
field artillery
480th Mtr.Regt., 47th Gds Rocket Art.Regt.
others
25th, 38th Eng.Bn., 680th, 1070th AT Regt., 93rd Tank Bde., 39th Tank Regt., 23rd AA Div.

FORTY-SEVENTH ARMY (Maj Gen P.M. Kozlov)
21st, 23rd Rifle Corps
Army Troops
field artillery
460th Mtr. Regt., 83rd Gds Rocket Art.Regt.
others
91st Eng. Bn., 269th, 1593rd AT Regt., 21st AA Div

FIFTY-THIRD ARMY (Lt Gen I.M. Mangarov)
28th Gds, 84th, 116th, 214th, 233rd, 252nd, 299th Rifle Div.
Army Troops
field artillery
461st Mtr. Regt., 89th Gds Rocket Art. Regt.
others
11th, 17th Eng. Bn., 232nd, 1316th AT Regt., 34th, 35th Tank Regt., 30th AA Div

FIFTH GUARDS TANK ARMY (Lt Gen P.A. Rotmistrov)
5th Gds Mech. Corps, 29th Tank Corps
Army Troops
field artillery
678th How.Art.Regt., 76th Gds Rocket Regt.
others
377th Eng.Bn., 994th Light Bomber Regiment, 689th AT Regt., 53rd Gds Tank Bde., 1549th SU Regt., 1st Gds MC Regt., 6th AA Div

FRONT RESERVES
35th Rifle Corps (HQ only), 3rd, 5th, 7th Gds Cavalry Corps, 4th Gds Tank Corps, 3rd Gds Mech. Corps, 1st, 2nd Mech. Corps
Support Troops
engineers
8th Eng.Sapper Bde., 27th Special Purposes Eng.Bde., 7th, 19th, 40th Pontoon Bn., 246th, 247th, 248th, 250th, 284th Eng.Bn.
others
78th MC Bn., 11th AA Div.

AIR ARMIES SUPPORTING THE SOVIET FORCES
2nd Air Army (Voronezh Front), 5th Air Army (Steppe Front), 16th Air Army (Central Front), 17th Air Army (Southwestern Front)

GERMAN FORCES

HITLER

OBERKOMMANDO DER HEERES

ARMY GROUP SOUTH (Field Marshal von Manstein)

4TH PANZER ARMY (Col. General Hoth)
LII CORPS (Gen Ott)
57th, 255th, 332nd Inf. Div.
Corps Troops
field artillery
 Arko 137, I/108th Field Art.Bn. (RSO),
 3rd/731st 15cm Gun Battery, 1st Hvy.Rocket Art.Regt.
others
 677th Eng.Regt., 74th Eng.Bn., 217th Constr.Bn., 23rd,
 80th Bridge Column Bn.,
 226th Bicycle Security Bn. (minus 1 Coy.)

II SS-PANZER CORPS (Obergruppenführer Hausser)
SS-Totenkopf, SS-Das Reich and SS-Leibstandarte Pz. Gren. Div.
Corps Troops
field artillery
 Arko 122, 861st, III/818th Field Art.Bn. (RSO),
 Commander of Smoke Troops 3, 55th Rocket Art.Regt.,
 1st Lehr Rocket Art.Regt., SS-Corps Rocket Art Bn.
engineers
 680th Eng.Regt., 627th, 666th Eng.Bn. (m), Bridging Staff 929,
 Commander of Constr. Troops 8., 26th Bridge Constr.Bn.,
 508th Lt.Bicycle Road Constr.Bn., 410th Constr.Bn.
Army Troops
 Higher Arko 312, Higher Constr. Staff 14,
 Commander for Constr. Forces 14, 155th Constr.Bn. (K),
 305th Const.Bn., Bridging Staff 922

ARMY DETACHMENT KEMPF (General Kempf)

III PANZER CORPS (Gen Breith)
168th Inf. Div., 6th, 7th, 19th Pz. Div.
Corps Troops
field artillery
 Arko 3, 612th Art.Regt., 857th 21cm How.Bn.,
 II/62nd Field Art.Bn., II/71st Hvy.Field Art.Bn.,
 228th Assault Gun Bn., 54th Rocket Art. Regt.
others
 601st, 674th Eng.Regt. (m), 70th, 651st Eng.Bn. (m),
 127.Eng Bn. (m) (minus 1 Coy.), 531st,
 925th Bridge Constr. Bn., 503rd Hvy Tank Bn., 99th,
 153rd AA Regt.

XI CORPS (Gen Raus)
106th, 320th Inf. Div.
Corps Troops
field artillery
 Arko 153, I/77th, I/213th, II/54th Field Art.Bn.,
 31st Lt.Art.Obsv.Bn., 905th Assault Gun Bn.,
 393rd Assault Gun Battery, II/1st Hvy.Rocket-Launcher Regt.,
 52nd Rocket Art. Regt.
others
 18th, 52nd Eng.Bn. (m), 923rd, 41st Bridge Constr.Bn.,
 246 Constr.Bn., 4th, 7th, 48th AA Regt.

XLII CORPS (Gen Mattenklott)
39th, 161st, 282nd Inf. Div.
Corps Troops
field artillery
 Arko 107, 2nd/800th 15cm Gun Bty., 13th Art.Obsv.Bn.
others
 620th Mtn.Eng.Regt. (m), 26th Constr. Regt., 219th,
 112th Constr. Bn. (U), 153rd Constr. Bn. (K), AT Bn. C.,
 560th Hvy. AT Bn. (Nashorn), 18th Penal Bn.
Army Troops
 Higher Arko 310, Commander of Smoketroops 1,
 781st Art. Regt. Staff, 22nd Constr. Bde., 21st Bridge Constr. Bn.,
 538th, 676th Hvy.Road Constr. Bn.

NINTH ARMY (Col. General Model)

XX CORPS (Gen Freiherr von Roman)
45th, 72nd, 137th, 251st Inf. Div.
Corps Troops
field artillery
 Arko 129, 860th Field Art.Bn., 15th Lt.Art.Obsv.Bn.
engineers
 512th Eng.Regt.Staff, 4th Eng.Regt. staff, 750th Eng.Bn.,
 Bridge Column B 626, 44th, 418th, 80th Constr.Bn.,
 244th Constr.Bn. (K)

XLVI PANZER CORPS (Gen Zorn)
7th, 31st, 102nd, 258th Inf. Div.
Corps Troops
field artillery
 Arko 1, 609th Art.Regt.Staff, 909th Assault Gun Bn.,
 430th Field Art.Bn., 611th 10cm Gun Bn.,
 II/47th Mixed Art.Bn., 3rd/637th 21cm How.Bty.,
 3rd/620th 15cm Gun Bty., 1st Recoilless Gun Bn.
 (with 423, 433 and 443 Bty.), 18th Hvy.Mtr.Bn.
others
 752nd Eng.Bn., Bridge Column B 12, 29, Bridging Staff 930,
 Commander of Constr.Forces 33, 584th Road Constr.Bn.,
 Group von Manteuffel (9th, 10th, 11th Jaeger Bn.)

XLVII PANZER CORPS (Gen Lemelson)
6th Inf. Div., 2nd, 9th, 20th Pz. Div.
Corps Troops
field artillery
 Arko 130, 904th, 245th Assault Gun Bn., II/63rd,
 II/67th Hvy.Field Bn., 637th 21cm How.Bn. (minus 3rd Bty.),
 1st/620th 15cm Gun Bty, 2nd Hvy.Rocket-Launcher Regt.
others
 678th Eng.Regt.Staff, 2nd Training Eng.Bn.,
 145th Bridge Constr.Bn., Bridging Staff 928,
 505th Hvy.Tank Bn. (minus 3rd Coy.), 312nd Pz. Coy. (Fkl)

XLI PANZER CORPS (Gen Harpe)
86th, 292nd Inf. Div. and 18th Pz. Div.
Corps Troops
field artillery
 Arko 35, 69th Art.Regt.Staff, 177th, 244th Assault Gun Bn.,
 616th, 425th, II/64th Field Art.Bn., 427th 10cm Gun Bn.,
 II/61st Hvy.Field Art.Bn., 604th 21cm How.Bn.,
 2nd/620th 15cm Gun Bty., 53rd Rocket Art.Regt.,
 19th Hvy.Mtr.Bn.
others
 104th Eng.Regt.Staff, 42nd Eng.Bn. (m), Bridging Staff 932
 (Bridge Column B 2/409, 606), 407th Constr. Bn.,
 656th Tank Destroyer Regt.

XXIII CORPS
216th, 383rd Inf. Div., 87th Gren. Regt (from 36th ID)
and 78th Assault Div.
Corps Troops
field artillery
 Arko 112, 109th, 41st, 774th Art. Regt. Staff, 185th,
 189th Assault Gun Bn., II/59th, 426th, 851st Field Art.Bn.,
 79th 10cm Gun Bn., 4th/69th 10cm Gun Bty.,
 422nd Mixed Art.Bn., 848th, II/66th Hvy.Field Art.Bn., 859th,
 1st, 2nd/635th 21cm How.Bty., 1st/817th 17cm Gun Bty.,
 22nd Lt.Art.Obsv.Bn., 51st Rocket Art. Regt.
others
 623rd Eng.Regt.Staff, 746th Eng.Bn., 85th Mtn.Eng.Bn.,
 Bridge Column B 88, 78th Road Constr.Bn., 811th,
 813th Armd Eng.Coy., 8th, 13th Jaeger Bn.
Army Troops
 442nd Div. Staff, Cmndr of Smoke Troops 4, 654th Eng.Bn., 751st
 Eng.Bn., 42nd, 539th Bridge Constr.Bn.,
 Bridge Column B 1/430th, 535th, Cmdr of Constr. Forces 42,
 544th, 576th, 580th Road Constr.Bn., Higher Constr.Staff 10,
 889th Sec.Bn.

LUFTWAFFE
 VIIIth AIR CORPS (Luftflotte 4) supporting Army Group South.
 1st AIR DIVISION (Luftflotte 6) supporting Army Group Centre.

BIBLIOGRAPHY

ABBOT, PETER AND NIGEL THOMAS. *Germany's Eastern Front Allies 1941–45*. London: Osprey Publishing, 1982.

BEEVOR, ANTONY. *Berlin the Downfall 1945*. London: Viking, Penguin Books Ltd, 2002.

BEKKER, CAJUS. *The Luftwaffe War Diaries*. London: Macdonald, 1964.

CARELL, PAUL. *The Scorched Earth*. London: Harrap, 1966.

CHANEY, OTTO. *Zhukov*. Newton Abbot: David and Charles, 1972.

CHAMBERLAIN, PETER AND CHRIS ELLIS. *Soviet Combat Tanks*. London: Almark Publishing, 1970.

DEAR, I.C.B. *The Oxford Companion to the Second World War*. Oxford: Oxford University Press, 1995.

DUNNIGAN, JAMES F. (EDITOR). *The Russian Front*. London: Arms and Armour Press, 1978.

ELLIS, JOHN. *The World War II Databook*. London: BCA, 1993.

ERICKSON, JOHN. *The Road to Berlin*. London: Weidenfeld and Nicolson, 1983.

GEHLEN, GENERAL REINHARD. *The Gehlen Memoirs*. London: William Collins, 1972.

GLANTZ, COLONEL DAVID M. *CSI Report No. 11 Soviet Defensive Tactics at Kursk, July 1943*. U.S. Army Command and General Staff College, September 1986.

GLANTZ, DAVID M. AND JONATHAN M. HOUSE. *The Battle of Kursk*. Lawrence, Kansas: University Press of Kansas, 2000.

GRUNBERGER, RICHARD. *A Social History of the Third Reich*. London: Weidenfeld & Nicholson, 1971.

GUDERIAN, GENERAL HEINZ. *Panzer Leader*. London: Michael Joseph, 1952.

HAUPT, WERNER. *Army Group South: The Wehrmacht in Russia 1941–1945*. Atglen, Pennsylvania: Schiffer Military History, 1998.

HEALY, MARK. *Kursk 1943: The tide turns in the East*. Oxford: Osprey Publishing, 1993.

HÖHNE, HEINZ. *The Order of the Death's Head*. London: Secker & Warburg, 1969.

Images of War. London: Marshall Cavendish Partworks, 1990.

KARPOV, VLADIMIR. *Russia at War 1941–45*. London: Century Hutchinson, 1987.

KUROWSKI, FRANZ. *Panzer Aces*. Winnipeg, Canada: J.J. Fedorowicz Publishing Inc, 2000.

LANDAU. S.H. *Goodbye Transylvania*. UK: Breedon Books, 1985.

LUCAS, JAMES. *Germany's Elite Panzer Force: Grossdeutschland*. London: Macdonald and Janes, 1978.

LUCAS, JAMES. *War on the Eastern Front*. London: Greenhill Books, 1979.

_____ AND MATHEW COOPER. *Hitler's Elite Leibstandarte SS*. London: Macdonald and Janes, 1975.

MANSTEIN, GENERAL ERICH VON. *Lost Victories*. London: Methuen & Co, 1958.

MARSHAL, S.L.A. (EDITOR). *The Simon and Schuster Encyclopedia of World War II*. New York: Simon and Schuster, 1978.

MAYER, S.L. (EDITOR). *The Russian War Machine*. London: Bison Books, 1977.

MELLENTHIN, F.W. *Panzer Battles 1939–1945*. London: Cassell & Company, 1955.

MITCHAM, SAMUEL W. JR. *Hitler's Field Marshals*. London: William Heinemann Ltd, 1988.

PAROTKIN, MAJOR-GENERAL IVAN (EDITOR). *The Battle of Kursk*. Moscow: Progress Publishers, 1974

PIEKALKIEWICZ, JANUSZ. *Krieg der Panzer 1939–1945*. Munich: Südwest Verlag GmbH & Co, KG, 1981.

PRICE, DR ALFRED. *Luftwaffe Handbook*. London: Ian Allan, 1977.

RUDEL, HANS-ULRICH. *Stuka Pilot*. London: Euphorion Books, 1952.

SEATON, ALBERT. *The Russo-German War 1941–45*. Novato, California: Presidio Press, 1971.

SHALITO, ANTON, ILYA SAVCHENKOV AND ANDREW MOLLO. *Red Army Uniforms of World War II*. London: Windrow and Greene, 1993.

SOLOVYOV, BORIS. *The Battle of Kursk*. Moscow: Novosti Press Agency, 1973.

SYDNOR, CHARLES W. JR. *Soldiers of Destruction*. New Jersey: Princetown University Press, 1977.

TAYLOR, BRIAN. *Barbarossa to Berlin, Volume Two*. Staplehurst: Spellmount, 2003;

TM.E 30.451 *Handbook on German Military Forces*. Washington, D.C.: US War Department, 1945

WILLIAMSON, GORDON. *Loyalty is my Honour*. London: Brown Packaging Ltd, 1995.

World War II Day by Day. London: Dorling Kindersley, 1990.

ZALOGA, STEVEN. *The Red Army of the Great Patriotic War 1941–5*. London: Osprey Publishing, 1989.

ZHUKOV, MARSHAL GEORGI. *The Memoires of Marshal Zhukov*. London: Jonathan Cape, 1971.

WEBSITES

German Armed Forces 1919–1945 (The), http://www.feldgrau.com

Historical Accuracy and ASL, http://www.uni.edu/~licari/HASL.htm

Kursk – Day by Day, http://dspace.dial.pipex.com

Kursk Reconsidered Germany's Lost Victory, George M. Nipe, Jr: www.thehistorynet.com/

Russian Battlefield, http://www.battlefield.ru/

The Battle of Kursk: Myths and Reality, http://www.uni.edu/~licari/citadel.htm

The Voice of Russia, http://www.vor.ru

Third Reich Factbook, http://www.skalman.ru/third-reich/index.htm

Tiger Battalions! http://www.chsk.com/steppenwolf/tigers.htm

INDEX

Page numbers in *italics* refer to illustrations.